Full Stack Development with MongoDB

Covers Backend, Frontend, APIs, and Mobile App Development Using PHP, NodeJS, ExpressJS, Python and React Native

Manu Sharma

www.bpbonline.com

FIRST EDITION 2022
Copyright © BPB Publications, India
ISBN: 978-93-55510-143

LIMITS OF LIABILITY AND DISCLAIMER OF WARRANTY

To View Complete
BPB Publications Catalogue
Scan the QR Code:

Dedicated to

All Family and Friends

My Grandmother:

Smt. Pushpa Devi Sharma

My Parents:

Sh. Vijay Sharma *and* **Smt. Neelam Sharma**

My Wife: **Anu Sharma**

My Sister: **Neha Sharma**

&

Especially to My Angel Daughter: **Siya Sharma**

About the Author

 **Manu Sharma** (MPhil) has more than 17 years of industry experience in software development at the architect level, web administration, project management and execution, product development, and team management. He has worked for various multinational companies, small to mid-sized organizations, universities as well as one of the biggest conglomerates of India. He is also the founder, architect, and developer of two open-source projects. In his free time, he loves to spend his time with his family and his daughter. His other interests are singing and arts. During some weekends you can find him singing and recording music in the studios, playing the flute, or painting with brushes in his hands.

About the Reviewers

❖ **Dheeraj Chhabra** is a Strategic-level professional working as Program Director in Happiest Minds Technologies Limited. He holds Masters in Computer Applications (MCA) from Indira Gandhi National Open University (IGNOU). Dheeraj has more than 18 years of work experience in IT and has worked in different established organizations at various levels from Software Developer to Program Management. He has worked on various technologies including Java Swings, Servlets, JSP, EJB, Asp, VB.Net, C#.Net, ASP.Net, SQL Server, Oracle, and more. He has played various important roles including, but not limited to, Software Engineer, Team Lead, Project Lead, Project Manager, Enterprise Solution Architect, Product Manager, and Program Manager. Dheeraj is a firm believer as well as a strong follower of Servant Leadership, Empowerment, and Continuous Integrated Development.

Dheeraj has earned various certifications such as PSM, TOGAF, PMP, PMI-ACP, SAFe 4 & 5, EXIN ASM, and is currently following his passion of continuous learning and development focused on a couple of more technical and leadership skills-oriented certifications. He is detail-oriented with a key focus on end-to-end project/program planning, execution, and delivery. He keeps a close eye to Run, Protect and Change the business.

❖ **Rohit Agarwal** is an IT professional with rich experience in Data Technologies. His expertise circle around Data Engineering, Architecture, and Analytics providing end-to-end solutions to business units by creating data pipelines and building business intelligence systems to help organizations take critical business decisions based on data. He earned his Master's degree in Information Systems from Northeastern University, Boston in the year 2017. He has a keen interest in Entrepreneurship and Innovation and has also learned the same from Harvard Extension School, Boston.

❖ **Mamoon Mushtaque** is a technically accomplished IT professional with 9+ years of experience in service-based as well as product-based organizations with insightful experience in various aspects of UI development using multiple technologies. He is currently working as Lead Software Engineer at Spiralyze LLC.

❖ **Harish Kumar Buttolia** has an M.Sc. (IT) from the Punjab Technical University. He worked for various Government and Private organizations. He possesses 18 years of experience in IT with a good knowledge of software and application development using open source technologies. He is having articles/publications published in renowned India/International Journals. He is always keen to learn new technologies. He is also interested in writing, reading, music, and travel.

Acknowledgement

First of all, I am thankful to almighty God for providing me with the opportunity to write a book. I am very thankful to Mr. Nrip Jain (Head, Business Development Group, BPB Publications) for believing in me and offering me to write this book.

I am also thankful to all my Gurus and Teachers in life for their teachings and blessings.

My special thanks to my daughter "Siya" for supporting me during the book journey.

I feel great to have some friends; most of them are still in touch with me including my college buddies, from ET&T as well as a few other friends – Chandrashekhar Kalia, Kapil Bharadwaj, Ankur Sood, Anugrag Sharma, Suresh Kumar, Umang Mathur, Nisha Jayna, Deepak Kumar Taank, Dhirendra Kumar, Joseph Vamsavardhan Gurja - Thank You All

I am very thankful to my uncle and neighbor – Prof. Jyoti Kumar Sharma for his guidance while I was about to start writing my first book and for encouraging me always.

I would like to thank few of my colleagues from my present organization (Spiralyze LLC) for their support, admiration, and appreciation:

Gajan Retnasaba, Yaseen Shaik, Sophie D'Souza, Dheeraj Sareen, Mitko Cabevski, Hassan Ahmad, Mamoon Mushtaque, Nikunjkumar Balar, Yuriy Kycha-Kolot, Bhavesh Vavadiya, Dhaval Balar, Sohil Hunani, Riyaz Lohiya, Jaya Prakash, Mohammad Subhani, Vaibhav Anchal, Kushal Borda, Abhishek Mohata, Himujjal Upadhyaya, Sonu Rana, Sergy Babich, Donatas Jasiunas, Cris Balano, Bash Simplicio, Rachelle Olvida, Sonali Rasane, Angelica Marbella, Quirino Lacambra IV – You people are awesome!

I would like to also thank a few people from my previous organizations: Rajesh Goyal, Santosh Kumar (@ Infopro) Amit Kumar Sen, Shahid Reza, Paarul Madaan, Sachin Chandra, Santosh Negi, Sandeep Kumar, Sunil Patnaik, Nishant Singh, Aniruddha Ratnaparkhi, Manish Singh, Sandeep Sugra (@ Shri Ram New Horizons)

Anupam Srivastava, Rohit Agarwal, Daljeet Singh, Ashok Kumar, Abhishek Kumar, Ajay Kumar, Puneet Sehgal, Vikrant Singh, Abhishek Verma, Aarfi Siddique, Deepak Gautam, Naveen Jeengar, Randhir Sharma, Sushil Kumar Prajapati, Priyanshu Singh, Jyoti Deep (@ Miracle Corporate Solutions Pvt. Ltd.) Shiw Kumar Prasad, Vidushi Sasan, Yashdeep Gupta, Gaurav Mukhija (JBi Digital) Amit Puri, Dhananjay Kumar Yadav, Dheeraj Yadav, Rahul Singh Yadav, Amitesh Maurya, Saurabh Sharma (@TSI India)

My gratitude also goes to the entire team at BPB Publications for being always supportive during the entire Book Journey and whenever I need their help they were always available to help me.

Last but not least I am very thankful to all the technical reviewers of this book, I really appreciate their hard work during technical review and am thankful to them whenever they have corrected me in some places which required changes.

Preface

This book is intended for the people who want to learn MongoDB at an Advanced Level and then want to scale their knowledge to the Full Stack Software Application Development both for Web and Mobile using MongoDB.

The readers should possess some basic understanding of the Database Concepts such as MongoDB and some intermediate understanding of Programming Concepts, Programming Languages like PHP, JavaScript, Node.js, React Native, and Python.

While we cover all in very practical and step by step Full Stack Application Development using MongoDB with Chapters Features Step by Step use of MongoDB with Programming Languages like PHP, JavaScript, Node.js, React Native and Python So even if the reader have a basic programming knowledge then also reader would be able to understand these Chapters easily. Every Concept has been explained in a manner that once you start the practical development while reading this book at the end you will be more experienced in Software Development both in Web and Mobile Technologies.

This Book Covers the Step by Step Practical Development along with Screenshots for almost every Step, You will learn to develop the following 4 Software Applications using 4 Different Languages –

One Database – 4 Apps

- Backend Catalog of a Publication House – CRUD Functionality with PHP and MongoDB

- REST API Development – Creating a RESTful Web Services of a Publication House – API Development using Node.js and MongoDB

- Mobile App Development – Creating a Mobile App of a Publication House – Data-Driven Dynamic Mobile App Development using React Native and MongoDB using API Calls

- Frontend Development – Creating a Website of a Publication House – Frontend Development using Python's Django Framework and MongoDB

The main programming languages used in this book:

- PHP
- Node.js
- JavaScript
- React Native (For Mobile Application Development)
- Python

Other languages/components used in this book:

- HTML
- CSS
- React Native Stylesheet Component

Software/modules/libraries/terms used in this book:

- Full-Stack Software Development
- Backend Software Development
- Frontend Software Development
- WAMP Stack / WAMP Server
- MERN Stack
- API Development
- MongoDB Compass
- NPM Modules
- Express.js
- CORS
- Postman
- PIP

- PyPI

- Django Framework

- PyMongo

- and Many More ....

Chapter 1 covers the concepts related to the client-side and server-side. You will learn the difference between the client and server and how the interactions happen between client and server. In the later part of this chapter, we would be also learning the client and server-side concepts in which a database like MongoDB is also involved. We would be exploring how the dynamic sites which are using databases like MongoDB work, how the server processes these requests and sends them back to the client. In the last section of this chapter we would be covering the MongoDB drivers and why they are used, what are the programming languages that are currently supported by MongoDB, and the MongoDB community availability of drivers.

Chapter 2 covers the data entry part using MongoDB Compass after creating the database and collection using MongoDB Compass so that we can have some real data to work with our next chapters.

Chapter 3 covers the introduction to PHP programming with MongoDB and how we can use PHP with MongoDB. In order to run PHP with MongoDB server, we should be having the right environment in place. So this chapter covers how we can set up the right environment to run PHP codes. In this chapter, we will learn what WAMP server is and how to install WAMP server. Later in this chapter, we will cover how we can set up MongoDB with PHP and WAMP server. In the last section of this book, we would be doing some coding and running some practical examples to connect and work with MongoDB server using PHP.

Chapter 4 covers the introduction to JavaScript programming language. We will learn Node.js programming with MongoDB and how we can use Node.js with MongoDB. In order to run Node.js with MongoDB server, we should be having the right environment in place. So this chapter covers how we can set up the right environment to run Node.js codes. In this chapter, we will learn what Node.js is and how to install Node.js. Later in this chapter, we will cover how we can set up MongoDB with Node.js. In the last section of this book, we would be doing some coding and running some practical examples to connect and work with MongoDB server using Node.js.

Chapter 5 covers the introduction to React Native Mobile Framework and then we will learn how we can build Mobile-based Apps using React Native with MongoDB programming with MongoDB and how we can use Node.js with MongoDB. In order to run React Native and build Mobile Apps with MongoDB we should be having the right environment in place. So this chapter covers how we can set up the right environment to run React Native codes. In this chapter, we will learn what React Native is and how to install React Native. In the last section of this book, we would be doing some coding and running some practical examples to connect and work with MongoDB Server using React Native.

Chapter 6 covers the introduction to Python programming language and Python programming with MongoDB and how we can use Python with MongoDB. In order to run Python with MongoDB server, we should be having the right environment in place. So this chapter covers how we can set up the right environment to run Python codes. In this chapter, we will learn what Python is and how to install Python. Later in this chapter, we will cover how we can set up MongoDB with Python. In the last section of this book, we would be doing some coding and running some practical examples to connect and work with MongoDB server using Python.

Chapter 7 covers the topics related to real application development as we are now going to start with the step by step web and mobile application development part involving various languages and frameworks like PHP, JavaScript (Node.js), Python, and React Native along with MongoDB. In this chapter, we would be learning about the application and software development terms like frontend, backend, and full stack development and try to understand the various technologies, frameworks, and stacks that are used in these various types of applications. In the later part of this chapter, we will cover the applications that we are going to develop in our next chapters and at last, we will cover an overview of various technologies and tools that we would be using to develop our web and mobile apps in our next chapters. So this chapter would be interesting for an overall overview of the next chapters which are related with the step by step full stack web and mobile application development of this book.

Chapter 8 covers the practical step by step development of CRUD based backend application using PHP and MongoDB along with frontend languages like HTML,

CSS, and JavaScript. In this chapter, we will learn how to create a backend catalog of a Publication House. This chapter starts with the Overview of our web application development using PHP and MongoDB, basic requirements, and some pre-development steps which are required to be performed before we start developing our application. Later in this chapter, we will learn how we can create a dashboard for our application and various other related functionalities required for the overall development of the catalog management system for a Publication House. In this chapter, all the sections have been explained in step by step practical manner so that by the end of this chapter you feel more confident in PHP and MongoDB application development.

Chapter 9 covers the practical step by step development of REST Based APIs using Node.js, Express.js, and MongoDB along with Node.js extensions like Body Parser. In this chapter, we will learn how to create APIs for a Publication House. This chapter starts with the overview of our API development using Node.js, Express.js, and MongoDB, basic requirements, and some pre-development steps which are required to be performed before we start developing our web services. Later in this chapter, we will learn how we can use various REST-based methods and various other related functionalities required for the overall development of APIs for a Publication House. In this chapter, all the sections have been explained in step by step practical manner so that by the end of this chapter you feel more confident in Node.js, Express.js, and MongoDB web services and API development.

Chapter 10 covers the practical step-by-step development of a mobile app developed using React Native and MongoDB. We will learn how to create a mobile app for a publication house and will start with the overview of our mobile app development using React Native, Expo, Expo CLI, Node.js, Express.js, and MongoDB. We will learn how to add the "Thumbs Up" and "Thumbs Down" functionality and how to store their counts in the MongoDB database using the API calls. In this chapter, all the sections have been covered step by step and detailed manner.

Chapter 11 covers the practical step by step development of frontend application developed using Python and MongoDB. In this chapter, we will learn how to create a website for a Publication House. This chapter starts with the overview of our frontend development using Python, Django, PyMongo, and MongoDB. We will start this chapter with basic requirements. Later in this chapter, we will learn how we can build the various functionalities of the frontend application like displaying the book catalogue list and displaying the book cover images, total number of "Thumbs

The four applications covered in this book
A Sneak Preview

This book covers the step-by-step practical development along with screenshots for almost every step. You will learn to develop the following 4 software applications using 4 different languages.

One Database – 4 Apps

Backend Catalogue of a Publication House – CRUD Functionality with PHP and MongoDB

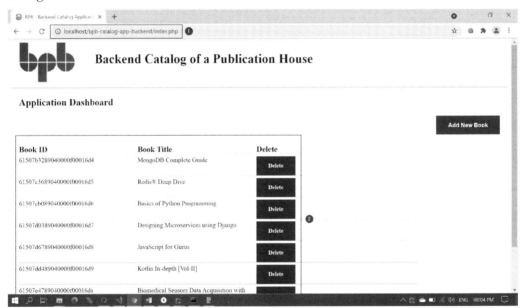

Figure 0.1: Application Dashboard Page

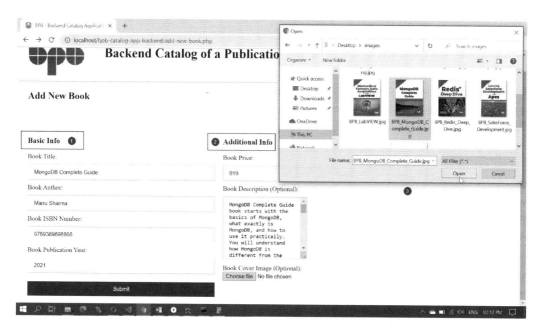

Figure 0.2: Add new book page

REST API Development – Creating a RESTful Web Services of a Publication House – API Development using Node.js and MongoDB

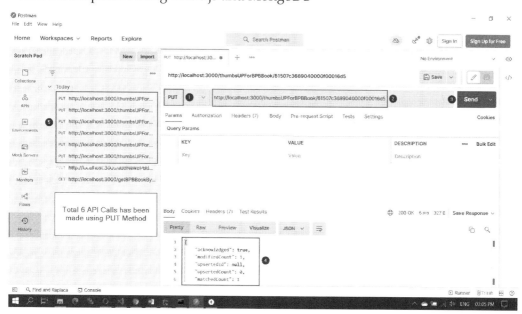

Figure 0.3: API Calls using Postman

Figure 0.4: MongoDB Compass—verifying the documents updated by our API calls

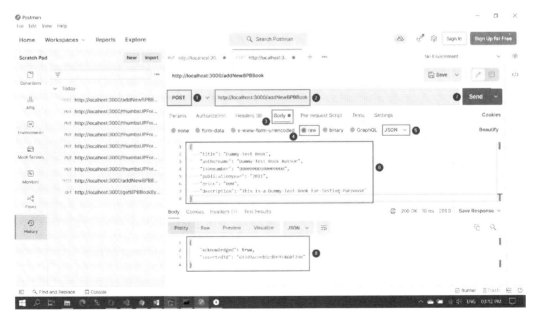

Figure 0.5: Adding dummy book with our API

Mobile App Development – Creating a Mobile App of a Publication House – Data Driven Dynamic Mobile App Development using React Native and MongoDB using API Calls

Figure 0.6: Thumbs Up and Thumbs Down Functionality

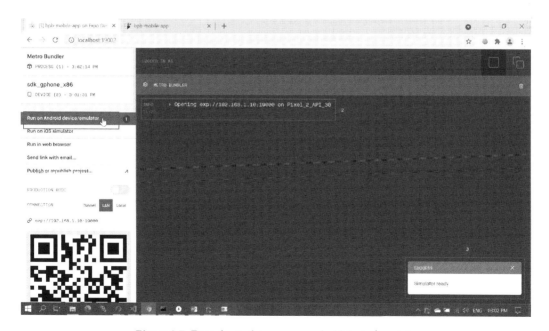

Figure 0.7: Expo dev tools > run on android device/emulator

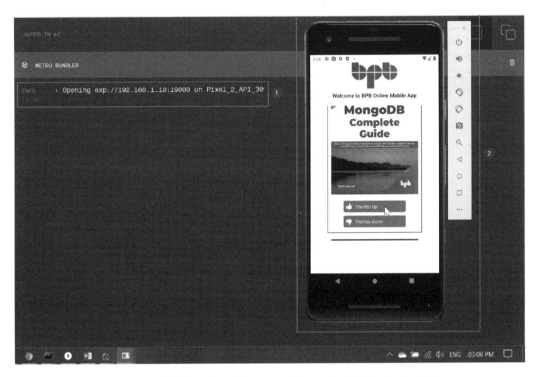

Figure 0.8: Mobile App Running successfully on Android device/emulator

Frontend Development – Creating a Website of a Publication House – Frontend Development using Python's Django Framework and MongoDB

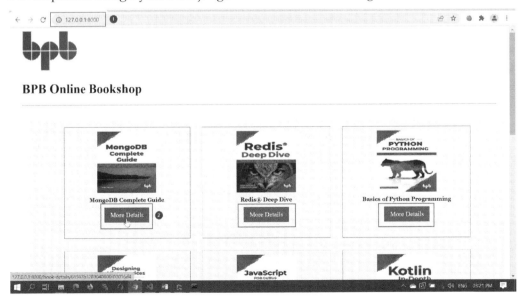

Figure 0.9: Django Frontend Application home page

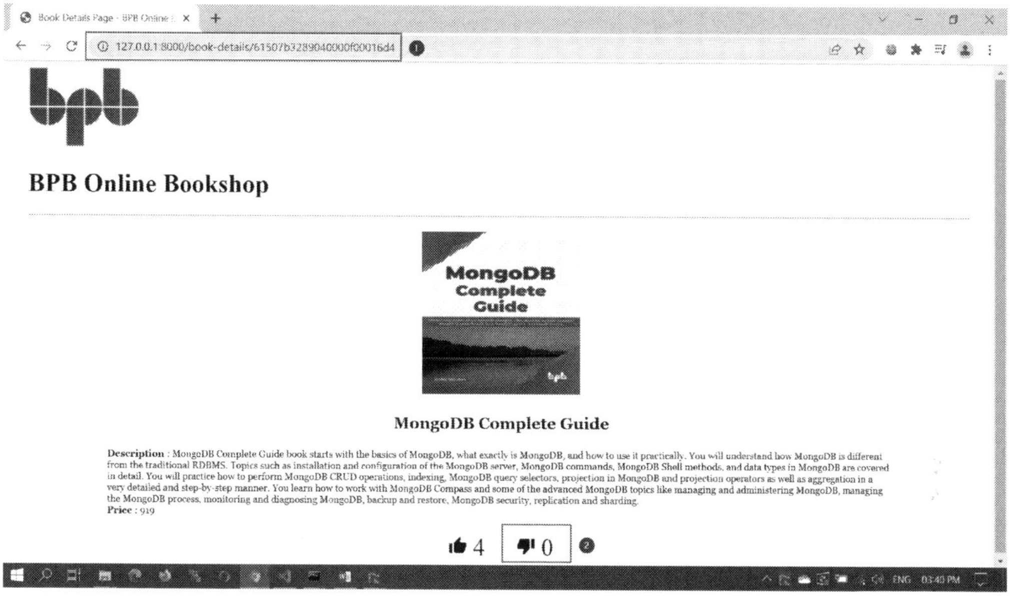

Figure 0.10: *Frontend - More Details Page – Thumbs Up and Thumbs Down*

Code Bundle and Coloured Images

Please follow the link to download the
Code Bundle and the *Coloured Images* of the book:

https://rebrand.ly/pi581cf

The code bundle for the book is also hosted on GitHub at **https://github.com/bpbpublications/Full-Stack-Development-with-MongoDB**. In case there's an update to the code, it will be updated on the existing GitHub repository.

We have code bundles from our rich catalogue of books and videos available at **https://github.com/bpbpublications**. Check them out!

Errata

We take immense pride in our work at BPB Publications and follow best practices to ensure the accuracy of our content to provide with an indulging reading experience to our subscribers. Our readers are our mirrors, and we use their inputs to reflect and improve upon human errors, if any, that may have occurred during the publishing processes involved. To let us maintain the quality and help us reach out to any readers who might be having difficulties due to any unforeseen errors, please write to us at :

errata@bpbonline.com

Your support, suggestions and feedbacks are highly appreciated by the BPB Publications' Family.

Did you know that BPB offers eBook versions of every book published, with PDF and ePub files available? You can upgrade to the eBook version at www.bpbonline.com and as a print book customer, you are entitled to a discount on the eBook copy. Get in touch with us at :

business@bpbonline.com for more details.

At **www.bpbonline.com**, you can also read a collection of free technical articles, sign up for a range of free newsletters, and receive exclusive discounts and offers on BPB books and eBooks.

Piracy

If you come across any illegal copies of our works in any form on the internet, we would be grateful if you would provide us with the location address or website name. Please contact us at **business@bpbonline.com** with a link to the material.

If you are interested in becoming an author

If there is a topic that you have expertise in, and you are interested in either writing or contributing to a book, please visit **www.bpbonline.com**. We have worked with thousands of developers and tech professionals, just like you, to help them share their insights with the global tech community. You can make a general application, apply for a specific hot topic that we are recruiting an author for, or submit your own idea.

Reviews

Please leave a review. Once you have read and used this book, why not leave a review on the site that you purchased it from? Potential readers can then see and use your unbiased opinion to make purchase decisions. We at BPB can understand what you think about our products, and our authors can see your feedback on their book. Thank you!

For more information about BPB, please visit **www.bpbonline.com**.

Table of Contents

CHAPTER 1
Client and Server-Side Concepts and Introduction to MongoDB Drivers

In the real-world scenario, when we request any information over the network or internet, then the client and server interact with each other to pass the requested information. In this chapter, you will be learning the concepts related to client-side and server-side and how the interactions happen between them. In the later sections of this chapter, we will be covering these concepts in relation to the databases like MongoDB, and we will learn how the dynamic sites which use the databases like MongoDB work.

Structure

In this chapter, we will discuss the following topics:

- Client and server-side concepts
- Client and server-side DB concepts
- Introduction to MongoDB drivers

Objectives

After studying this chapter, the reader will be able to understand the client-side and server-side concepts and learn the difference between the client and server. The reader will also learn the client- and server-side concepts in which a database like

MongoDB is involved. This chapter will also cover the MongoDB drivers and their uses, the programming languages that are currently supported by MongoDB, and the MongoDB community availability of drivers.

Client and server-side concepts

Before we move on to the programming part of this chapter and the book, let us define a few concepts related to the client and server.

Clients are those who send the requests to the server to perform specific tasks. The server receives the commands sent by the clients and performs the tasks. Once the tasks are executed and completed, the server sends the results back to the client.

There are many different types of clients as well as servers. Each of them performs specific tasks. For example, there are Web servers and Web clients. A simple example of a Web server is Apache HTTP Web server, Microsoft IIS Web server, or NGINX Web server.

Similarly, we have Web clients, which we use every day on our PCs, laptops, mobiles, tablets, and so on. So, we might be able to realize that they are Web browsers such as Google Chrome, Microsoft Edge, Mozilla Firefox, Mac Safari, Opera, and many more.

So what happens here? You will type some URL of a website that you would like to visit, like "**https://bpbonline.com**", which is one of the best places to buy online IT and technology books. When you type the URL in the browser, the browser acts as a client and sends this request to the Web server on which the website of BPB Publication is running. The Web server accepts this request from the client and executes it at its end, and after that, it passes the request back as an HTML page that the browser understands easily, as shown in *figure 1.1*.

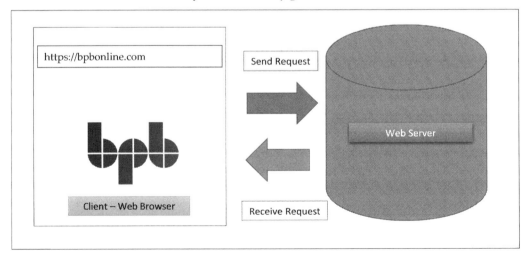

Figure 1.1: Client–server architecture

Now, let us understand this example in a more interesting manner.

So, you visit the BPB Publication Online website by typing the URL "**https://bpbonline.com**" on your browser. Now, you want to purchase a book, and you go to the shopping cart of the website, pay the amount, and you are done. During all these steps, your client (who is your browser) and the server (on which the BPB Publication Online website is hosted) have been communicating with each other. This is the one side of the coin.

Now, let us understand what could be happening on the server-side. As you know, e-commerce websites and portals like "BPB Publication Online" run with some sophisticated technologies, and those websites are dynamic. Here, dynamic means that the content and the features on these websites keep changing as new book titles arrive every week or every day. These websites update their content instantly. You are lucky sometimes when you reach these websites during a discount period or promotional offer.

A few questions here are how do these dynamic things happen? Is something happening at only the Web server end?

The answer is No! The Web server cannot alone do such dynamic things without the help of other technologies. The internet consists of different types of technology. Each website is unique in terms of its technology stack.

To run these dynamic portals and websites, server-side programming languages such as PHP, Node JS (a server-side JavaScript environment), and Python are used. There are many other server-side programming languages available such as Java, C#, ASP.NET (.NET framework), and **Ruby on Rails (RoR)**, but for this chapter and the upcoming chapters, we will be using examples from programming languages such as PHP, JavaScript (Node JS), and Python only.

Where was MongoDB until now? Few of us are now thinking about where MongoDB or any other database fits in the client-server picture.

Let us now understand the client and server concept in terms of database.

Client and server-side DB concepts

In the previous section, we have understood what client and server are in general terms. Now, let us move one step ahead and understand the concept of client and server where the database like MongoDB acts like a server.

MongoDB is a database server, as you all know. It also executes the requests that it receives from the clients. As a browser, it acts as a Web client for a Web server. We have MongoDB clients like MongoDB Compass, which is the official client for MongoDB, and a few others like Robo 3T that are helpful in connecting to the MongoDB server.

Whenever you install MongoDB on any OS, you need some client to connect and talk to the MongoDB Server. So, MongoDB client is a program that helps us to connect and perform various operations like the execution of the MongoDB queries and DB operations.

If you remember, we have used MongoDB Shell many times in the previous chapters, and also, we have learned about MongoDB Compass in the last chapter of that book. These are MongoDB clients who are used to connect and communicate with the MongoDB server. Here, the MongoDB client requests the MongoDB server to execute some query or command, and this is somewhat a similar manner in which a Web client requests a Web server to deliver some Web page or URL, as shown in *figure 1.2*.

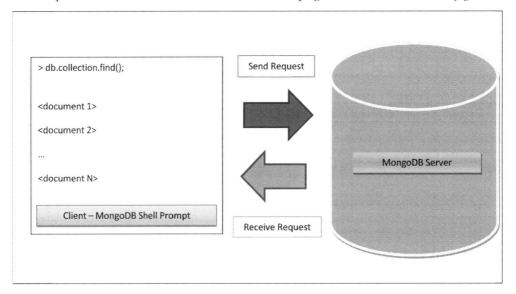

Figure 1.2: *Client–server DB architecture*

But many of you may still be thinking about how the dynamic websites and portals work with databases like MongoDB to present the dynamic data on the Web as we are not using these clients on the websites. Actually, this happens with the help of server-side programming languages such as PHP, Node JS, or Python. These programming languages have built-in drives which interact with MongoDB on the server-side.

In the next section, we will be learning about the MongoDB drivers, and later we will cover the MongoDB drivers for programming languages.

Introduction to MongoDB drivers

Database drivers are client-side libraries that are used to connect and communicate with databases. In our scenario, the MongoDB drivers work as if they are software libraries that run from the client-side and communicate with the MongoDB server. The purpose of the drivers is to provide the interface between the client-side environment and MongoDB server.

The client-side environment varies according to the programming languages they use. Any MongoDB client which interacts with the MongoDB server does this with the help of drivers. Even MongoDB Shell, which uses JavaScript language for querying the database, uses drivers to connect to the MongoDB server.

So, whether it is any desktop-based application such as MongoDB Compass, Command, shell-based application like Mongo Shell, website which is developed using MongoDB as a database server, or any mobile application which uses REST APIs to communicate with MongoDB database via some backend process, all of these use drivers, which act as an interpreter between them and MongoDB server, as shown in *figure 1.3*.

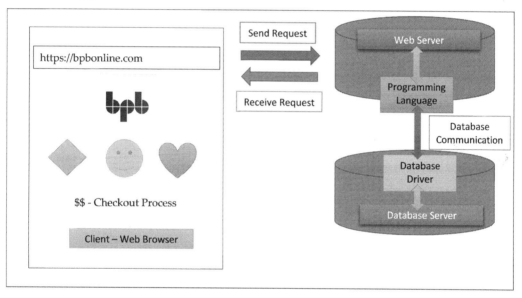

Figure 1.3: *Client-server DB architecture—programming languages and database drivers—communication and interactions*

Any application or website that interacts with MongoDB can do this using some programming language such as PHP, Node JS, or Python, and these programming languages then interact with MongoDB using their own drivers.

Every programming language has its own MongoDB drivers to connect and communicate with the MongoDB server. MongoDB supports all major programming languages, and the list is huge. You can visit the MongoDB drivers page to view the list of all the drivers' libraries for programming languages that are supported officially by MongoDB Inc., as shown in *figure 1.4*.

For more details, visit: **https://docs.mongodb.com/drivers/**

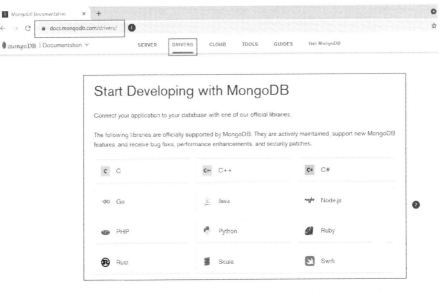

Figure 1.4: *MongoDB drivers—list of officially supported drivers libraries*

MongoDB also supports more programming languages which are supported by the MongoDB community. If you are developing any application that is not listed on the official driver's page. In that case, you can look at the community page to check if your language is listed on the community page or not at: **https://docs.mongodb.com/drivers/community-supported-drivers**, as shown in *figure 1.5*.

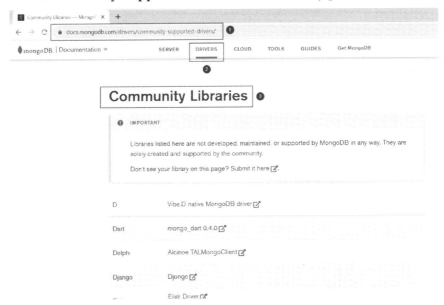

Figure 1.5: *MongoDB drivers – list of community-supported drivers libraries*

MongoDB drivers for programming languages (PHP, JavaScript, and Python)

Before we start with the programming part, please note that in order to use MongoDB with these programming languages, you must have a workable environment ready so that you can easily run the examples provided in the further chapters, which are related to programming and application development.

We will be covering the step-by-step method for each programming language, PHP, Node JS, and Python, in the upcoming chapters, by first creating the right environment on our machines to run the practical examples of the programming.

Conclusion

In this chapter, we have learned about the concepts related to client-side and server-side and how the interactions happen between them. We have also learned these concepts in relation to the databases like MongoDB and how the dynamic sites that use the databases like MongoDB work. In the last section of this chapter, we have covered the MongoDB drivers and the programming languages that are currently supported by MongoDB and also the MongoDB community drivers. In the upcoming chapter of this book, we will use MongoDB Compass to create a database and collection, and insert some dummy data using MongoDB Compass, which will help us to work with different programming languages, such as PHP, Node.js, React Native, and Python, used along with MongoDB in this book.

Questions

1. What do you understand by client-side and server-side? Give some examples.

2. Is the browser a client-side or server-side application?

3. What do you think the websites which are dynamic in nature use to present the dynamic content?

4. How does MongoDB fit in terms of client and server concepts, and how does the communication happen?

5. What are database drivers?

6. List some programming languages which have official MongoDB driver support.

CHAPTER 2
Data Addition Using MongoDB Compass

Before we start with the real programming and software-related part using MongoDB and programming languages, we need some data to start with. In this chapter, we will be doing some data entry using MongoDB Compass after creating the database and collection using MongoDB Compass so that we can have some real data to work with, in our upcoming chapters.

Structure

In this chapter, we will discuss the following topics:

- MongoDB Compass
- Launching MongoDB Compass and connecting to MongoDB server using MongoDB Compass
- Creating a MongoDB database and collection using MongoDB Compass
- Data addition using MongoDB Compass (creating some documents in our MongoDB collection)

Objectives

After studying this chapter, the reader will be able to enter some data in the MongoDB database, which we will require before we start with our upcoming chapters related to programming and software development. In this chapter, we will be using the MongoDB Official GUI, which is MongoDB Compass, to add some real data (adding some documents) in the MongoDB Collection.

About MongoDB Compass

MongoDB Compass is the **Graphical User Interface** (**GUI**) tool that helps us to connect with the MongoDB server very easily and do a lot of things using GUI that takes a lot of time if we do them via commands or queries. MongoDB Compass also provides many features that are helpful in visualizing the data, as well as manipulating the data in the collections. MongoDB Compass is more than a visual GUI client or data manipulation tool.

MongoDB Compass has been explained in a step-by-step manner starting from how to install it and how to use it in the BPB Publications book titled—"*MongoDB Complete Guide*" written by *Manu Sharma*. In case you want to understand MongoDB basics and MongoDB Compass basics, you can refer to the book mentioned.

Note
1. This current book assumes that the reader has a basic knowledge of MongoDB and MongoDB Compass.

2. It also assumes that MongoDB and MongoDB Compass has been already installed on the reader's machine.

3. As this is an advanced book, covering the basics is out of the scope of this book.

Launching MongoDB Compass and connecting to MongoDB server using MongoDB Compass

Let us now try to connect to MongoDB using MongoDB Compass from your Windows machine. To connect to MongoDB from your Windows machine, you can follow these steps:

1. Click Search Area of your Task Bar and type "**Compass**". You will see that the Compass app will appear along with the details. Click **Open,** or you can open it using the **Run as Administrator**. This will open MongoDB Compass with administrative privileges, as shown in *figure 2.1*.

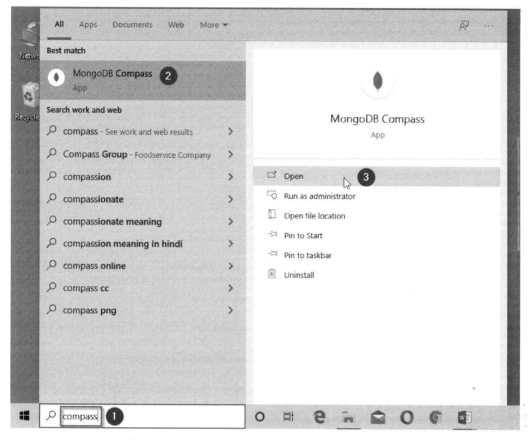

Figure 2.1: *MongoDB Compass—open MongoDB Compass*

2. For a new connection, click the link in the MongoDB Compass GUI Interface under the New Connection link, which says `Fill in connection fields individually,` as shown in *figure 2.2.*

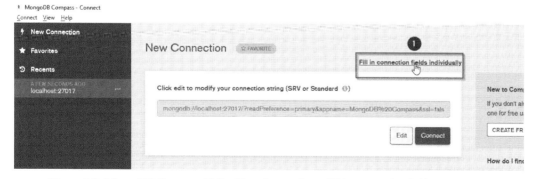

Figure 2.2: *MongoDB Compass GUI—New Connection—fill in connection fields individually*

3. Now, enter Hostname as "`localhost`", Port as "`27017`" (Default Settings), and click the **Connect** button to connect to the MongoDB server, as shown in *figure 2.3*.

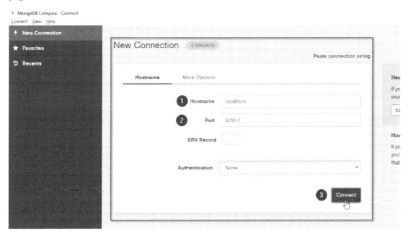

Figure 2.3: *MongoDB Compass GUI—connect to MongoDB Server using default settings*

Creating a MongoDB database and collection using MongoDB Compass

Let us now try to create a MongoDB database and collection using MongoDB Compass so that we can add our data to the MongoDB collection (adding new documents). To create a MongoDB database and collection using MongoDB Compass, you can follow these steps:

1. Once you are connected to the MongoDB server, you can see the button on the top section of the MongoDB Compass GUI, which says "**CREATE DATABASE**". Click this button as shown in *figure 2.4*.

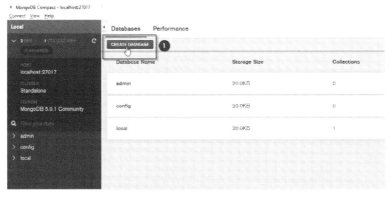

Figure 2.4: *MongoDB Compass GUI—create database*

2. Once you click the "**CREATE DATABASE**" button, it will open a new popup window to add the details. In the "`Database Name`" field, type "**BPBOnlineBooksDB**", and in the "`Collection Name`" field, type "**BPBOnlineBooksCollection**", and then click "`Create Database`", as shown in *figure 2.5*.

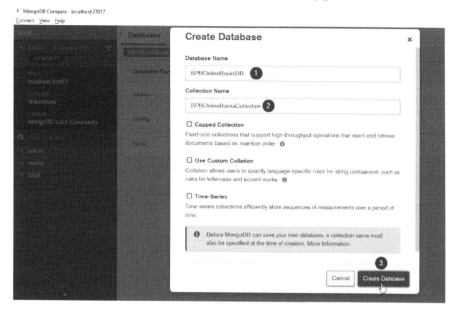

Figure 2.5: *MongoDB Compass GUI—create database popup window*

3. Once you click the "`Create Database`" button with the required details as mentioned in the previous step, you will see that your MongoDB database, as well as collection, has been successfully created by MongoDB Compass, as shown in *figure 2.6*.

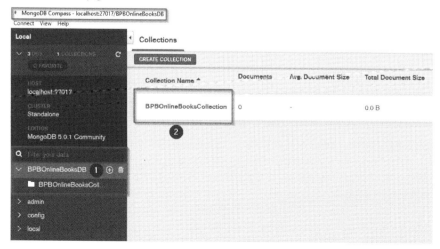

Figure 2.6: *MongoDB Compass GUI—MongoDB database and collection is created successfully*

Data addition using MongoDB Compass (creating some documents in our MongoDB collection)

Let us now try to add our data to the MongoDB Collection (adding new documents). To add new data to the database, we need to create documents in our collection. Let us take an example of some books published by BPB Publications and add their details to the MongoDB database using the following table, which contains the list of books and their details:

Book Title	Book Author	Book ISBN	Book Pages	Book Brief Description
MongoDB Complete Guide	Manu Sharma	9789389898866	470	Master MongoDB—the widely used modern database in a step-by-step, practical, and easy-to-understand approach covering all major topics.
Redis® Deep Dive	Suyog Dilip Kale, Chinmay Kulkarni	9788194837763	228	This book begins with teaching you to set up your own Redis environment, followed by Redis data structures, their architecture, and use cases.
ITIL® 2011 The Story Continues	Dr. Pratul Sharma	9789388176736	82	This book describes the ITIL service lifecycle and standards for service design and development. An explanation is given in untraditional layman's language, with easy-to-follow examples and Explores issues of creating and maintaining value for clients through monitoring.
Decoding JavaScript	Rushabh Mulraj Shah	9789390684816	370	Mastering advanced JavaScript to build modern next-generation Web applications.

Book Title	Book Author	Book ISBN	Book Pages	Book Brief Description
Python In-Depth	Ahidjo Ayeva, Kamon Ayeva, Aiman Saed	9789389328424	364	"Python In-Depth" gives you a detailed presentation of the possibilities for solving everyday problems, even complex ones using Python.
Designing User Interfaces	Dario Calonaci	9789389898743	230	Think about UIs using design thinking principles from an award-winning graphic designer.
Advanced Web Development with React	Mehul Mohan	9789389423594	204	The book starts by introducing the reader to react, what it is, and why you need a library like react to work with medium to large scale applications.

Table 2.1: *Sample data to be added into MongoDB database*
(data for creating the MongoDB documents in MongoDB collection)

Now, let us do some data entry using MongoDB Compass. MongoDB Compass gives us various ways to insert the data using JSON, CSV, or manual data entry.

1. Click the link, and this shows the **Collection Name** to add the documents into this **Collections** as shown in *figure 2.7*.

Figure 2.7: *MongoDB Compass GUI—collection link*

2. Once you are into the collection, you will see the option to add new data. Click the drop-down button which says "**Add Data**", and then select the "**Insert Document**" to add data manually in this step. We will check the JSON method too in our next steps, as shown in *figure 2.8*.

Figure 2.8: *MongoDB Compass GUI—Collection—Add data*

3. Once you click the drop-down button that says "**Add Data**" and then select the "**Insert Document**" to add data, it will open a popup window to add the data manually. We will select **List View** instead of Code View to add the Data and will keep Document ID Value "_id" as it is, which is generated by default by MongoDB. Just hover over the "_id" field and click the plus symbol "+" to add a new record, as shown in *figure 2.9*.

Figure 2.9: *MongoDB Compass GUI—Collection—Add Data*

4. We will be keeping the following structure of the document fields (key and values), and we will take the values from *table 2.1* to add these values. Let us first define the keys of our document. Refer to the following table (*Table 2.2*).

Key using the Heading from Table 2.1 (Row 1 Example)	Value from the respective data using Table 2.1 (Row 1 Example)
Book-title	MongoDB Complete Guide
Book-author	Manu Sharma
Book-ISBN	9789389898866
Book-pages	470
Book-brief-description	Master MongoDB—the widely used modern database in a step-by-step, practical, and easy-to-understand approach covering all major topics

Table 2.2: *Add sample data referring to Table 2.1 using MongoDB Compass*

5. Now, in this step, we will be referring to the key-value pairs from *table 2.2* and will use the Plus symbol to add all the data. After you are done with all the fields (key-value pairs), you can click the "**Insert**" button to add the data to the MongoDB Collection. This will result in creating the new MongoDB document under the collection (as shown in *figure 2.10*).

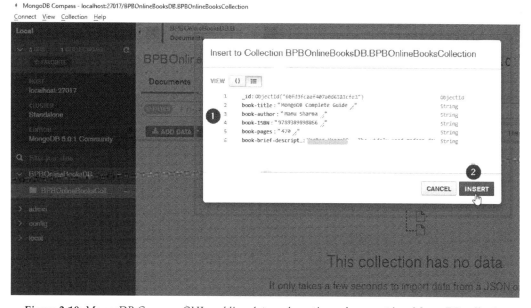

Figure 2.10: *MongoDB Compass GUI—adding data and creating a document in a MongoDB collection*

6. After the data is entered as described in the previous step, we can see the whole document in the MongoDB collection. You can insert all seven documents in *table 2.1* like we added the first record. But, in case you would like to try the JSON method, you can delete this document and use the JSON method explained in the next steps, as shown in *figure 2.11*.

Figure 2.11: MongoDB Compass GUI—adding data and creating a document in a MongoDB collection

7. You can use the below JSON to add all seven documents at once. Copy the following JSON code. From the collection area of MongoDB Compass, select **Add Data**. Now, instead of list view, we will use the code view to copy and paste the following data into the database:

```
[{
  "_id": {
    "$oid": "60fd3fcaaf407a0d6383cfe3"
  },
  "book-title": "MongoDB Complete Guide",
  "book-author": "Manu Sharma",
  "book-ISBN": "9789389898866",
  "book-pages": "470",
  "book-brief-description": "Master MongoDB - The widely used modern database in a step-by-step,  practical, and easy-to-understand approach covering all major topics"
},{
```

```
 "_id": {

  "$oid": "60fd485daf407a0d6383cfe4"

 },

 "book-title": "Redis® Deep Dive",

 "book-author": "Suyog Dilip Kale, Chinmay Kulkarni»,

 "book-ISBN": "9788194837763",

 "book-pages": "228",

   "book-brief-description":  "This   book  begins   with   teach-
ing  you  to  set  up  your  own  Redis  environment,  followed  by  Re-
dis data structures, their architecture, and use cases"

 },{

 "_id": {

  "$oid": "60fd4975af407a0d6383cfe6"

 },

 "book-title": "ITIL® 2011 The Story Continues",

 "book-author": "Dr. Pratul Sharma»,

 "book-ISBN": "9789388176736",

 "book-pages": "82",

 "book-brief-description": "Describes  the  ITIL  service  lifecy-
cle  and  standards  for  service  design  and  development An  explana-
tion  is  given  in  untraditional  Layman's  language,  with  easy  to  fol-
low  examples  Explores  issues  of  creating  and  maintaining  val-
ue for clients through monitoring"

 },{

 "_id": {

  "$oid": "60fd49cdaf407a0d6383cfe7"

 },

 "book-title": "Decoding JavaScript",

 "book-author": "Rushabh Mulraj Shah»,

 "book-ISBN": "9789390684816",
```

```
  "book-pages": "370",

    "book-brief-description":    "Mastering    advanced    JavaS-
cript to build modern next-generation web applications."

},{

 "_id": {

  "$oid": "60fd4a12af407a0d6383cfe8"

 },

 "book-title": "Python In - Depth",

 "book-author": "Ahidjo Ayeva, Kamon Ayeva, Aiman Saed",

 "book-ISBN": "9789389328424",

 "book-pages": "364",

 "book-brief-description": ""Python In-Depth" gives you a de-
tailed  presentation  of  the  possibilities  for  solving  every-
day problems, even complex ones using Python."

},{

 "_id": {

  "$oid": "60fd4a59af407a0d6383cfe9"

 },

 "book-title": "Designing User Interfaces",

 "book-author": "Dario Calonaci",

 "book-ISBN": "9789389898743",

 "book-pages": "230",

 "book-brief-description": "Think  about  UIs  using  design  think-
ing principles from an award-winning graphic designer"

},{

 "_id": {

  "$oid": "60fd4ab8af407a0d6383cfea"

 },

 "book-title": "Advanced Web Development with React",
```

```
"book-author": "Mehul Mohan",

"book-ISBN": "9789389423594",

"book-pages": "204",

  "book-brief-description": "The  Book  Starts  By  Introduc-
ing The Reader To React, What It Is And Why You Need A Li-
brary Like React To Work With Medium To Large Scale Applications."

}]
```

8. Click the "**Insert**" button as shown in *figure 2.12*.

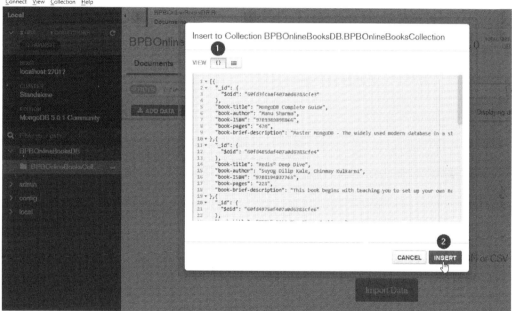

Figure 2.12: MongoDB Compass GUI—adding data and creating multiple documents in a MongoDB collection using JSON method.

9. After you click the "**Insert**" button in the previous step, you will see all the seven documents inserted in the collection using the JSON method, as shown in *figure 2.13*.

Figure 2.13: MongoDB Compass GUI — collection — add data using JSON method — added multiple documents

Conclusion

In this chapter, we have entered some real data in the MongoDB database. We have used MongoDB Compass to add some data (adding some documents) in the MongoDB Collection using Manual and with JSON method. In the upcoming chapter, we will start with the basic programming with PHP and MongoDB, where we will be learning how we set up the necessary environment to use PHP with MongoDB and how we can use PHP programming language to connect with MongoDB.

Questions

1. What is MongoDB Compass?

2. Give an example to connect to MongoDB server using MongoDB Compass.

3. Write the steps to create MongoDB collection.

4. How can you create a MongoDB document in the collection using MongoDB Compass?

5. Is it possible to add multiple documents using MongoDB Compass?

## CHAPTER 3

Starting Up Programming with MongoDB and PHP

PHP is one of the widely used programming languages, many of the open sources are built with PHP, and it is one of the most popular languages used for Web development, so in this chapter, we will cover the introduction to PHP Programming with MongoDB. We are going to learn how we can use PHP with MongoDB. We will also learn how to set up MongoDB with PHP and WAMP server. As we move on to the last section of this chapter, we will be doing some coding and running practical examples to connect and work with MongoDB Server using PHP.

Structure

In this chapter, we will discuss the following topics:

- Using PHP with MongoDB
- Installing WAMP server and setting up the environment for PHP
- Setting Up Mongo DB with PHP and WAMP server
- Connecting and working with MongoDB Server using PHP

Objectives

After studying this chapter, the reader will be able to understand how to use PHP with MongoDB. This chapter will cover the installation of the WAMP server and set up the environment ready for PHP programming with MongoDB. Later in this chapter reader will also learn about how to connect and work with MongoDB Server using PHP programmatically.

Using PHP with MongoDB

PHP is a widely used and one of the most popular server-side programming languages, and it has been around 25 years now since its first version came. A lot of open-source software and projects are developed in PHP, which includes WordPress, Drupal, Joomla, Magento, and many more.

There are many different ways to run PHP with MongoDB on various operating systems such as Windows, Linux, and Mac OS. To cover them all is out of the scope of this chapter and book. But we are going to use some easiest methods by which we can have our environment ready to work with PHP and MongoDB. Let us start with some steps so that we are able to run our codes with PHP and MongoDB.

Installing WAMP server on Windows operating system

WAMP server is a software stack available for Windows operating system. It is one of the widely used software which is useful in installing PHP, Apache Web Server, and MySQL database. We are not using the MySQL database in this book, but we will be adding the MongoDB extension with the WAMP server and using it instead of MySQL. The only reason that we are using WAMP is that it is simple to install and use, and we do not have to install PHP and Apache Web servers separately as the WAMP server installs them both. Also, it is easier to manage this software using the WAMP server.

We will be using the default installation method to install the WAMP server on the machines that will run Windows operating system. For this chapter, we are using Windows operating system. If you want to use other operating systems such as Linux or Mac OS; in that case, you can set up your environment with the help of other stack software such as XAMPP (for Linux operating system) and MAMP (for Mac operating system).

The following are the links for various stacks available for different operating systems:

- For Windows OS: WAMP Stack: **https://www.wampserver.com/**
- For Linux OS: XAMPP Stack: **https://www.apachefriends.org/**
- For Mac OS: MAMP Stack: **https://www.mamp.info/**

We will show you how to install WAMP on Windows operating system.

Installation steps

Let us start with the installation of the WAMP stack on our machine. The following are the steps that are required to be performed to install the WAMP stack or WAMP server:

Step 1—Download WAMP server

1. Open the WAMP server official website—**https://www.wampserver.com/** in your favorite browser, click the download link. This will take you to the download screen where you have two options available, one is for 64 Bit operating system, and another one is for 32 Bit operating system. Click the one based on your machine architecture, as shown in *figure 3.1*.

Figure 3.1: *WAMP server official website home page*

2. Once the download starts, you can easily see the download process with the download icon and progress on your browser, as shown in *figure 3.2*.

This progress shows differently in every browser. The screenshot is from Google:

Figure 3.2: *WAMP server download screen—download progress*

3. Once the download is 100% completed, you can follow the next steps. (As shown in *figure 3.3*.)

   In Step 1, we have covered how to download the WAMP server from the official website, and the next steps are related to the Installation Process, so we have covered this separately in step 2 of the WAMP server Installation Process.

Step 2—install WAMP server on your Windows machine

Once the download is complete and the installer file is fully downloaded, it will show a download complete icon as shown in *figure 3.3*, and you can proceed further.

Figure 3.3: *WAMP server download screen—download 100% complete—next steps*

1. Now, open this installer file, and it will start the WAMP server setup wizard, which will guide you to complete the installation of the WAMP server in your machine, as shown in *figure 3.4*.

Figure 3.4: *WAMP server download screen—download 100% complete—open installer file*

2. Now, open this installer file, and it will start the WAMP server setup wizard, which will guide you to complete the installation of the WAMP server in your machine. We are not going to cover all steps here as it is out of scope for this chapter. Please follow the setup process, and it will install the WAMP server on your Windows machine, as shown in *figure 3.5*. Also, during the installation process, the setup will ask you to accept the license agreement. It is recommended to read the license agreement and other terms and conditions.

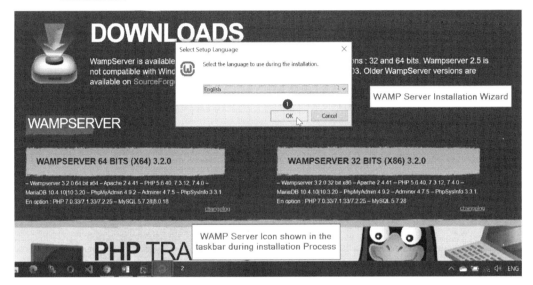

Figure 3.5: WAMP server setup wizard

3. The installer will ask you to select components that are different versions of the software, such as PHP, MySQL, MariaDB, and so on. If you wish, you can install any latest versions. But, it is recommended to go with the default installation, as shown in *figure 3.6*.

***Figure 3.6**: WAMP server setup wizard—selecting components*

4. Once the installation is 100% complete, click the "**Finish**" button to exit the Setup Wizard, as shown in *figure 3.7*.

***Figure 3.7**: WAMP server setup wizard—installation complete*

Step 3—starting and using the WAMP server on your Windows machine

Once the installation is done, you should start the WAMP server by typing "**wamp**" on the search area of the taskbar and opening the WAMP server, which will launch the WAMP server on your Windows machine, as shown in *figure 3.8*.

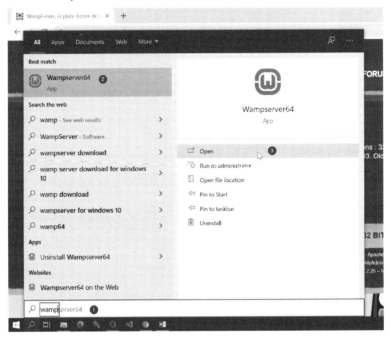

Figure 3.8: Launching WAMP server

1. Once the WAMP server has been successfully started, you will see the WAMP server icon (in green) in the Task Bar tray. When you run the WAMP server, it usually takes a few seconds to start all the services such as Apache, MySQL, and so on, and the icon changes from red to orange and finally green. If the WAMP icon is green, it means that all the services have been successfully started, and now you can use the WAMP server, as shown in *figure 3.9*.

Figure 3.9: WAMP server—all services have been started successfully

2. You can click on the green icon, and it will open up a small menu that has a lot of options from where you can do many things like starting/stopping/restarting the WAMP server, changing the settings of PHP, Apache Server, and so on. We are not going to cover all these in this chapter as this is out of the scope of this chapter. If you wish, you can explore these settings from your machine, as shown in *figure 3.10*.

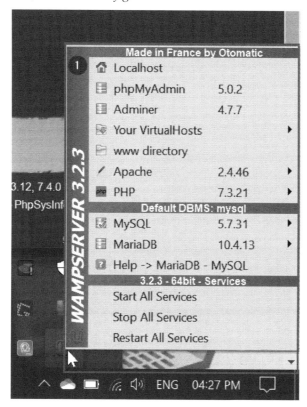

Figure 3.10: WAMP server menu with a lot of options

Step 4—running localhost

Once the WAMP server has started on your machine, you can now start working with the local server, which has Apache and PHP installed. So, as we have the required environment ready, we can run localhost.

1. To run localhost, just open your favorite browser like Google Chrome and type: **http://localhost/** and press *Enter*. This will open up a new page, and you will be shown the WAMP server page default page on your localhost. Here, you will get all the information about the version of the WAMP server, server configurations that have a list of various software running in the

background, along with their version details such as Apache Web Server and PHP, as shown in *figure 3.11*.

Figure 3.11: *WAMP server — localhost*

If you are able to see this page, it means that most of the things which are required to start the application development with PHP are ready except MongoDB, which we will cover in our next step.

Step 5—setting up MongoDB extension with PHP

In this step, we are going to set up the MongoDB extension with PHP. There are different ways to do it. Some methods prefer doing this with "*Composer*", which is the Dependency Manager for PHP, but we will do it the other way. Please follow the following steps to set up the MongoDB extension with PHP.

1. Open **PHP Extension Community Library (PECL)** home page for MongoDB in your favorite browser by entering the URL: **https://pecl.php.net/package/ mongodb** in your browser address bar. This will open up the PECL MongoDB home page. Browse the latest available stable version of the extension and click the DLL link just after the Windows icon, as shown in *figure 3.12*.

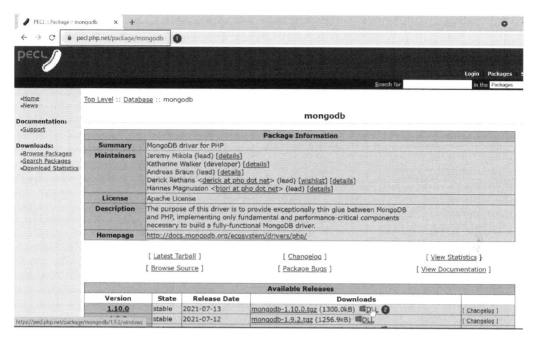

Figure 3.12: PECL MongoDB home page

2. This will open a new page that will have the DLL lists available for various PHP versions. As we are running PHP 7.3 with WAMP, we will be downloading that. The other option we should be checking here is the *"Thread Safe"* and *"Machine Architecture"*. Machine Architecture can be 32 Bit or 64 Bit which depends on your computer hardware. If you want to check if Thread Safety is enabled in your PHP version, you can open the command prompt and then navigate to your PHP folder, which is similar to "**D:\wamp64\bin\php\php7.3.21**" and run the following command as shown in *figure 3.13*.

```
php -i|findstr "Thread"
```

You may also check the same from the **phpinfo()** under the Tools section of your WAMP localhost home page, where you will get all the details related to PHP installed on your system.

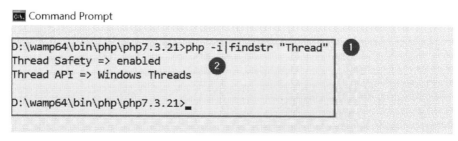

Figure 3.13: Checking thread safe

3. After you click the right DLL file, the download will start, and after the download gets finished, you should open this ZIP file and extract the DLL from the ZIP file. After that, you should copy this DLL file in the extension directory of your PHP version (in our case, as we are running PHP version 7.3 on WAMP and WAMP is installed on D: drive), the location of the PHP extensions directory would be somewhat similar to: **D:\wamp64\bin\php\ php7.3.21\ext**. You can see a lot of other DLL files present in this folder, as shown in *figure 3.14*.

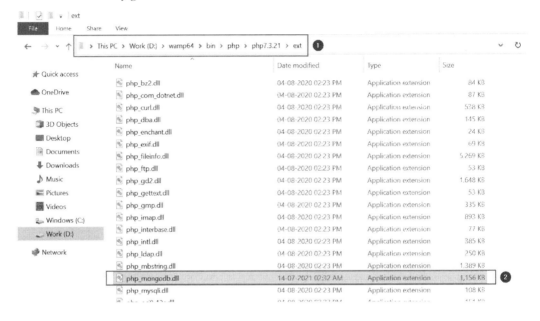

Figure 3.14: *Copying PHP MongoDB extension DLL to PHP extensions directory on WAMP*

4. Once you are done with this step, go to the WAMP server manager by clicking the WAMP server green icon in your Windows taskbar tray and then navigate to the PHP menu and click **php.ini**. This will open the **php.ini** file in which we are going to add the following line under the PHP extensions section, as shown in *figure 3.15*.

```
extension=php_mongodb
```

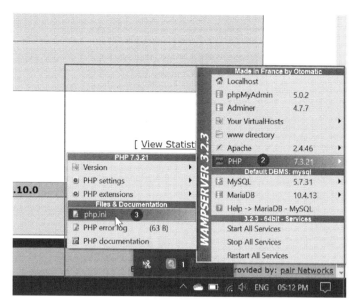

Figure 3.15: Opening *php.ini* file

5. The previous step will open the **php.ini** file. Navigate to the PHP extension section of this file and add the line mentioned in the previous step. After that, save this file. You may enter this line towards the end or anywhere in the extension section of this file. In our example, we have just added this after the MySQL extension, as shown in *figure 3.16*.

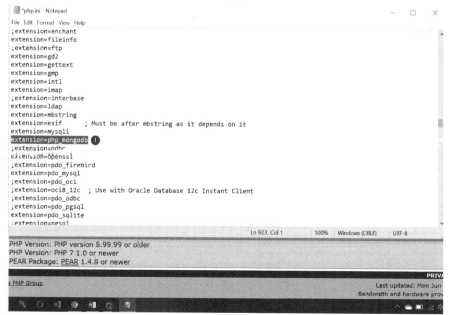

Figure 3.16: Adding MongoDB extension to php.ini file

6. After you added the MongoDB extension code in the **php.ini** file and saved it, close this file and go to the WAMP server manager by clicking the green icon on the Windows taskbar tray and restart all the services. It will take a few seconds for WAMP to restart all the services, as shown in *figure 3.17*.

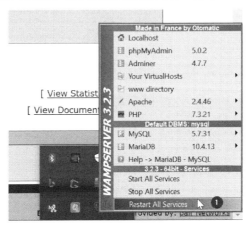

Figure 3.17: *WAMP—restarting all services*

7. After WAMP has finished restarting all the services, open the WAMP home page from your browser and scroll to the tools section which is at the end of the page. Click **phpinfo()**. This will open up a new page with the details of PHP. Scroll to the middle of the page, where you will see the details of the PHP extensions. You will see now that the MongoDB extension has been installed and set up for PHP, as shown in *figure 3.18*.

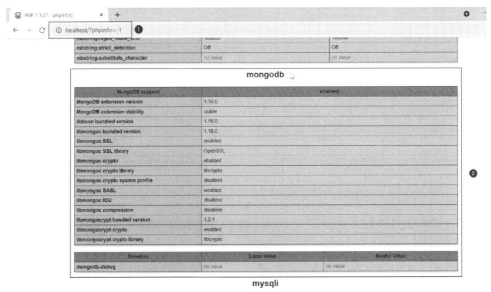

Figure 3.18: *phpinfo()—MongoDB extension*

As we are done with the setup of our environment with MongoDB and PHP, we will now start the programming part.

Programming with PHP and MongoDB

In the previous section of this chapter, we have set up our environment to run PHP with MongoDB. Now, let us start our programming part. Before we start with the programming and coding part, let us do one more thing as you have been doing progress from the previous chapter. We always started MongoDB with the command prompt. Now, as you have understood the basic concepts, you can now automate a few things, including the MongoDB server starting. In Windows operating systems, whenever you install MongoDB, the installer creates MongoDB service automatically, and you can start or stop the MongoDB server using Windows service manager.

Let us start MongoDB using Windows service manager.

Starting MongoDB server from Windows service manager

To start MongoDB using Windows service manager, follow these steps:

1. In the search section of your Task Bar, type "**services**" and open it, as shown in *figure 3.19*.

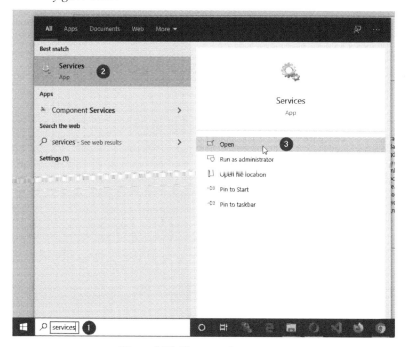

Figure 3.19: Open services manager

2. This will open Windows services manager. You will see all the services that are installed on your Windows machine. Navigate to MongoDB Server (MongoDB). Click this service and start it (in case it is not yet started), or you may leave this step if it is already started, as shown in *figure 3.20*.

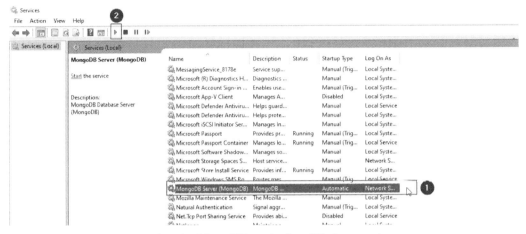

Figure 3.20: Starting MongoDB service from Windows service manager

Now comes the programming part. Let us now try to write a code in PHP that does the small task of connecting to the database. Here, we would be writing a small piece of code in PHP with the help of the PHP MongoDB extension, which we have installed and set up in our previous step.

Note that as we are using PHP and writing PHP code, it is recommended to use some code editor or **Integrated Development Environment** (**IDE**) like Microsoft Visual Studio Code. You can download and install Microsoft Visual Studio Code from this link: **https://code.visualstudio.com**.

Microsoft Visual Studio Code is open-source and free software and is available for almost all operating systems.

It is also recommended that you should create some folders under your WAMP www folder for this purpose and save your files under that folder. The path could be somewhat like this: **D:\wamp64\www\mongodb-examples,** as shown in *figure 3.21*.

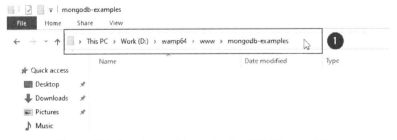

Figure 3.21: Creating a folder under the WAMP www folder

Example 1—connecting to MongoDB Server using PHP

In our example, we have used the "**$mongoDBClientConnection**" variable, which is assigned as an object for the "**MongoClient()**" class. We have saved this file as "**mongodb-connection.php**" under the path: **D:\wamp64\www\mongodb-examples**. The following *figure 3.22* shows the code for the same.

Code 1

```php
<?php

    $mongoDBClientConnection = new MongoDB\Driver\Manager("mongodb://localhost:27017");


  echo "We have Successfully Connected to MongoDB Server using PHP";

?>
```

The following is the screenshot for the same in Visual Studio Code:

Figure 3.22: *Working with PHP files using Microsoft Visual Studio Code*

Now, let us run this example. Open your browser and type **http://localhost/mongodb-examples/mongodb-connection.php**. You will see we have connected successfully to the MongoDB server using PHP, as shown in *figure 3.23*.

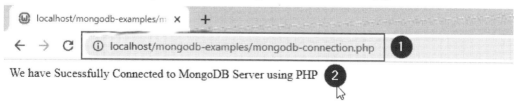

Figure 3.23: *Localhost—connecting to MongoDB Server using PHP*

Example 2—fetching MongoDB Documents using PHP

In our example, we have used the "**$mongoDBClientConnection**" variable, which is assigned as an object for the "**MongoClient()**" class, and then we have used the "**$query**" object, which is an instance of the MongoDB Query class. Then, we pass this object in the "**executeQuery**" method as a second parameter. The first parameter of this method is the <Database-Name>.<Collection-Name>. We have saved this file as "**fetching-documents.php**" under the path: **D:\wamp64\www\ mongodb-examples**. The following is the code for the same:

Code 1

```php
<?php
    $mongoDBClientConnection = new MongoDB\Driver\Manager("mongodb://
localhost:27017");

  echo 'We have Sucessfully Connected to MongoDB Server using PHP';

  echo '<hr />';

  $query = new MongoDB\Driver\Query([]);

    $rows = $mongoDBClientConnection->executeQuery("BPBOnlineBooksDB.
BPBOnlineBooksCollection", $query);

  foreach ($rows as $row) {
  echo $row->_id .' => '. $row->{'book-title'} . ' [By : '. $row->{'book-
author'} . ']';
  echo '<br />';

  }

?>
```

Now, let us run this example. Open your browser and type: **http://localhost/ mongodb-examples/fetching-documents.php**. You will see that we have connected successfully to the MongoDB server using PHP, and we have also got the documents from the collection, as shown in *figure 3.24*.

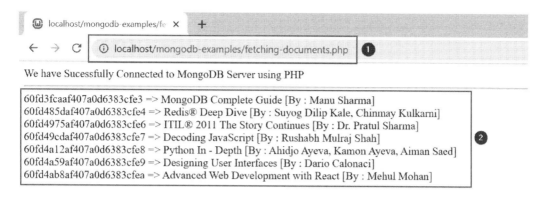

Figure 3.24: Localhost—connecting to MongoDB Server and fetching the documents from collection using PHP

Conclusion

In this chapter, we have covered the introduction to PHP programming with MongoDB. We have also learned that in order to run PHP with MongoDB server, we should have the right environment in place. We have learned how we can set up the right environment to run PHP codes. Later in this chapter, we have also learned what a WAMP server is and how to install a WAMP server. In the last section of this chapter, we have done some coding and run some practical examples to connect and work with the MongoDB server using PHP. In the upcoming chapter of this book, we will learn about Node.js and how we can use Node.js with the MongoDB database.

Questions

1. What is PHP?

2. List two most popular open-source software which runs on PHP.

3. What is WAMP?

4. How can we install PHP MongoDB Extension? Explain the process.

5. Give an example to connect to MongoDB server with PHP.

CHAPTER 4
Starting Up Programming with MongoDB and JavaScript (Node.js)

Node.js, which is based on JavaScript engine-based programming language, is the most happening programming language these days; many of the modern applications are running using Node.js. In this chapter, we will cover the introduction to JavaScript programming language, and then, we will learn Node.js programming with MongoDB and how we can use Node.js with MongoDB. This chapter covers how we can set up the right environment to run Node.js codes. Later in this chapter, we will be doing some coding and running some practical examples to connect and work with MongoDB Server using Node.js.

Structure

In this chapter, we will discuss the following topics:

- Using JavaScript (Node.js) with MongoDB

- Installing Node.js and setting up the environment for server-side JavaScript

- Installing and setting up the NPM MongoDB library

- Connecting and working with MongoDB server using Node.js

Objectives

After studying this chapter, the reader will be able to understand how to use Node.js with MongoDB. This chapter will also cover how to install Node.js and MongoDB driver for Node.js to set up the environment ready for development. Later in this chapter, we will be doing some coding and learning how to connect MongoDB using the Node.js official MongoDB Driver.

Using JavaScript (Node.js) with MongoDB

JavaScript is one of the most popular and widely used server-side as well as client-side programming languages, and its client-side variant has been around from the start of the internet. The server-side JavaScript has gained popularity among developers as well as software companies after the launch of Node.js in the year 2009. A lot of open-source software and projects are developed in Node.js, and it is the base framework or environment for many other frameworks like Express JS and as well as Full Stack frameworks like Meteor JS.

There are many different ways to run Node.js with MongoDB on various operating systems such as Windows, Linux, and Mac OS. To cover them all is out of the scope of this chapter and the book, but we are going to use some of the easiest and official methods by which we can have our environment ready to work with Node.js and MongoDB. Let us start with some steps so that we are able to run our codes with Node.js and MongoDB.

Installing Node.js on Windows operating system

Let us install Node.js on Windows operating system by following the step-by-step installation method.

Installation steps

Let us start with the installation of Node.js on our machine. Following are the steps that are required to be performed to install WAMP Stack or Node.js:

Step 1—download Node.js

1. Open the Node.js official website—**https://nodejs.org** in your favorite browser, browse to the middle section of the home page and click the download link, where you have two options available, one is recommended version, and another one is the latest version. For this chapter and book, we will download and install the recommended version, as shown in *figure 4.1*:

Figure 4.1: Node.js official website Home Page

2. Once the download starts, you can easily see the download process with the download icon and progress on your browser (this progress shows differently in every browser, the screenshot is of Google Chrome browser, every browser shows this in a different manner). You should wait till it is 100% complete, as shown in *figure 4.2*:

Figure 4.2: Node.js download screen—download progress

3. Once the download is 100% completed, you can follow the next steps (as shown in *figure 4.3*).

   In Step 1, we have covered how to download Node.js from the official website. The next steps are related to the installation process, so we have covered this separately in Step 2 of the Node.js installation process.

Step 2—install Node.js on your Windows machine.

Once the download is complete and the installer file is fully downloaded, it will show a download complete Icon (as shown in *figure 4.3*), and you can proceed further.

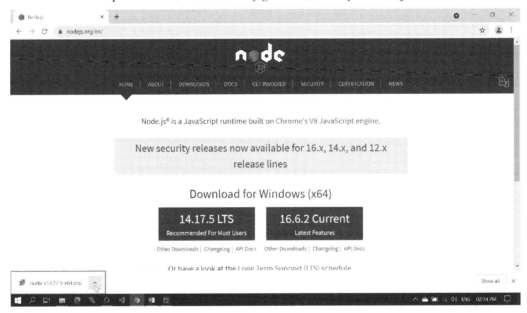

Figure 4.3: *Node.js download screen—download 100% Complete—next steps*

1. Now open this installer file, and it will start the Node.js setup wizard, with will guide you to complete the installation of Node.js in your machine, as shown in *figure 4.4*:

Figure 4.4: Node.js download screen—download 100% Complete—open installer file

2. Now open this installer file, and it will start the Node.js setup wizard, with will guide you to complete the installation of Node.js in your machine. We are not going to cover all steps here as it is out of the scope of this chapter. Please follow the setup process, and it will install Node.js on your Windows machine (as shown in *figure 4.5*). Also, during the installation process, the setup will ask you to accept the License Agreement. It is recommended to read the License Agreement and other Terms and Conditions.

Figure 4.5: Node.js setup wizard

3. The installer will ask you to select the installation location to install this software on your Windows machine and also give the list of other software like NPM package manager. If you want, you can change the installation location you can change it or else go with the default installation. But it is recommended to select all the other features by default. Also, it is recommended to install the tools for a native module that setup may ask you to install during the setup process, as shown in *figure 4.6*:

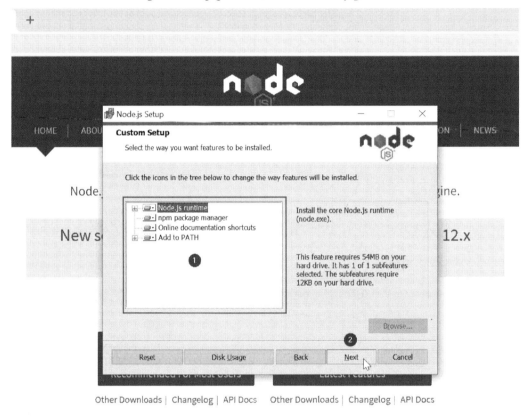

Figure 4.6: *Node.js setup wizard—selecting all the features*

4. You can optionally install the tools for a native module that setup may ask you to install during the setup process. You may install these tools later too by following the installation instructions from the URL: **https://github.com/ nodejs/node-gyp**, as shown in *figure 4.7*:

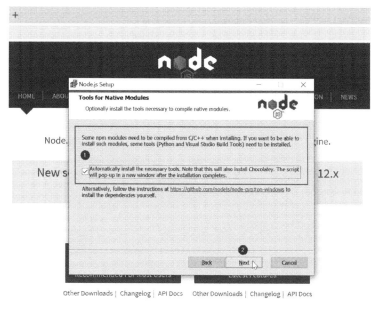

Figure 4.7: *Node.js setup wizard—tools for native modules*

5. Once the installation is 100% complete, click the "**Finish**" button to exit the Setup Wizard, as shown in *figure 4.8*:

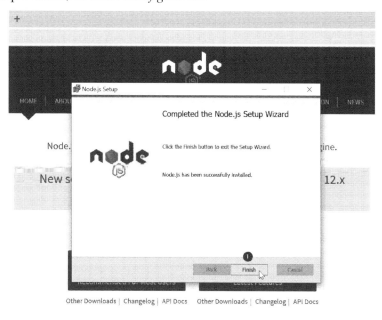

Figure 4.8: *Node.js setup wizard—installation complete*

Step 3—post-installation steps and verifying Node.js on your Windows machine

Once the installation is done, you should first verify Node.js and NPM (Node package manager or package manager for JavaScript programming language). In order to verify this two software on your Windows machine, open Command Prompt by typing "**cmd**" from the Search Bar located in the Taskbar, as shown in *figure 4.9*:

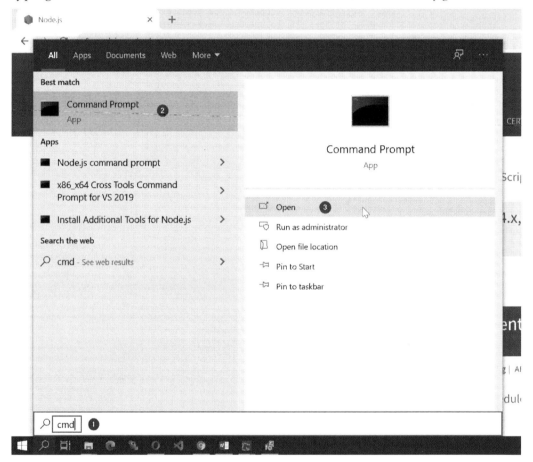

Figure 4.9: Post-installation verification steps for Node.js and NPM

6. Type the following two commands one by one to verify Node.js and NPM installation in the command prompt, as shown in *figure 4.10*:

    ```
    node --version

    npm --version
    ```

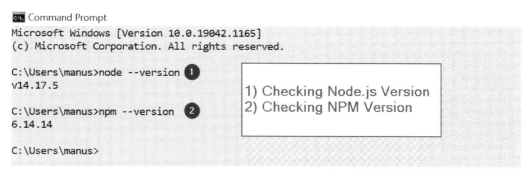

Figure 4.10: Command prompt—verifying Node.js and NPM version on Windows

As you can see, both Node.js and NPM have been correctly installed on your Windows machine. Now, we can start with the development part of this chapter and start to use MongoDB with Node.js. In the next section, we will cover how to use MongoDB with Node.js applications. But before that, there is one last step we have to follow before we code. It is covered in Step 4.

Step 4—installing the MongoDB driver for Node.js using NPM

Once Node.js and NPM have been correctly installed on your Windows machine; now, we can install the MongoDB Driver using **Node Package Manager** (**NPM**).

1. To install the official driver for MongoDB just open your favorite browser like Google Chrome and type: **https://www.npmjs.com/package/mongodb** and then press *Enter*. This will open up the official page for MongoDB on the NPM website, and you will be shown a lot of information about this driver, including how to install it using NPM and how to use it, as shown in *figure 4.11*:

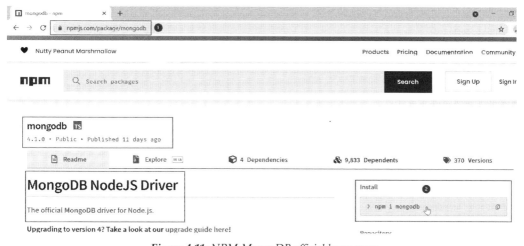

Figure 4.11: NPM MongoDB official home page

2. Now, as we know what is the right command to install the official MongoDB driver for Node.js, choose any location on your machine and create a new folder or directory named "**mongodb-nodejs**", as shown in *figure 4.12*:

Figure 4.12: Create a new directory named "mongodb-nodejs" on your Windows machine

3. Now open up your command prompt and navigate to this directory "**mongodb-nodejs**", as shown in *figure 4.13*:

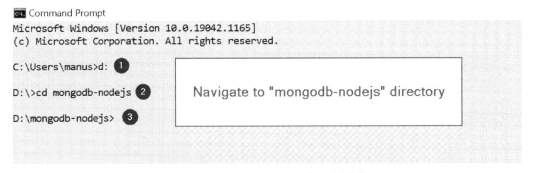

Figure 4.13: Navigating to "mongodb-nodejs" directory

4. Now run any of the following commands that have been mentioned on the MongoDB Driver home page of the NPM website. This will install MongoDB Driver for Node.js to our directory, where we are now going to create our Node.js application along with MongoDB, as shown in *figure 4.14*:

npm i mongodb

OR

npm install mongodb

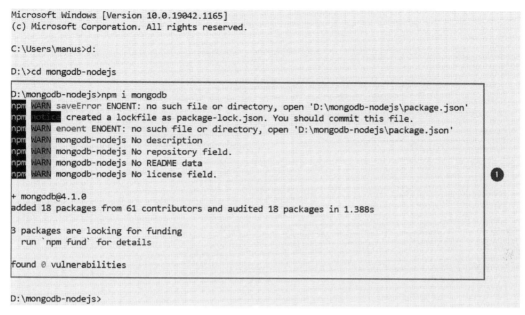

Figure 4.14: *Installing MongoDB driver for Node.js*

If you open your "**mongodb-nodejs**" folder (or directory), you will find that a folder named "**node_modules**" has been created automatically by this process, along with a file named "**package-lock.json**". Basically, whenever you install any node module in Node.js it will create a folder named "**node_modules**" where it will download and copy all the node modules which are required by a specific module (like here we are installing MongoDB Driver for Node.js), or we can say those Node.js modules on which this MongoDB Driver is dependent plus its own files, as shown in *figure 4.15*:

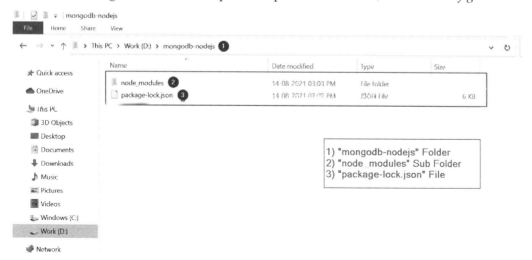

Figure 4.15: *"node_modules" Folder and "package-lock.json"*
File is automatically created by the MongoDB driver for Node.js installation process

You may also open the "**node_modules**" folder and could see the other modules which are downloaded by the installation process, as shown in *figure 4.16*:

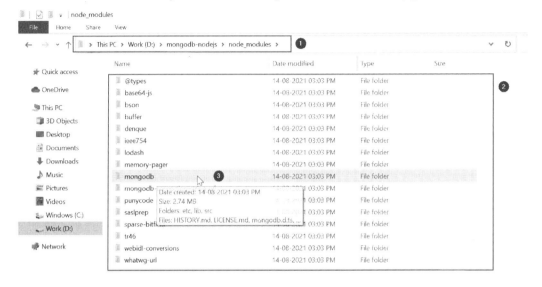

Figure 4.16: *MongoDB driver has been installed along with the other dependencies*

The "**package-lock.json**" is a file where the module and its dependencies are displayed in JSON tree format. For more information about "**package-lock.json**", you can visit this URL: **https://docs.npmjs.com/configuring-npm/package-lock-json.html**

We would also be covering another JSON file, "**package.json**", which is used in Node.js application in our upcoming chapters, where we would cover advanced application development using Node.js.

As we have completed the setup of our environment with MongoDB and Node.js, now we can start with the programming part.

Connecting and working with Node.js and MongoDB

In the previous section of this chapter, we have set up our environment to run Node. js with MongoDB. Now let us start our programming part.

Let us now try to write a code in Node.js that does the small task of connecting to the database. Here we would be writing a small piece of code in Node.js with the help of the Node.js MongoDB driver, which we have installed and set up in our previous step.

Note that as we are using Node.js and writing Node.js code, it is recommended to use some Code Editor or **Integrated Development Environment (IDE)** like Microsoft Visual Studio Code or any Code Editor of your choice. You can download and install Microsoft Visual Studio Code from this link: **https://code.visualstudio.com**. Microsoft Visual Studio Code is an Open Source and free software and is available for almost all operating systems.

Example 1—connecting to MongoDB server using Node.js

In our example, we have used the "**MongoDBClient**" constant that is assigned as an object for the "**MongoClient**" class. Then we have called the connect method using this object. We have saved this file as "**mongodb-connection.js**" under this path: **D:\mongodb-nodejs** and the following is the code for the same (as shown in *figure 4.17*).

Code 1

```
const MongoDBClient = require('mongodb').MongoClient;


// Connection URL String
const url = 'mongodb://localhost:27017';


// Connecting to MongoDB Server using connect Method
MongoDBClient.
connect(url, { useUnifiedTopology: true }, function(err, client) {
 if(err){
  console.log("Some Error While Connecting to MongoDB Server" + err);
 }else{
  console.log("Connected Sucessfully to MongoDB Server using Node.
js Driver for MongoDB");
 }
 // Close the Server Connection
 client.close();
});
```

Following is the screenshot of Microsoft Visual Studio Code:

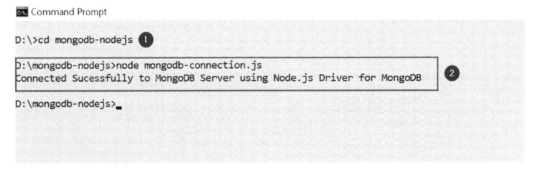

Figure 4.17: *Working with Node.js files using Microsoft Visual Studio Code*

Now, let us run this example. Open the command prompt and navigate to the **"mongodb-nodejs"** folder where you have saved this file and type the following command to run this code:

```
node mongodb-connection.js
```

You will see that we have connected successfully to MongoDB Server using Node. js, as shown in *figure 4.18*:

▣ Command Prompt

```
D:\>cd mongodb-nodejs  ❶

D:\mongodb-nodejs>node mongodb-connection.js
Connected Sucessfully to MongoDB Server using Node.js Driver for MongoDB  ❷

D:\mongodb-nodejs>_
```

Figure 4.18: *Command prompt—connecting to MongoDB server using Node.js*

Example 2—fetching MongoDB documents using Node.js

In our example, we have used the **"MongoDBClient"** constant that is assigned as an object for the **"MongoClient"** class. Then we have called the connect method using this object. After that, we have selected a DB **"BPBOnlineBooksDB"**, and then we have selected the collection as **"BPBOnlineBooksCollection"**, and at last, we have used the **"collection.find().toArray()"** method to get all the documents from the collection and then printed them on console and closed the server connection. We have saved this file as "**mongodb-list-documents.js**" under this path: **D:\ mongodb-nodejs** and the following is the code for the same:

Code 2

```
const MongoDBClient = require('mongodb').MongoClient;

// Connection URL String
const url = 'mongodb://localhost:27017';

// Connecting to MongoDB Server using connect Method
MongoDBClient.
connect(url, { useUnifiedTopology: true }, function(err, client) {
  if(err){
    console.log("Some Error While Connecting to MongoDB Server" + err);
  }else{
    console.log("Connected Sucessfully to MongoDB Server using Node.
js Driver for MongoDB");
  }

  // Select DB
 const dbname = "BPBOnlineBooksDB";
 const db = client.db(dbname);

  // Get the "BPBOnlineBooksCollection" Collection
  const collection = db.collection('BPBOnlineBooksCollection');
  // Find All Documents in "BPBOnlineBooksCollection" Collection
  collection.find().toArray(function(err, docs) {
    if(err){
      console.log("Some Error While Executing the Script" + err);
    }else{
      console.log("Our Node.js Script Found All these records:");
      console.log(docs);
    }
      // Close the Server Connection
      client.close();
  });

});
```

Now let us run this example. Open the command prompt and navigate to the "**mongodb-nodejs**" folder where you have saved this file and type the following command to run this code:

```
node mongodb-list-documents.js
```

You will see that we have connected successfully to the MongoDB server using Node.js, and then this script has also displayed all the documents in the MongoDB collection, as shown in *figure 4.19*:

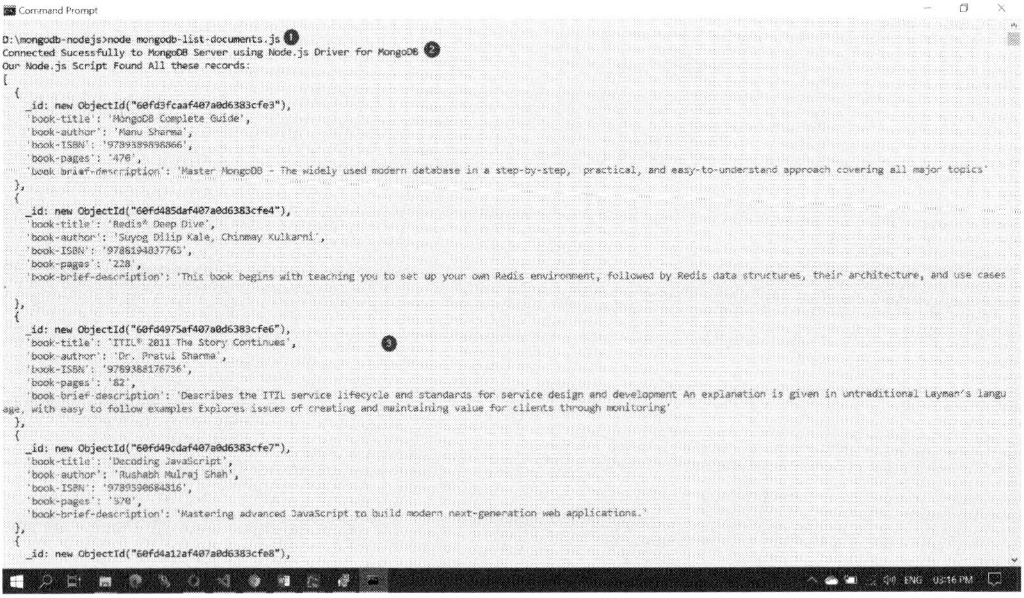

Figure 4.19: *Command prompt—connecting to MongoDB Server and fetching the documents from the collection using Node.js*

Conclusion

In this chapter, we have covered the introduction to JavaScript and Node.js programming and how we can use Node.js with MongoDB. We have also learned how to set up the right environment to run Node.js codes. In the last section of this chapter, we have done some coding and run some practical examples to connect and work with MongoDB Server using Node.js. In the upcoming chapter of this book, we will learn about React Native programming and setting up the right environment before starting with the real *data-driven mobile app development* using React Native and MongoDB using APIs developed using Node.js and Express.js in the later advanced chapter of this book.

Questions

1. Can we use JavaScript for both server side as well as client-side?

2. What is Node.js?

3. Can you name any modern frameworks which use Node.js to build applications?

4. What does NPM stand for?

5. What is the command to install the official MongoDB driver for Node.js?

6. Give an example to connect to MongoDB server with Node.js.

CHAPTER 5

Starting Up Programming with MongoDB and React Native

Mobile users are growing all over the world, and so that mobile app development, in this dynamic world, we are using many mobile apps on our mobile phones, and mobile app development is one of the interesting topics among developers. React Native is one of the most popular mobile app development frameworks today, and this chapter covers the introduction to React Native mobile framework. We should have the right environment in place. So, this chapter covers how we can set up the right environment to run React Native codes. We will also cover how we can view our App on various platforms such as mobile, Emulator, and browser. In the last section of this chapter, we will do some coding and running some practical examples to show how we can actually start with mobile app development.

Structure

In this chapter, we will discuss the following topics:

- Introduction to React Native
- Pre-development steps
    - Check Node.js and NPM on your system
    - Installing Android Studio
    - Installing Android SDK

- o   Setting up the environment variables

- o   Installing Expo CLI using NPM

- o   About Expo and Expo CLI

- o   Creating our mobile App using Expo and Expo CLI

- o   Running our mobile App using Expo and Expo CLI

- o   Opening and viewing App in mobile device using Expo app

- o   Opening and viewing app in Android Emulator

- • Programming with React Native

- o   Practical examples

- • A brief introduction to programming with React Native and MongoDB

Objectives

After studying this chapter, the reader will be able to understand what React Native is. This chapter covers the introduction to various tools used during the development of the mobile App. Here, the reader will learn how to install Android Studio and Android SDK by setting up the environment ready for development and understanding what Expo and Expo CLI are. The reader will also learn how to set up Expo and Expo CLI. In the last section of this chapter, the reader will learn how to develop React Native mobile App with step by step practical examples, and the reader will also get a brief idea on how to use MongoDB with React Native and how we are going to develop our dynamic mobile App using MongoDB in the later advanced chapter of this book.

Introduction to React Native

React Native is a widely used and one of the most popular frameworks based on React.js used to create mobile applications for all the major platforms such as Android, iOS, **Universal Windows Platform** (**UWP**,) and even can be used for building Web apps.

Both React Native and its base Library React are created by Facebook Inc., and both are getting very popular these days due to their features, which include the rendering of the right components when the application data changes. React uses the component-based approach where the components manage their own state.

The main difference between React.js and React Native is that React.js uses the Virtual **Document Object Model** (**DOM**) to render the browser code but React Native uses the Native APIs to render components on mobile.

React Native allows us to build Cross-Platform native mobile apps, which gives these apps a native feel.

There are some differences in React Native related to the use of HTML and CSS. Unlike Web applications, React Native uses some different ways to use HTML and CSS that we will look at later in this chapter.

Pre-development steps

There are many different ways to create mobile apps with React Native and MongoDB. To cover them all is out of the scope of this chapter and book, but we are going to use some of the easiest and official methods by which we can have our environment ready to work with React Native and MongoDB. Let us start with some steps so that we are able to run our codes with React Native and MongoDB.

In our previous chapter, where we have given the introduction about getting started with MongoDB and JavaScript (Node.js), we have already covered how to install the Node.js and **Node Package Manager** (**NPM**). Follow the following steps before we start to code:

Step 1—check Node.js and NPM on your system

You should first verify that Node.js and NPM. In order to verify these two software on your Windows machine, open the command prompt by typing "**cod**" from the Search Bar located in the Taskbar, as shown in *figure 5.1*:

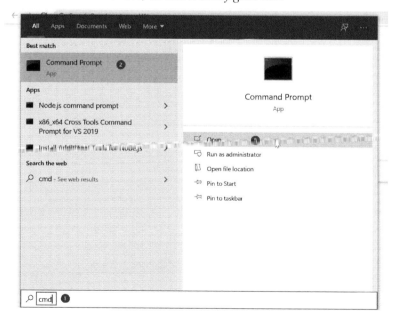

Figure 5.1: *Open command prompt*

1. Type the following two commands one by one to verify Node.js and NPM installation in the command prompt, as shown in *figure 5.2*:

```
node --version
```

```
npm --version
```

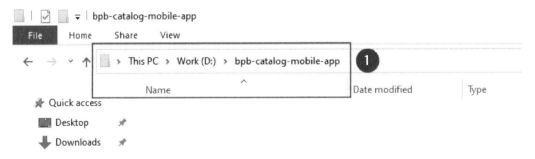

Figure 5.2: *Command prompt—verifying Node.js and NPM version on Windows*

As you can see, both Node.js and NPM have been correctly installed on your Windows machine.

Step 2—creating a project folder in your system

Choose any location on your machine and create a new folder or directory named "**bpb-catalog-mobile-app**" the location could be similar to **D:\ bpb-catalog-mobile-app**, as shown in *figure 5.3*:

Figure 5.3: *Create a new directory named "bpb-catalog-mobile-app" on your Windows Machine*

Step 3—installing Android Studio

1. We need to have Android Emulator to run our React Native mobile app scripts on Windows. For this purpose, we need to download and install. Visit: **https://developer.android.com/studio** in your favorite browsers such as Google Chrome and click the **Download** button, as shown in *figure 5.4*:

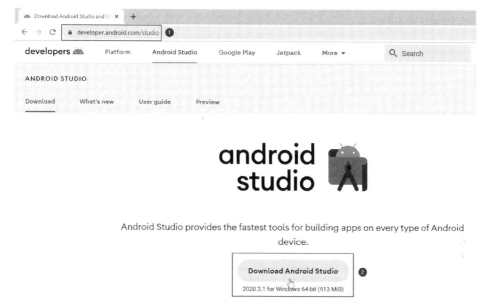

Figure 5.4: Android Studio Home Page

2. After you click "**Download Android Studio**", it will open a popup having *"Terms and Conditions"*, It is recommended to read terms and conditions before downloading the Android Studio. Click the "**Download Android Studio For Windows**" button; after you click this button, the download will start in your browser, and you can see the download progress, as shown in *figure 5.5*:

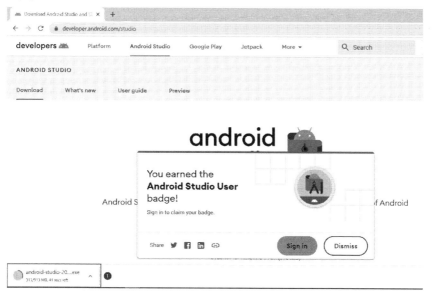

Figure 5.5: Android Studio download screen

3. After the download is 100% complete, you can open the installer file, and it will launch the Setup Wizard for Android Studio. Click the **Next** button to start the setup process, as shown in *figure 5.6*:

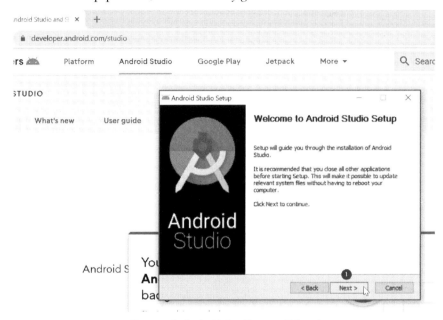

Figure 5.6: *Android Studio setup Wizard*

4. During the setup process, it will show you the screen in which you have the option to select "**Android Virtual Device**". Please note that you need to select this option so that we are able to use "**Android Virtual Device**" or Android Emulator, as shown in *figure 5.7*:

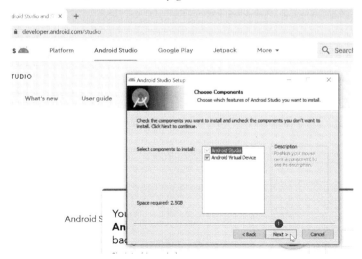

Figure 5.7: *Android Studio Setup Wizard—choose components screen*

5. During the setup process, you can change the location of the software where you need this software to get installed on your machine, as shown in *figure 5.8*:

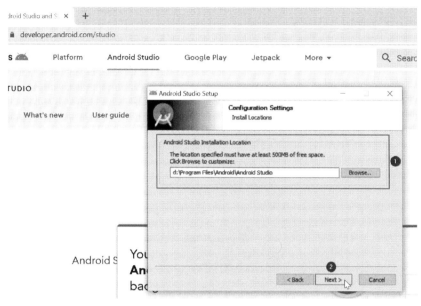

Figure 5.8: *Android Studio Setup Wizard—installation location*

6. You can see the setup installation progress, and once it is done, you can press the "**Next**" button, as shown in *figure 5.9*:

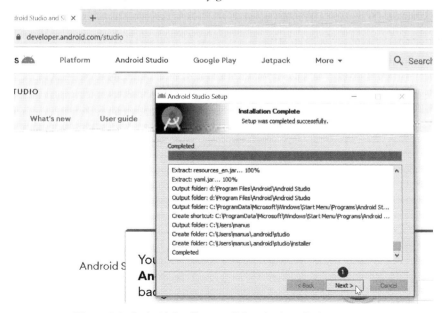

Figure 5.9: *Android Studio setup Wizard—installation progress*

7. After the setup is complete, you will see the last screen of the wizard, as we do not need to launch the Android Studio. We can uncheck the "**Start Android Studio**" checkbox and then click the "**Finish**" button to exit the setup wizard, as shown in *figure 5.10*:

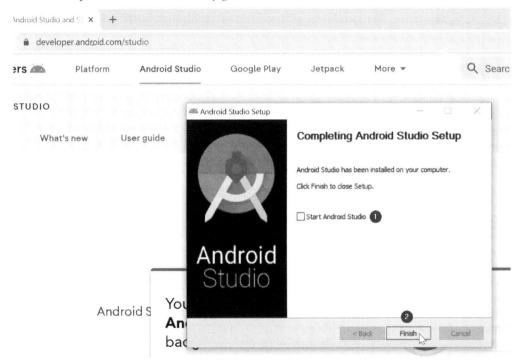

Figure 5.10: Android studio setup Wizard – installation complete

Step 4—installing Android SDK

1. If you open your Android Studio first time (as we skipped to launch Android Studio in Step 3 purposely, to cover the "*Installing Android SDK (Software Development Kit)*"), in the Search Bar under the taskbar of Windows, type "*android*" and you will see the Android Studio will appear as we have installed it in our previous step, as shown in *figure 5.11*:

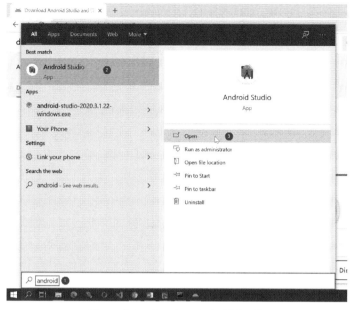

Figure 5.11: Opening Android Studio

2. This will launch the Android Studio as we have not Installed Android SDK yet. The message will appear once the Android Studio is launched the first time, which says something like this: "Your Android SDK is missing, out of date, or corrupted", You need to click on the button that says: "**Open SDK Manager**". You might leave this step if the Android SDK is already installed on your machine, as shown in *figure 5.12:*

Figure 5.12: *Android Studio—SDK problem Alert Box*

3. After you click the "**Open SDK Manager**" button, it will launch the SDK Manager window, and you will see that "**Android SDK location**" is empty. In order to resolve this, we need to install the Android SDK, which will be downloaded from the Internet. You might skip this step if the Android SDK is already installed on your machine, as shown in *figure 5.13*:

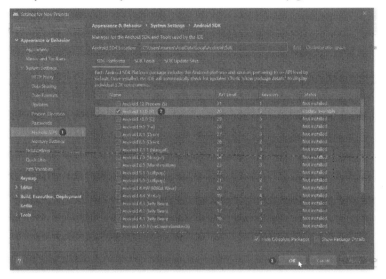

Figure 5.13: *Android Studio—SDK Manager*

4. To install the Android SDK, click the edit link under the Android SDK location. This will launch another window from where we can install the latest version of Android SDK. You might leave this step if the Android SDK is already installed on your machine, as shown in *figure 5.14*:

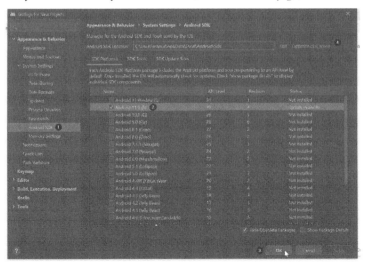

Figure 5.14: *Android Studio—SDK location—Click Edit Link*

Step 5—setting up the environment variables

We need to set up the environment variables paths on our Windows Machine for Java **Software Development Kit** (**SDK**) and Android SDK. Both of these environment variables and their paths are required so that our application and Android Emulator will run properly on Windows. To set up these environment variables paths, follow the following points:

1. In your Windows search menu under taskbar, type "**environment variables**" and when it shows the option "**Edit the system environment variables**". Open it, as shown in *figure 5.15*:

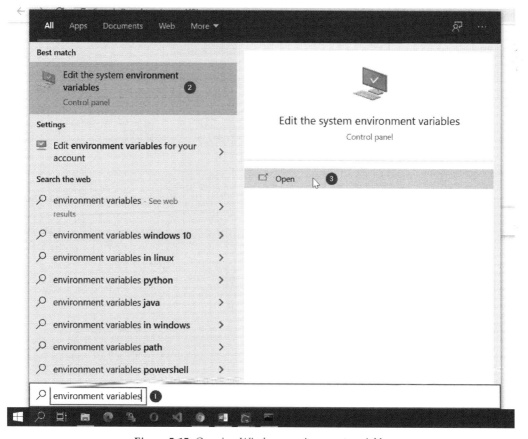

Figure 5.15: Opening Windows environment variables

2. This will open the system properties window, and under this, you will see the "**Environment Variables**" button. Click this button, and it will open

a new window where you can add new environment variables, as shown in *figure 5.16*:

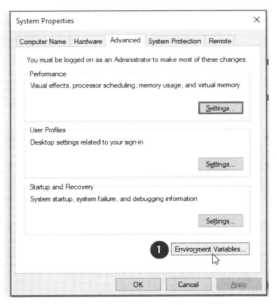

Figure 5.16: *System properties screen*

3. This will open the **System Properties** window, and under this, you will see the "**Environment Variables**" button. Click this button, and it will open a new window where you can add new environment variables. You need to create "**User Variables**". Click the "**New**" button under the **User Variables** section. This will open a new window where you can find new user environment variables, as shown in *figure 5.17*:

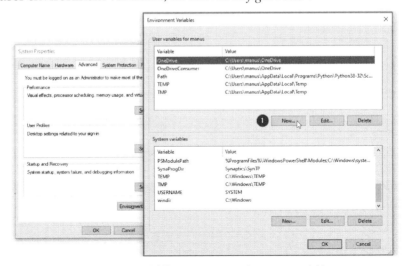

Figure 5.17: *Adding new user environment variable*

4. Once you click the "**New**" button, it will open another window where you need to add "**Variable name**" and "**Variable value**". Please enter the following value for "**JAVA_HOME**". Note that this path may vary according to the "Android Studio" installation path in your machine. In order to enter the correct details, you can use the "**Browse Directory**" option (as shown in *figure 5.18*).

   • **Variable Name**: `JAVA_HOME`

   • **Variable Path**: `D:\Program Files\Android\Android Studio\ jre\jre`
     (this path varies according to your machine where you have installed your Android Studio).

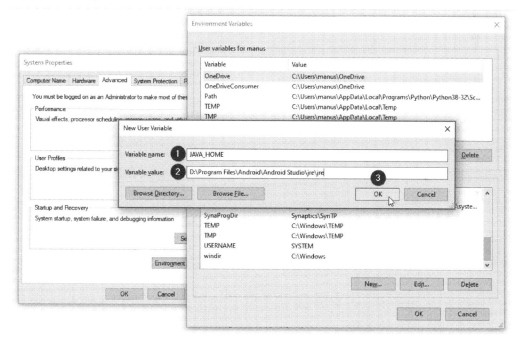

Figure 5.18: *Adding new user environment variable—JAVA_HOME*

5. Repeat the last step to enter one more variable for "**ANDROID_HOME**". Note that this path may vary according to the "Android SDK" installation path in your machine. So, in order to enter the correct details, you can use the "**Browse Directory**" option after you enter these details (as shown in *figure 5.19*).

   • **Variable Name**: `ANDROID_HOME`

   • **Variable path**: `C:\Users\manus\AppData\Local\Android\Sdk` (this path varies according to your machine, where you have installed your Android SDK).

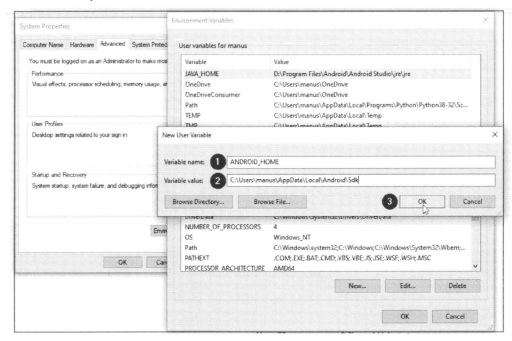

Figure 5.19: Adding new user environment variable — ANDROID_HOME

Step 6—installing Expo CLI using NPM

Expo is a framework to build React Native applications. It has inbuilt tools and libraries which are very helpful while we build our applications using React Native.

Expo CLI is the Expo's Command Line Interface, which is used to create React Native Projects using Expo.

1. Open up your command prompt and navigate to your project directory that is: "**D:\bpb-catalog-mobile-app**" in our case (as shown in *figure 5.20*):

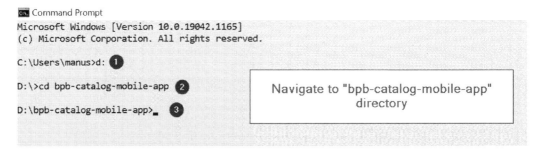

Figure 5.20: Navigating to "bpb-catalog-mobile-app" directory

2. Open your favorite browser like Google Chrome, and in the address bar, type: **https://expo.dev/** and press *Enter*. This will open the "**Expo**" home page. Here, you will see all the details about Expo and Expo CLI, including the command to install them in your project. Click the "**Get Started**" link on the top navigation bar of the home page. This will open up the "Quick Starter Guide" page, as shown in *figure 5.21*:

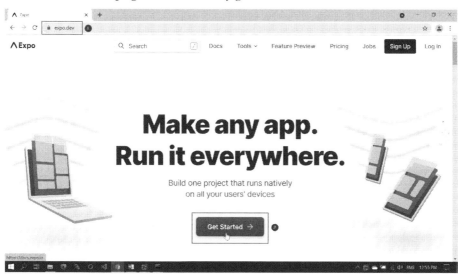

Figure 5.21: *Expo Home Page*

3. As we have already installed Node.js in our previous chapters, we can skip steps to install Node.js and simply move to Step 3 and install Expo CLI in our project, as shown in *figure 5.22*:

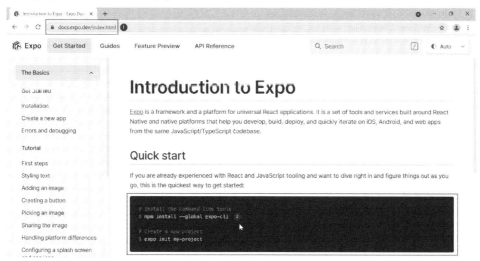

Figure 5.22: *Expo get started page*

4. Now run the following command that has been mentioned on the Expo "Quick Starter Guide" page. This will install Expo CLI using **Node Package Manager** (**NPM**) to our project directory, where we are now going to create our React Native application along with MongoDB, as shown in *figure 5.23*:

```
npm install --global  expo-cli
```

Here "--global" means that Expo CLI will be installed globally in your computer so that you can use it anywhere when you might be working with Expo CLI again.

Figure 5.23: Installing Expo CLI

As we have installed Expo using the "--global" parameter, it has been installed globally under the following locations:

```
C:\Users\manus\AppData\Roaming\npm\expo -> C:\Users\manus\AppData\
Roaming\npm\node_modules\expo-cli\bin\expo.js
```

```
C:\Users\manus\AppData\Roaming\npm\expo-cli   ->   C:\Users\manus\
AppData\Roaming\npm\node_modules\expo-cli\bin\expo.js
```

5. We can verify this by navigating to the "**npm**" folder under "**AppData**", as shown in *figure 5.24*:

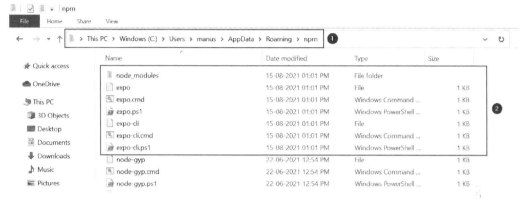

Figure 5.24: *AppData global NPM installation*

Step 7—creating our mobile App using Expo and Expo CLI

1. Open the command prompt and navigate to your project directory, which is: "**D:\bpb-catalog-mobile-app**" in our case and type the following command, as shown in *figure 5.25*:

```
expo init bpb-mobile-app --npm
```

We have given --npm parameter here to open our App using NPM instead of Yarn (which is a default option).

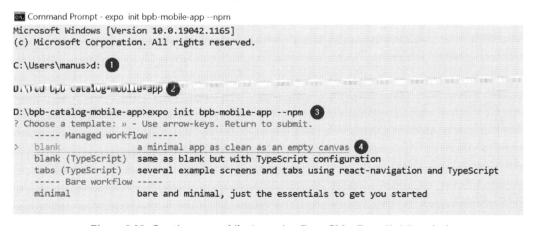

Figure 5.25: *Creating our mobile App using Expo CLI—Expo "init" method*

2. After we run the command as mentioned previously. Expo CLI will prompt us to "**Choose a Template**". For our example, we will choose the "blank" template and press *Enter* again. After you press *Enter* key, the Expo CLI will start creating our mobile application using NPM, as shown in *figure 5.26*:

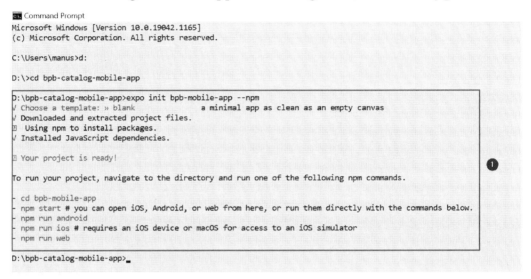

Figure 5.26: *Creating our mobile App using Expo CLI—app structure created for development*

3. We can browse our project folder and can see a new folder with an app name that we have given during our EXPO CLI initialization Command in Point 1. The same folder has been created under our project folder with the Expo files and other Node Modules, as shown in *figure 5.27*:

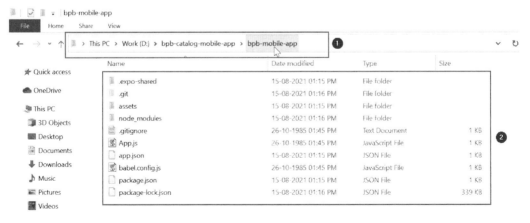

Figure 5.27: *App folder and files created by Expo CLI*

Step 8—running our mobile App using Expo and Expo CLI

1. Open the command prompt and navigate to your project directory and then to our application directory, which is: "**D:\bpb-catalog-mobile-app\bpb-mobile-app**" in our case, and type the following command, as shown in *figure 5.28*:

   `npm start`

   When we run the above command, Expo CLI will start our application, and we can see that it will start after some time. Please remember that you should not close this command prompt window as doing this will stop our App. You should keep it running.

Figure 5.28: *Starting our mobile App with Expo Start Command—"expo start"*

2. Once the App gets ready, Expo will try to automatically launch this App in the default browser. If it does not happen, then you can now open your favorite browsers such as Google Chrome and type: **http://localhost:19002/** in the URL bar and press *Enter*. This will Open Expo Developer tools in the browser where we can have work on app settings and options in the browser with the help of Node Metro Bundler, which is a JavaScript Bundler for React Native. We can also see many ways to view and run our App in browsers, emulators, or real devices (as shown in *figure 5.29*).

For more details about React Native Bundler, you can visit:

- https://www.npmjs.com/package/metro-bundler
- https://github.com/facebook/metro

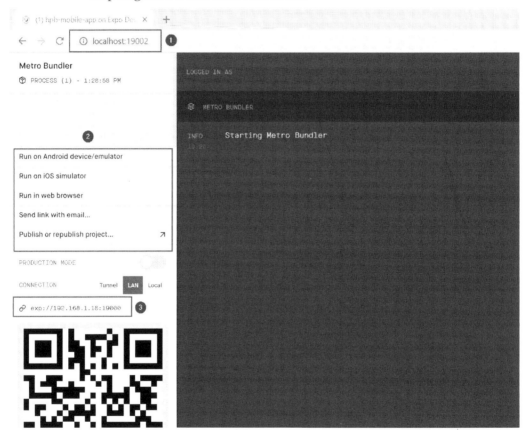

Figure 5.29: Expo developer tools

3. There are many other ways to open and view our application using the following methods:

    *   Using Web Browser

    *   Using the QR Code with the Expo app (Android)

    *   Using the QR Code with the Camera app (iOS)

    *   Using Android Emulator

Let us explore some of these methods. If we want to run our application in the browser, then we need to simply click the "**Run in web browser**". Once you do this, it will try to create our App ready for the browser, and you can see the process in the background in the command prompt where your App was started using Expo CLI (as shown in *figure 5.30*).

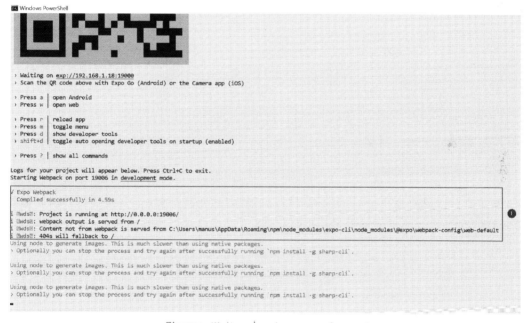

Figure 5.30: Expo logs in command prompt

4. The previous step will automatically launch our App in the new tab of the browser. If it does not happen automatically, then you can now open a new tab in the browser and type: **http://localhost:19006/** in the URL bar and press *Enter*. This will open our App where we can also see the changes as we develop our mobile App in the next steps, as shown in *figure 5.31*:

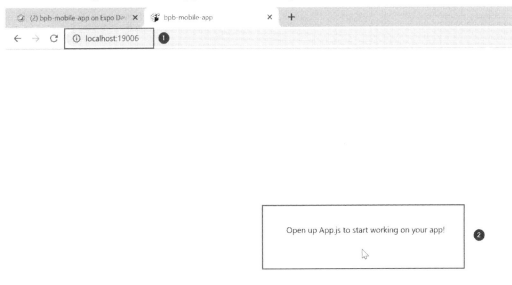

Figure 5.31: *Our App Home Screen in Browser*

Step 9—opening and viewing an app in mobile device using Expo app

1. Open Google Play Store on your Android Mobile and search for Expo App for React Native. Once you get the search results, click on the right App and install the Expo app on your mobile phone, as shown in *figure 5.32*:

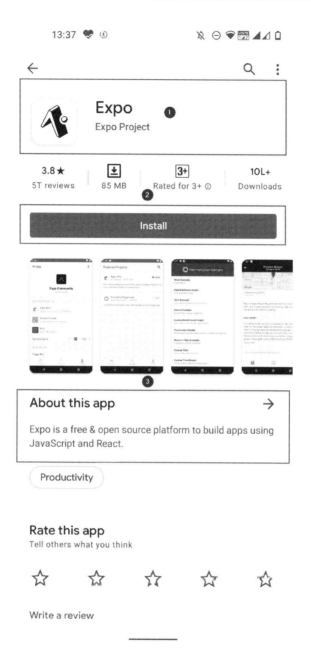

Figure 5.32: *Installing Expo App in your mobile (Android Device)*

2. After you have installed this App open this App on your mobile phone. This App requires some permissions to "*take pictures and record videos*" because we need to scan the QR code on our mobile using this App. Allow this App to take pictures, as shown in *figure 5.33*:

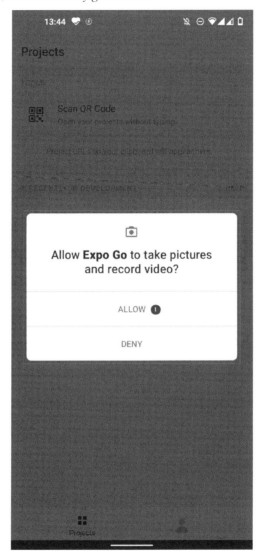

Figure 5.33: *Allow permissions for Expo App in your device*

3. Now click the scan QR Code and point your mobile camera to the QR Code that you either see in your command prompt where you have started your App with Expo CLI or your Web browser under Node Metro Builder, as shown in *figure 5.34*:

Figure 5.34*: Scan the bar code shown in your browser or command prompt using the Expo App*

4. Once your QR code has been correctly scanned by your mobile, you will see that after some time, your App will be displayed under the **Projects,** and you can open this App from your mobile phone, as shown in *figure 5.35*:

Figure 5.35: *Expo launches our App in mobile device*

5. Once you click over your App in the Expo projects, it will open this App on your mobile, and we can see the default screen of our App in Android mobile, which is a real device, as shown in *figure 5.36*:

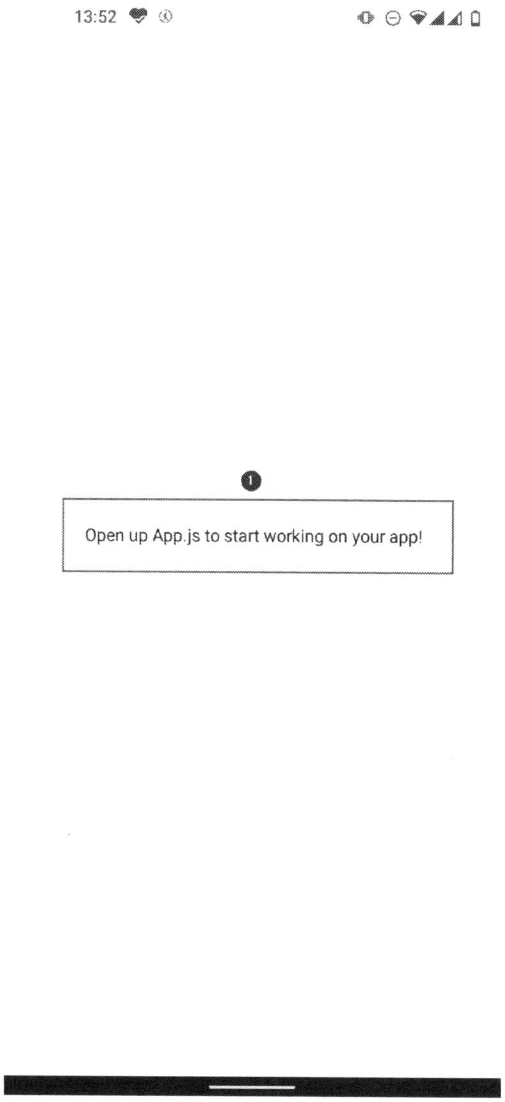

13:52 ♥ ⊛   ⬤ ⊖ ▼◢◢ ▯

❶

Open up App.js to start working on your app!

Figure 5.36: *Our App Home screen in real device*

6. You may also see the logs messages that will be shown both under your command prompt where you have started your App using Expo CLI as well as in your browser where Expo Dev Tools and Node Metro Builder is opened, as shown in *figure 5.37*:

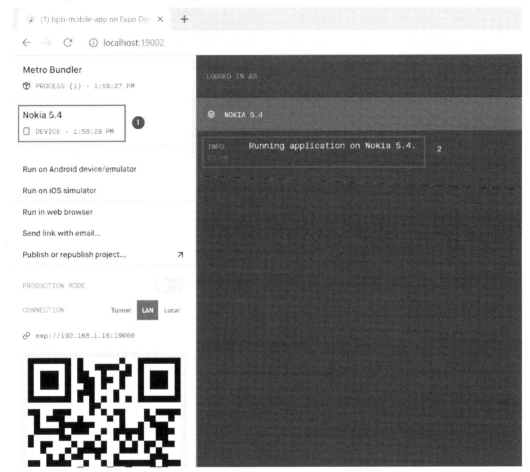

Figure 5.37: *Expo Developer tools—logs*

Step 10—opening and viewing app in Android Emulator

If you try to open your App using "**Run on Android device/emulator**" you might get an error message if your Android Emulator is not set up correctly in your Windows machine. To solve this issue, we need to first set up the Android Emulator with the help of Android Studio, as shown in *figure 5.38*:

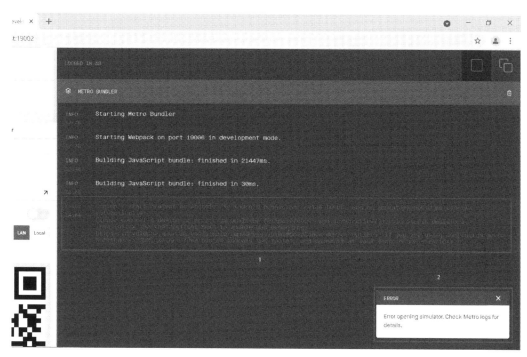

Figure 5.38: *Error message—could not launch Emulator*

1. Open Android Studio and click **"More Actions"**. It will show many options after clicking it, as shown in *figure 5.39*:

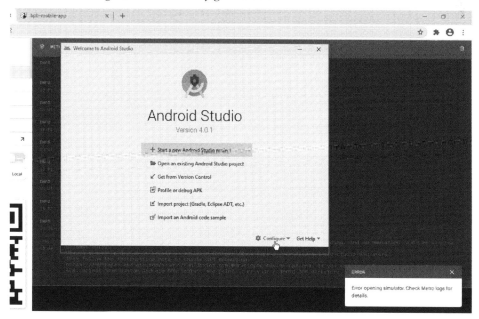

Figure 5.39: *Android Studio—Configure*

2. Now click **Android Virtual Device (AVD)** Manager to open the AVD Manager window, as shown in *figure 5.40*:

Figure 5.40: *Selecting AVD Manager from Android Studio Configure*

3. In your AVD Manager screen, click the "`Create Virtual Device`" button, as shown in *figure 5.41*:

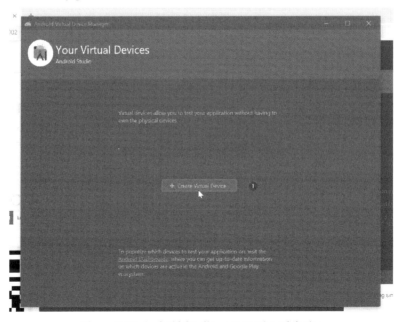

Figure 5.41: *Android Studio—create virtual device*

4. In the Hardware screen, select any phone device (in our example, we have selected Pixel 2 mobile device with Play Store and click **Next**, as shown in *figure 5.42*:

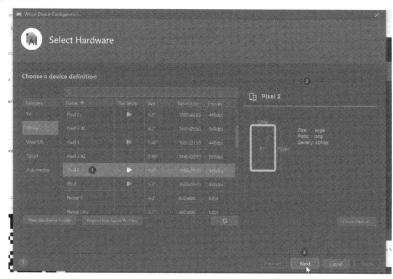

Figure 5.42: *Creating virtual device—select hardware*

5. In the **Select a system image** section, choose any recommended image and download it (in our example, we have chosen 30 API version). You might need to accept the Terms and Conditions while downloading the new image and related software. It is recommended to read the Terms and Conditions before downloading, as shown in *figure 5.43*:

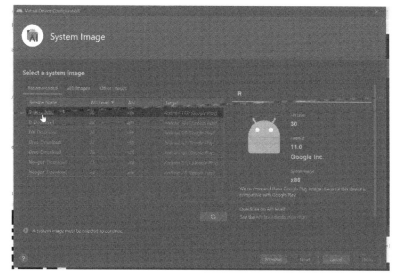

Figure 5.43: *Android virtual device configuration—selecting the image*

6. After we are done with all the above points, we can then choose the name of our Android Virtual Device and click the "**Finish**" button, as shown in *figure 5.44*:

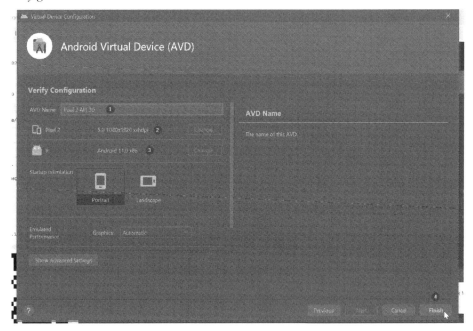

Figure 5.44: *Android virtual device configuration—verify configuration*

7. This AVD will be shown in the virtual devices in the Android Studio. Click the "**Play**" button to launch this AVD, as shown in *figure 5.45*:

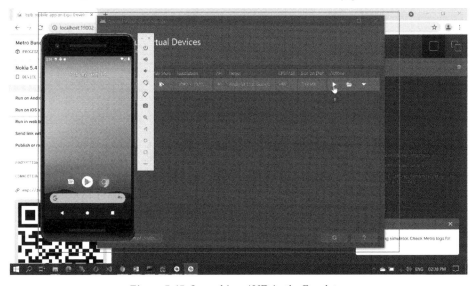

Figure 5.45: *Launching AVD in the Emulator*

8. Now click the "**Run on Android device emulator**", and it will open our App in Android Emulator, as shown in *figure 5.46*:

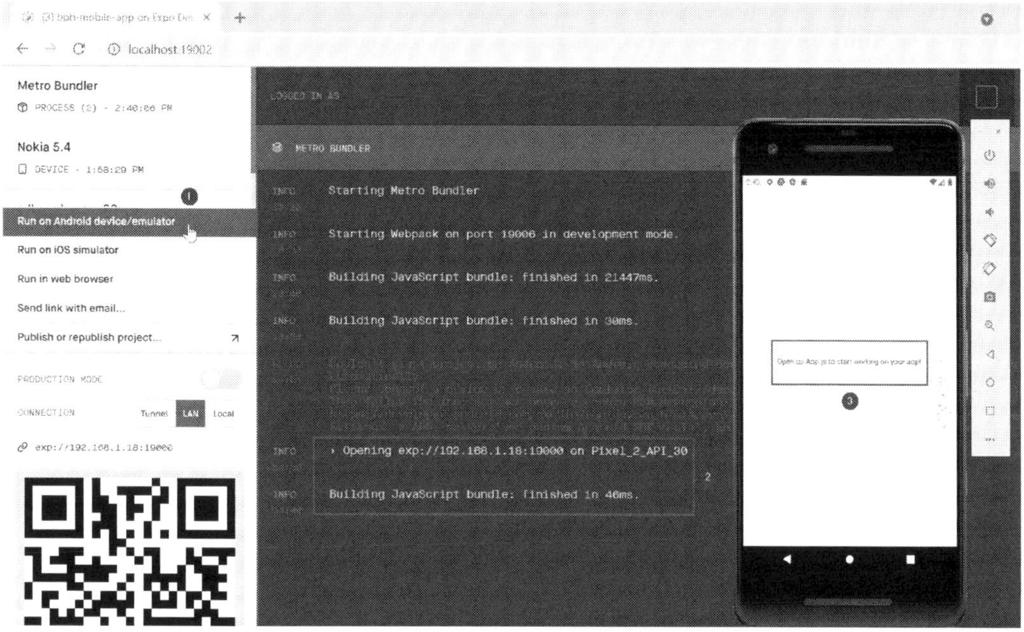

Figure 5.46: Expo Dev tools—launching our App in Android Emulator

Programming with React Native

In the previous section of this chapter, we have set up our environment to run React Native with MongoDB. Now, let us start our programming part.

Let us now try to write a code in React Native that does a small task of connecting to the database. Here, we would be writing a small piece of code in React Native, which will communicate with MongoDB with the help of API that we have created in our previous chapter, where we have learned to create APIs using Node.js and Express.Js.

Note that as we are using React Native and writing React Native Code, it is recommended to use some code editor or **Integrated Development Environment (IDE)** like Microsoft Visual Studio Code or any code editor of your choice. You can download and install Microsoft Visual Studio Code from this link: **https://code.visualstudio.com**. Microsoft Visual Studio Code is open-source and free software and is available for almost all operating systems.

Example 1—changing the text in our mobile App

Following is the default "**App.js**" code, which is created by Expo CLI. This code includes some files from Expo, React, and React Native, and the components (or objects) such as "**StatusBar**", "**React**", "**StyleSheet**", "**Text**", and "**Views**" have been created. In React Native, we use CSS in a different manner using the "**StyleSheet**" component to create our styles, and here, we generally use Flexbox CSS properties for styling but it applies to **<View>** component only. **<Text>** component in React Native does not use Flex to organize its content. We can use "**numberOfLines**" prop, etc.

<View> component can have any number of child elements, and it can contain nested **<Views>**, **<Text>**, and **<Image>** components, and so on.

In our default code, there is a default function **App(),** which returns some "**Text**" and shows it to the screen, as shown in *figure 5.47*:

Code 1

```
import { StatusBar } from 'expo-status-bar';
import React from 'react';
import { StyleSheet, Text, View } from 'react-native';


export default function App() {
  return (
    <View style={styles.container}>
      <Text>Open up App.js to start working on your app!</Text>
      <StatusBar style="auto" />
    </View>
  );
}


const styles = StyleSheet.create({
  container: {
    flex: 1,
    backgroundColor: '#fff',
    alignItems: 'center',
    justifyContent: 'center',
  },
});
```

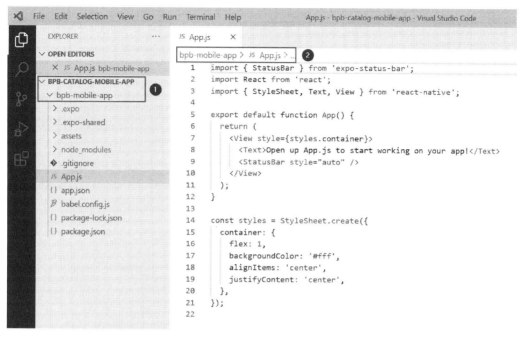

Figure 5.47: *Working with React Native files using Microsoft Visual Studio Code*

Now let us change the text message of our App, and the code of the same is as follows:

Code 2

```
import { StatusBar } from 'expo-status-bar';
import React from 'react';
import { StyleSheet, Text, View } from 'react-native';

export default function App() {
 return (
  <View style={styles.container}>
   <Text>Welcome to BPB Online Mobile App</Text>
   <StatusBar style="auto" />
  </View>
 );
}

const styles = StyleSheet.create({
 container: {
```

```
  flex: 1,
  backgroundColor: '#fff',
  alignItems: 'center',
  justifyContent: 'center',
 },
});
```

After the code change, run this App again. In case you have closed your App you can again run this App by using the following command after navigating to the correct location which is: "**D:\bpb-catalog-mobile-app\bpb-mobile-app**" in our case, as shown in *figure 5.48*:

npm start

Figure 5.48: Starting our App using Expo CLI

This will now start a "**Metro Bundler**" and open "**Expo Developer Tools**" in your browser. In case it is not launched automatically, open your browser and type: **http://localhost:19002**. You now need to click the option under "**Expo Developer Tools**", which says "**Run in Web Browser**", as shown in *figure 5.49*:

Figure 5.49: Expo Dev tools—launching our App in browser

Once you click the option under "**Expo Developer Tools**", which says "**Run in Web Browser**", it will start the process of launching your App in a browser, and after some time, it will open the App in the browser. If this does not happen automatically, then first check the logs under "**Metro Bundler**", and then you may try opening this URL: "**http://localhost:19006/**" in a new browser tab, as shown in *figure 5.50*:

Figure 5.50: Our App Home Screen shown in the browser

We have seen how we can easily change the text of our mobile app. Now let us add some Logo images to our app in our next example.

Example 2—adding logo image in our mobile App

In our example, we have created a separate header section and included it in the default **App()** function. We have also imported the **<Image>** component from "React Native" and then we have used this **<Image>** component to display the logo image in our App. If you remember that in our previous example we have learned that **<View>** components can include **<Image>** components as well as **<Text>** components. We have done the same thing here; we just created a separate code for the header section of our App, and the following is the code for the same.

Code 1

```
import { StatusBar } from 'expo-status-bar';

import React from 'react';

import { StyleSheet, Text, View, Image } from 'react-native'; // Imported the Image Component


export default function App() {

 return (

 <View style={styles.container}>

 {appHeaderSection}

 </View>

 );

}

//Style Sheet

const styles = StyleSheet.create({

 container: {

  flex: 1,

  backgroundColor: '#fff',

  alignItems: 'center',

  justifyContent: 'flex-start', /* Flex Start */

  marginTop: 10
```

```
},
});


// Header Section
const appHeaderSection = (
  <View style={styles.container}>
  <Image source={require('./images/bpb-logo.
png')} style={{height: 100, width: 150}} />
  <Text>Welcome to BPB Online Mobile App</Text>
  <StatusBar style="auto" />
  </View>
);
```

Also, note that once you do changes in your App, the Expo will automatically refresh your code and you can see the instant changes whatsoever you are doing in your code, as shown in *figure 5.51*:

Figure 5.51: Our App with changed text and logo shown in the browser

We have seen how we can easily add the logo image to our mobile App. Now let us open the same in The Android Emulator. For this, you need to open the Android Studio and follow the points as explained in the previous section of this chapter which is Step 10 under the pre development part of this chapter. Open AVD Manager and start the virtual device and wait for it to start and after that from the Expo

Developer Tool click "`Run on Android device /emulator`". This will open our App in the Android Emulator (Virtual Device), as shown in *figure 5.52*:

Figure 5.52*: Command prompt—connecting to MongoDB server using Node.js*

A brief introduction to programming with React Native and MongoDB

In this chapter, we have learned how we can create the right environment for mobile application development and have created a simple mobile app. Now, we need to create a dynamic app that uses MongoDB collection data for reading and updating. For all these operations we need some way so that our mobile App can communicate with the MongoDB database. For this purpose, we need **Application Programming Interfaces** (**APIs**), which would be helpful in the further development of our mobile application.

We will be covering more about API and API development in the next chapters of this book and will learn to create APIs using Node.js and Express.js (which is a framework for Node.js and it has a lot of features to create APIs along with MongoDB). A whole chapter is dedicated to this purpose, where you will learn how to create API and perform CRUD operations using API calls.

After we learn how to create APIs using Node.js and Express.js along with MongoDB, we will further resume our mobile application development in the advanced chapter, which is dedicated to creating the mobile application development for a publishing house where we will learn the following:

- How to connect MongoDB Server with the help of API using React Native

- How to show the list of books that we will add using the backend, which we will create in our upcoming chapter using PHP and MongoDB

- How to give a *"Thumbs Up"* and *"Thumbs Down"* rating to a book from a mobile application using API

Also, in this book, there will be a bonus chapter about "MongoDB Realm", which will give step by step introduction to MongoDB Realm and how we can work with MongoDB Realm along with React Native for developing mobile apps.

The upcoming chapters would be very helpful in making you learn many new things, and they will add good learning toward the full-stack development, which we will cover step by step in the next chapters.

Conclusion

In this chapter, we have covered the introduction to React Native mobile framework. We have learned that in order to run React Native and create mobile apps, we should have the right environment in place. We have seen how we can view our App on various platforms like mobile, Emulator as well as in a browser. In the last section of this chapter, we have done some coding and run some practical examples, and learned how we can actually start with the mobile app development. In the upcoming chapter, we will be learning how we can use Python programming language with MongoDB and in the later advanced chapters of this book, we will be also covering how to use APIs built with Node.js and Express.js with React Native mobile app and connect to MongoDB these topics are covered in a detailed manner in the advanced chapters of this book in which we will finally learn how to create a dynamic mobile app with React Native and MongoDB.

Questions

1. What is React Native?

2. What are the pre-development steps that you need in order to develop an App in React Native?

3. What is Expo and Expo CLI?

4. How can you create mobile app using Expo CLI?

5. What is the command used to launch our application with Expo CLI?

6. Name two React Native components that you have learned in this chapter?

CHAPTER 6
Starting Up Programming with MongoDB and Python

If we think about Data Science, Machine Learning, and AI, then one language that comes to our mind is Python. Python is one of the most popular languages today, and it has been used for the development of various software applications, including Web-based. This chapter covers the introduction to Python programming language and Python programming with MongoDB and how we can use Python with MongoDB. This chapter covers how we can set up the right environment to run Python codes. In the last section of this chapter, we will be doing some coding and running some practical examples to connect and work with the MongoDB server using Python.

Structure

In this chapter, we will discuss the following topics:

- Using Python with MongoDB
- Installing Python and setting up the environment for running Python scripts
- Installing and setting up MongoDB driver with PIP
- Connecting and working with MongoDB server using Python

Objectives

After studying this chapter, the reader will be able to understand how to use Python with MongoDB and how to install Python and set up the environment ready for development. This chapter also covers the coding part, where the reader will learn how to set up the right environment to use MongoDB along with Python and also how to connect and work with the MongoDB database using Python.

Using Python with MongoDB

Python is an interpreted, high-level, object-oriented programming language and one of the widely used and most popular programming languages these days due to its use in many areas and artificial intelligence. Python is a general-purpose programming language. Besides Web development, it is used in back-end development, software development, data sciences, and also writing system scripts.

There are many ways to run Python with MongoDB on various operating systems such as Windows, Linux, and Mac OS. To cover them all is out of the scope of this chapter and book. But we are going to use some of the easiest and official methods by which we can have our environment ready to work with Python and MongoDB. Let us start with some steps so that we are able to run our codes with Python and MongoDB.

Installing Python on Windows operating system

Let us install Python on Windows operating system by following the step-by-step installation method.

Installation steps

Let us start with the installation of Python on our machine. Following are the steps that are required to be performed to install Python.

Step 1—download Python

1. Open Python's official website—**https://www.python.org** in your favorite browser, point your mouse to the "**Downloads**" link on the top section of the home page and click the download link in which you will see the latest version of Python with its version number. Click this link, as shown in *figure 6.1*:

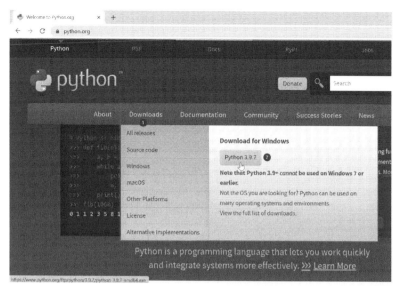

Figure 6.1: Python official website Home Page

2. Once the download starts, you can easily see the download process with the download icon and progress on your browser (this progress shows differently in each browser. The screenshot is of Google Chrome browser. Every browser shows this in a different manner), you should wait till it is 100% complete, as shown in *figure 6.2*:

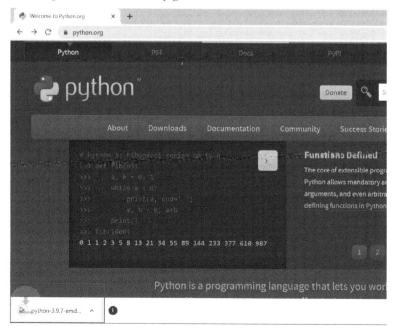

Figure 6.2: Python download screen—download progress

3. Once the download is 100% complete, you can follow the next steps (as shown in *figure 6.3*).

In Step 1, we have covered how to download Python from the official website. The next steps are related to the installation process, which we have covered separately in Step 2 of the Python installation process.

Step 2—install Python on your Windows Machine

Once the download is complete and the installer file is fully downloaded, it will show a download complete icon (as shown in *figure 6.3*), and you can proceed further.

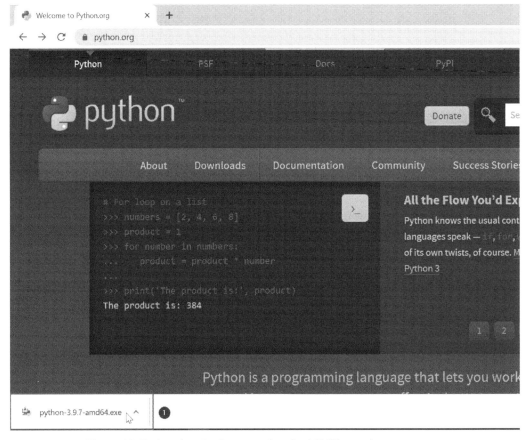

Figure 6.3: *Python download screen—download 100% complete—next steps*

1. Now open this installer file, and it will start the Python setup wizard guiding you to complete the installation of Python in your machine, as shown in *figure 6.4*:

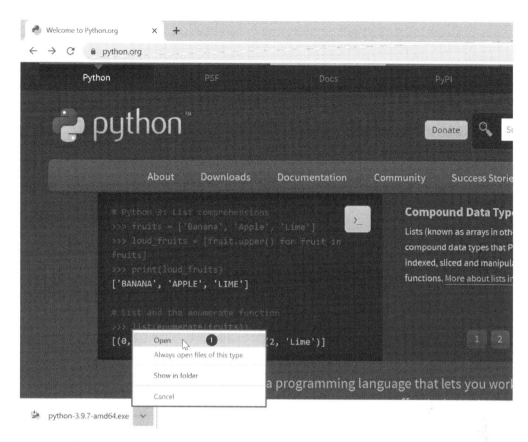

Figure 6.4: *Python download screen—download 100% complete—open Installer file*

2. Now open this installer file, and it will start the Python setup wizard guiding you to complete the installation of Python in your machine. It is recommended to check the checkbox that says "**Add Python to PATH**" so that it will add the path of the Python to the Windows environment variables, and we can run Python-related commands from everywhere. We are not going to cover all steps here as it is out of the scope of this chapter. Please follow the setup process, and it will install Python on your Windows machine (as shown in *figure 6.5*). Also, during the installation process, the setup may ask you to accept the License Agreement. It is recommended to read the License

Agreement and other Terms and Conditions. Click "**Install Now**" to start the installation process.

Figure 6.5: Python setup wizard

3. The installer also allows you to customize the installation of this software on your Windows machine. If you want, you can change the installation location or else go with the default installation. But it is recommended to select the default method. Once the installation gets started, you will see the setup progress, as shown in *figure 6.6*:

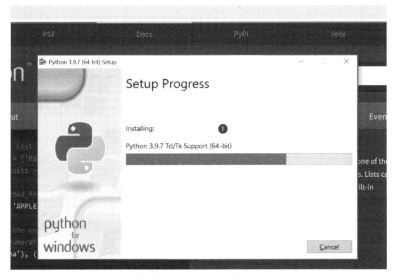

Figure 6.6: Python setup wizard—setup progress

4. After the installation is 100% complete, you will see the last screen of this wizard. Click on the "**Close**" button to finish the setup process, as shown in *figure 6.7*:

Figure 6.7: Python setup wizard—installation complete

Step 3—post-installation steps and verifying Python on your Windows Machine

Once the installation is done, you should first verify that Python and PIP (Python Package Installer that is a standard package manager for Python and is used to install and manage software packages written in Python Programming Language) is correctly installed on your machine. In order to verify these two software on your

Windows machine, open the command prompt by typing "**cmd**" from the search bar located in the taskbar, as shown in *figure 6.8*)

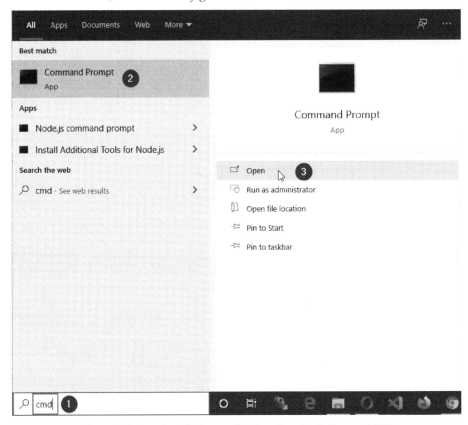

Figure 6.8: Post-installation verification steps for Python and PIP

1. Type the following two commands one by one to verify Python and PIP installation in the command prompt, as shown in *figure 6.9*:

```
python --version
```

```
pip --version
```

```
Command Prompt
Microsoft Windows [Version 10.0.19042.1165]
(c) Microsoft Corporation. All rights reserved.

C:\Users\manus>python --version     1
Python 3.9.7

C:\Users\manus>pip --version
pip 21.2.4 from C:\Users\manus\AppData\Local\Programs\Python\Python39\lib\site-packages\pip (python 3.9)   2

C:\Users\manus>_
```

1) Checking Python Version
2) Checking PIP Version

Figure 6.9: Command prompt—verifying Python and PIP version on Windows

As you can see, both Python and PIP have been correctly installed on your Windows machine. Now we can start with the development part of this chapter and start to use MongoDB with Python. In the next section, we will cover how to use MongoDB with Python applications. But before that, there is one last step we have to follow before we code. It is covered in Step 4.

Step 4—installing MongoDB driver for Python using Python Package Index (PyPI)

Once Python and PIP have been correctly installed on your Windows machine, we can install MongoDB driver using **Python Package Index** (**PyPI**), which is the repository for software and modules written in Python programming language).

1. To install the official driver for MongoDB just open your favorite browser like Google Chrome and type: **https://pypi.org/project/pymongo/** and then press *Enter*. This will open up the official page for MongoDB on the PIP website, and you will be shown a lot of information about this driver, including how to install it using PIP and how to use it. You can also see the latest release details of this driver, as shown in *figure 6.10*:

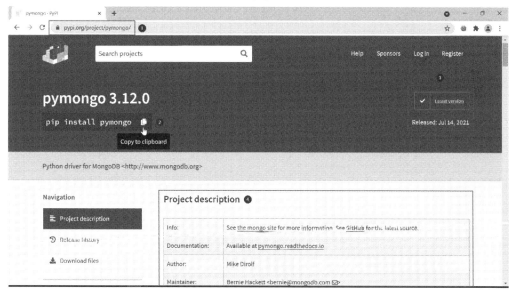

Figure 6.10: *PyPI MongoDB official Home Page*

2. Now, as we know what is the right command to install the official MongoDB driver for Python, choose any location on your machine and create a new folder or directory named "**mongodb-python**", as shown in *figure 6.11*:

Figure 6.11: *Create a new directory named "mongodb-python" on your Windows Machine*

3. Now open up your command prompt and navigate to this directory "**mongodb-python**", as shown in *figure 6.12*:

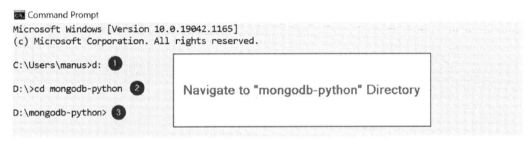

Figure 6.12: *Navigating to "mongodb-python" directory*

4. Now run any one of the following commands, which are mentioned on the MongoDB driver home page of the PyPI website. This will install MongoDB driver for Python to our directory where we are now going to create our Python application along with MongoDB, as shown in *figure 6.13*:

```
pip install pymongo
```

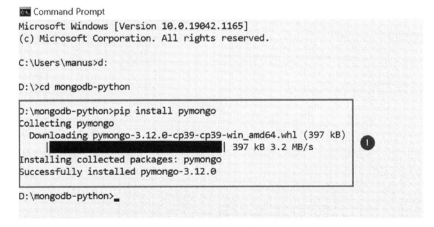

Figure 6.13: *Installing MongoDB driver for Python*

As we are finished with the setup of our environment with MongoDB and Python; now, we can start with the programming part.

Programming with Python and MongoDB

In the previous section of this chapter, we have set up our environment to run Python with MongoDB. Now let us start our programming part.

Let us now try to write a code in Python which do the small task of connecting to the database. Here, we will be writing a small piece of code in Python with the help of the Python MongoDB driver that we have installed and set up in our previous step.

Note that, as we are using Python and writing Python code, it is recommended to use some Code Editor or **Integrated Development Environment** (**IDE**) like Microsoft Visual Studio Code or any Code Editor of your choice. You can download and install Microsoft Visual Studio Code from this link: **https://code.visualstudio.com**. Microsoft Visual Studio Code is open-source and free software and is available for almost all operating systems.

Example 1—connecting to MongoDB server using Python

In our example, we have imported the "**pymongo**" which is a Python MongoDB driver module, used the "**MongoDBClient**" variable, which is assigned as an object for the "**MongoClient**" class, and passed the MongoDB connection string in the constructor. We have saved this file as "**mongodb-connection.py**" under this path: **D:\mongodb-python** and the following is the code for the same, as shown in *figure 6.14*:

Code 1

```
import pymongo

MongoDBClient = pymongo.MongoClient("mongodb://localhost:2/017/")

if MongoDBClient:

  print("Connected Sucessfully to MongoDB Server using Python Driver for MongoDB")

else:

  print("Some Error While Connecting to MongoDB Server")
```

The following is the screenshot of the same in Microsoft Visual Studio code:

Figure 6.14: Working with Python files using Microsoft Visual Studio Code

Now let us run this example. Open up your command prompt and navigate to the "**mongodb-python**" folder where you have saved this file and type the following command to run this code:

```
python mongodb-connection.py
```

You will see that we have connected successfully to the MongoDB server using Python, as shown in *figure 6.15*:

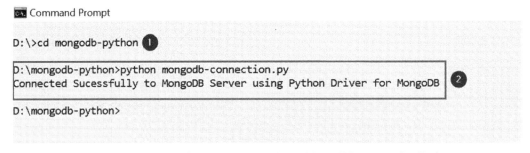

Figure 6.15: Command prompt—connecting to MongoDB server using Python

Example 2—fetching MongoDB documents using Python

In our example, we have imported the "**pymongo**", which is a Python MongoDB driver module, used the "**MongoDBClient**" variable, which is assigned as an object for the "**MongoClient**" class, and passed the MongoDB connection string in the constructor. Then we have created a variable DB, which has assigned our database "**BPBOnlineBooksDB**". After that, we have used the "**db. BPBOnlineBooksCollection.find()**" method in a for loop and printed all the documents in the "**BPBOnlineBooksCollection**" collection. We have saved this file as "**mongodb-list-documents.py**" under this path: **D:\mongodb-python** and the following is the code for the same:

Code 1

```
import pymongo

MongoDBClient = pymongo.MongoClient("mongodb://localhost:27017/")

if MongoDBClient:

  print("Connected Sucessfully to MongoDB Server using Python Driv-
er for MongoDB")

  db = MongoDBClient.BPBOnlineBooksDB

  if db:

    print("Our Python Script Found All these records:")

    for documents in db.BPBOnlineBooksCollection.find():

      print(documents)

  else:

    print("Some Error While Connecting to Database")

else:

  print("Some Error While Connecting to MongoDB Server")
```

Now let us run this example. Open up your command prompt and navigate to the **"mongodb-python"** folder where you have saved this file and type the following command to run this code:

python mongodb-list-documents.py

You will see that we have connected successfully to the MongoDB server using Python, and then this script has also displayed all the documents in the MongoDB collection, as shown in *figure 6.16*:

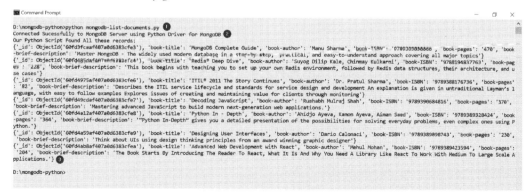

Figure 6.16: *Command prompt—connecting to MongoDB server and fetching the documents from collection using Python*

Conclusion

In this chapter, we have covered the introduction to Python programming with MongoDB and how we can use Python with MongoDB. We have also learned that in order to run Python with MongoDB server, we should have the right environment in place. We have also learned how we can set up MongoDB with Python. In the last section of this chapter, we have done some coding and run some practical examples to connect and work with the MongoDB server using Python. Till now in this book, we have learned how to set up the right environments and how to connect with MongoDB using various programming languages such as PHP, Node. js, React Native, and Python; from the upcoming chapters, we will start with the full-stack development with a complete software ecosystem of various applications. The upcoming chapters will be very interesting as we will learn how these apps connect with each other in a software ecosystem.

Questions

1. What is Python?

2. What is PIP, and its purpose?

3. What is PyPI?

4. What is the command to install the official MongoDB driver for Python?

5. Give an example to connect to MongoDB server with Python.

6. Give an example to connect to the MongoDB server and list the documents with Python.

CHAPTER 7

Full-Stack Development Using MongoDB

Starting with the step-by-step practical Web and mobile application development using MongoDB, PHP, JavaScript (Node.js), React Native, and Python.

What comes to your mind when you encounter the word "Full Stack"? Many of us have been doing it or could be a part of this during our day-to-day jobs. This chapter covers the instruction to various terms, which are used in software development, including the full-stack. This chapter covers topics related to application and software development and terms such as frontend, backend and full-stack development and understanding various technologies, frameworks, and stacks which are used in these various types of applications.

In the later part of this chapter, we will cover applications that we are going to develop in our next chapters. We will also cover an overview of various technologies and tools that we would be using to develop our Web and mobile apps. This chapter is an interesting one to get an overall overview of the upcoming chapters, which are related to the step-by-step full-stack Web and mobile application development of this book.

Structure

In this chapter, we will discuss the following topics:

- Introduction to full-stack development

- Frontend technologies and stack

- Backend technologies and stack

- Full-stack development and technologies

- Overview of applications that we will develop in our upcoming chapters

- Overview of various technologies and tools that we will use to develop our Web and mobile apps

Objectives

After studying this chapter reader will understand the full stack development covering both frontend and backend technologies and various other stacks. While going through this chapter reader will get a brief understanding of full-stack development and technologies and the applications that we are further going to develop in our next advanced chapters of this book.

Introduction to full-stack development

Many of you might be wondering what exactly this term "full-stack" means? Let us understand this term and why full-stack development is a trending topic these days, and why we have chosen this to be included for application development for this book. Before we understand what exactly the term "full-stack" means, let us understand a few other terms.

Frontend

The front end is usually the visible part of any application by which the user interacts with the application. Generally, it is the interface that is responsible for user interaction. These application interfaces are presented to the user so that users can interact with the system. Every frontend interface could be unique in terms of which technology they use. Some of the interfaces, like desktop apps, have their frontend interfaces written in programming languages, which are different than what we use in Web and mobile development.

For websites and mobile applications, their frontend relies on a few software like Web browsers or mobile OS in the case of native apps. For example, a frontend for a website or web app renders with the help of Web browsers such as Google Chrome or Mac Safari.

Normally, whenever any frontend is presented to users, it has various elements such as forms, buttons, text boxes, and so on, and using these frontend elements, the user can easily interact with the application.

Frontend technologies and stack

Front-end also refers to the client-side of the application. So, anything we are developing on the frontend is mostly the client-side development.

Client-side development can be Web-based (browser-based) or can use some mobile frameworks to present the frontend to the users.

If the frontend application uses the browser to display the application, then technologies or stack that is used in the development is mostly as follows:

- HTML
- CSS
- JavaScript
- CSS Frameworks like Bootstrap
- JavaScript Libraries like jQuery

Mostly if the front-end application uses mobile to display applications, then the technologies or stack that is used mostly depend on the type of application. These applications can be classified into two types:

- Native apps
- Hybrid apps

Native mobile apps

Native mobile apps are developed for a specific platform like Android or iOS. They are native in nature which means they are developed using technologies or programming languages that are related to these platforms. For example, if we write a Native app for Android, then the app will use Java as a programming language, and thus app developers should develop and code their app in the Native language for the Android platform, which is Java. The same thing applies to iOS-based Native apps. In the case of iOS apps, we need to develop these apps in their native language, which is Objective C.

Native apps have advantages in terms of the user experience, and they are also fast than hybrid mobile apps. But these are more costly to develop as we need to develop these apps for all the platforms; for example, an app needs to be developed separately for Android as well as iOS, which also costs time.

The major programming languages that are used to develop Native apps are as follows:

- Java

- Objective C

Hybrid mobile apps

Hybrid mobile apps are developed using the combined features of both Web and native technologies. Mostly these apps use the elements and components from both Web and native platforms.

Usually, hybrid apps are faster to develop and are also cross-platform compatible, which means that if we are developing a hybrid app, then it can be supported by different mobile platforms like Android and iOS.

Mostly hybrid apps work great on multi-platforms, and many new frameworks are coming up that help develop them. Most of these use Web-based technologies plus some features of the devices, which are native. These hybrid apps work on a Web view. Basically, a hybrid app runs like a Web app on mobile platforms and uses additional native features of mobile platforms.

Hybrid apps work on multi-platforms due to the wrapper which they use, which helps run these hybrid apps on different mobile platforms.

The major programming languages and frameworks which are used to develop hybrid apps are as follows:

- HTML

- CSS

- JavaScript

- jQuery mobile

- Ionic framework

- Facebook's React Native framework

- PhoneGap framework

- Google's Flutter framework

- Python Kivy framework

- Python BeeWare framework

Backend

The backend also refers to the server-side of the application. Anything we are developing on the server end is mostly server-side development. It uses various server-side applications and components to render the results to the client. Right from the request that is sent to the server by clients, the server then processes them using various services and programs, which are running on the server end, and these are hidden from the client-side.

Back-end technologies and stack

Backend technologies and stack can include Web servers such as Apache HTTP Server, database servers like MongoDB or MySQL, and server-side programming languages, applications, frameworks, and server app stacks such as PHP, Node.js, Express.js, Python, WAMP, LAMP, or MAMP.

Backend application uses various server stacks, technologies, programming languages, and backend frameworks to render results to the client. These could vary widely from one backend application to another, and these could include the following:

- Web servers such as Apache HTTP Server and Nginx Server.

- Server stacks such as—WAMP, LAMP, and so on.

- Server-side programming languages, such as PHP, Java, Node.js, Python, Ruby on Rails, C#, ASP.Net, and so on.

- Server-side frameworks, such as Express.js, Sails.js, Laravel, CodeIgniter, Symphony, Zend Framework, Django, and so on.

- Database servers, such as MongoDB, Redis, Firebase, ElasticSearch, Neo4j, OrientDB, MSSQL, Mysql, Oracle, and so on.

- Application servers such as—Apache Tomcat, JBoss, and so on.

Full-stack

Full-stack is a term used to donate the technology development part of an application or computer program that uses technologies related to the frontend as well as the backend. Full-stack combines various technologies, programming languages, frameworks, software libraries, and other technology stacks such as Web stack, mobile stack, hybrid stack, and so on to develop the entire ecosystem of the application.

Full-stack development and technologies

Full-stack development refers to the use of the right mix of both frontend and backend technologies to develop applications across Web, mobile, and various other devices such as tabs, smart TV, IoT, and so on.

There are various technologies that are listed in our previous sections, which cover technologies used in the frontend and backend. During any full-stack development, we may pick and use these technologies according to our requirements.

There are various stacks available today that we can use based on our requirements; these are combinations of various technologies and programming languages, such as:

- **MEAN stack:** MongoDB, Express.js, Angular JS and Node.js

- **MERN stack:** MongoDB, Express.js, React.js, and Node.js

- **MEVN stack:** MongoDB, Express.js, VUE.js, and Node.js

- **Meteor.js:** a full-stack framework based on Node.js and supports Angular. js and React.js for frontend development and has inbuilt support for MongoDB

There are many other stacks available that have the combination of various technologies, and those can be used along with MongoDB, such as:

- WAMP and LAMP Stack where we can use MongoDB

- Python with MongoDB

Full-stack developer

By going through and reading the above sections, many of you might be thinking that why we have mentioned so many technologies as we are learning MongoDB in this book? This list could be more, but in order to make you understand the use of MongoDB with the current technologies in today's modern applications, we have covered these technologies in this chapter.

We are not going to learn all of these technologies in this book as it is out of the scope of this book. The goal is to experience practical use of MongoDB with the help of the right mix of technologies that are trending and used by development companies widely across the globe. So you are able to understand that MongoDB is used widely and almost everywhere.

MongoDB is one of the first choices of developers and organizations today because of its availability and compatibility with most of the widely used programming languages, its developer friendliness, and flexibility.

A full-stack developer is a person who can develop an application in frontend as well as backend technologies by using the right mix of programming languages and frameworks.

The purpose of the next chapters in which we are going to create a *"full-stack application"* with a mix of various technologies is to make you understand how we can use MongoDB with various technologies and programming languages so that you can acquire a good knowledge of application development using MongoDB and you can use the same knowledge in your future development of various applications.

Our next chapters are related to the step-by-step application development using MongoDB and various client-side languages such as HTML, CSS, and JavaScript and server-side programming languages such as PHP, Node.js, and Python, which we are going to cover following by keeping MongoDB in the center of the whole ecosystem of various applications:

- Development of CRUD based backend Web application using PHP and MongoDB

- Development of RESTful APIs using Node.js and MongoDB

- Development of dynamic bookshop frontend using Node.js and MongoDB

- Development of mobile book review app using React Native and MongoDB

The whole ecosystem of Web and mobile applications, which we are going to create in our upcoming chapters, can be better understood by the following figure (*figure 7.1*):

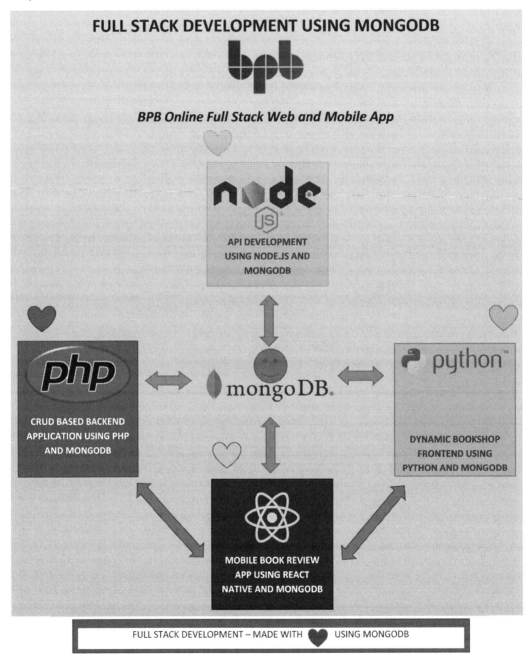

Figure 7.1: Full-stack development with MongoDB—eco system

Conclusion

In this chapter, we have covered topics related to application development and also learned about application and software development terms, such as frontend, backend, and full-stack development, and understood various technologies, frameworks, and stacks, which are used in these various types of applications. We have also learned about an overview of various technologies and tools that we would be using to develop our Web and mobile apps in our upcoming advanced chapters of this book.

In the upcoming chapter, we will cover the step-by-step method to develop a CRUD-based backend Web application using PHP and MongoDB, in which we will create a dynamic backend application.

Questions

1. What is a frontend?

2. Name some frontend programming languages.

3. What is a backend?

4. Can we use JavaScript for backend application development?

5. What do you understand by the term "full-stack"?

6. Name any full-stack framework.

CHAPTER 8

MongoDB Step by Step Practical Application Development Using PHP

Backend catalog of a publication house

Till now, in this book, we have been covered various programming languages, such as PHP, Node.js, React Native, and Python, and learned how to use these with MongoDB. In this chapter, we will cover the practical step-by-step development of CRUD-based backend application using PHP and MongoDB along with frontend languages such as HTML, CSS, and JavaScript. Later in this chapter, we will learn how we can create a dashboard for our application and various other related functionalities required for the overall development of the catalog management system for a publication house. All the sections have been explained in step-by-step practical manner so that by the end of this chapter you feel more confident in PHP and MongoDB application development.

Structure

In this chapter, we will discuss the following topics:

- Overview of our CRUD based Web application developed using PHP and MongoDB

- Requirements

- How our final application looks like

- Pre-development steps

- Backend catalog dashboard development

- Listing of catalog functionality

- Adding new book functionality

- Deleting functionality

Objectives

After studying this chapter, the reader will be able to understand how we can develop a CRUD-based Web application using PHP and MongoDB. Before we start with the coding and application development part, we will have a sneak preview of what our final application will look like and then understand and perform some pre-development steps. Later in this chapter, we will learn how to develop a backend catalog dashboard using PHP and MongoDB, including various other functionalities, such as the listing of catalog functionality, adding new book functionality, and deleting functionality, using PHP and MongoDB.

Overview of our Web application developed using PHP and MongoDB

In this chapter, we are going to develop a CRUD application using PHP, MongoDB, HTML, CSS, and JavaScript.

We are going to create an application in which we are able to create the backend catalog of a publication house such as BPB publications.

This backend application will have the following features:

- Ability to add (create) the book with its details

- Ability to list (read) all the books in the catalog

- Ability to modify (update) the details of existing book entry

- Ability to remove (delete) any existing book entry

In order to create this interface, we would be writing some codes using the following:

- **PHP**—to connect to MongoDB Server using the PHP driver and to do server-side CRUD operations and interacting with MongoDB.

- **HTML**—to present user interfaces such as forms and buttons so that users can interact with these pages to add, update, delete, or list the catalog.

- **CSS**—to add some nice styles to our forms and buttons so that they look a bit pretty.

- **JavaScript**—We would be using client-side JavaScript and jQuery (which is a very popular and widely used client-side JavaScript library) for form validations, modal windows, and performing some actions when some event occurs (event handling).

Requirements

The reader should have the basic knowledge and understanding of the following:

- PHP
- HTML
- CSS
- HTML Forms
- CSS Flexbox
- JavaScript
- jQuery (recommended, but optional for this chapter)

Final application

As we complete all the sections of this chapter, our final app will look something like this (as shown in *figure 8.1* and *figure 8.2*):

Application Dashboard Page

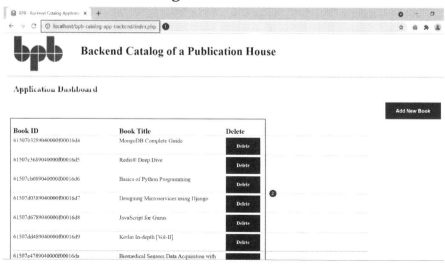

Figure 8.1: Application Dashboard page—preview

Add new book page

Figure 8.2: Add new book page—preview

Let us divide our application into the following sections so that we can then combine all these sections having all the features of this backend catalog application. Following are the sections that we would be working on:

- Backend catalog dashboard
- Listing of catalogs
- Adding new book functionality
- Deleting functionality
- Editing and updating functionality (code yourself)

Let us start now with the actual development part. To start with, let us first get ready with the real environment so that what we will code will reflect on the system.

Pre-development steps

In our previous chapter, where we have given the introduction about getting started with MongoDB and PHP, we have used MongoDB Extension and written our codes accordingly. It is possible to follow the same way in this chapter, where we can use the PHP MongoDB extension and code. But there is another better way to do it by using the MongoDB PHP library instead of the PHP MongoDB extension. MongoDB PHP library provides a high-level abstraction for the low-level API which PHP extension provides. So, we are going to install and use the MongoDB PHP library in this chapter before we start coding. Follow these steps before we start to code.

Step 1—install composer

1. Composer is the package and dependency manager for PHP, just like NPM for Node.js or PyPI for Python. So, in order to install the composer, visit: **https://getcomposer.org** and click the download link which will open the download page: **https://getcomposer.org/download/**, as shown in *figure 8.3*:

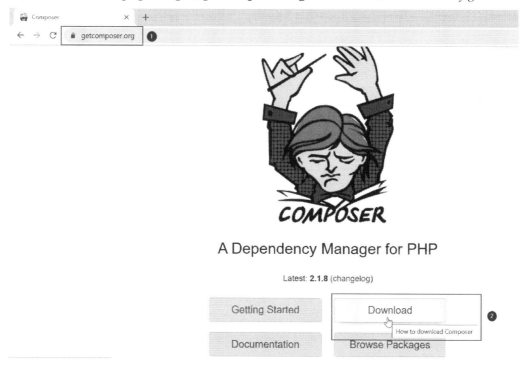

Figure 8.3: Composer Home page

2. You can download the composer installer and run it. Just follow the instructions given on the website and install the composer. The installation would be similar to the other software installers that you run on your Windows machine (in case you are using other operating systems such as Linux or Mac OS, please follow the related instructions for installing composer on these operating systems). Once you run the composer installer, the installation

wizard will appear, and it will install composer on your Windows machine, as shown in *figure 8.4*:

Figure 8.4: *Composer installation wizard*

3. During the installation, the composer will ask you to provide the location of the PHP as we are running a WAMP server and using PHP version 7.3.21 (this version will vary in case of new releases. So, you should check the correct version from your WAMP server by clicking the WAMP green icon in your Windows system tray). Just click the **Browse** button, navigate to the WAMP PHP directory and select "**php.exe**" from there, which has a similar path like: **D:\wamp64\bin\php\php7.3.21\php.exe**. You should also check the checkbox that says "**Add this PHP to your path?**" and then click the "**Next**" button, as shown in *figure 8.5*:

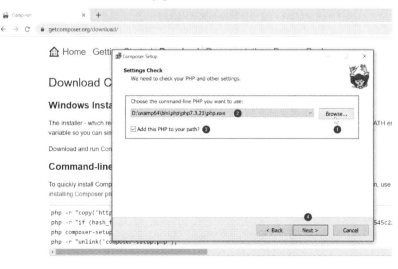

Figure 8.5: *Composer installation—PHP path*

4. Once the composer installation is completed by the installer wizard, read the important information provided by the installation wizard and then click the "**Next**" button to proceed to the finish screen, as shown in *figure 8.6*:

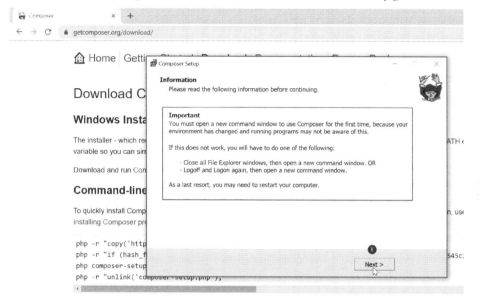

Figure 8.6: *Composer installation*

5. Click the **Finish** button, and we are done with the installation part, as shown in *figure 8.7*:

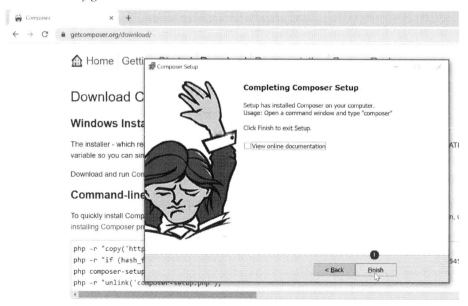

Figure 8.7: *Composer installation — completed*

Step 2—adding MongoDB Extension to php.ini file

As we have given the command line PHP path to: **D:\wamp64\bin\php\php7.3.21\ php.exe** while installing the composer, it will now take the reference of PHP using this path and use php.ini of this location. Make sure that you have enabled the MongoDB extension in this file if you have not done it yet (this step was explained in the previous chapter - *Chapter 3 (Starting Up Programming with MongoDB and PHP)* of this book, where we have given the basic introduction of PHP with MongoDB). To enable this extension for this location, just open the **php.ini** file in the location: **D:\ wamp64\bin\php\php7.3.21** (make sure this file is related to your PHP version and located on the right path, which is "**D:\wamp64\bin\php\php7.3.21\php. ini**", in our case. You can also navigate to this path and open this right "**php.ini**" using a text editor like Notepad). We will add the following line where you see other extensions like MySQL in this file, and after adding this line save this file and close it, as shown in *figure 8.8*:

extension=mongodb

```
php.ini - Notepad
File  Edit  Format  View  Help
; move to the new ('extension=<ext>) syntax.
;
; Notes for Windows environments :
;
; - Many DLL files are located in the extensions/ (PHP 4) or ext/ (PHP 5+)
;   extension folders as well as the separate PECL DLL download (PHP 5+).
;   Be sure to appropriately set the extension_dir directive.
;
extension=bz2
extension=curl
;extension=dba
;extension=com_dotnet
;extension=enchant
extension=fileinfo
;extension=ftp
extension=gd2
extension=gettext
extension=gmp
extension=intl
extension=imap
;extension=interbase
extension=ldap
extension=mbstring
extension=exif      ; Must be after mbstring as it depends on it
extension=mysqli
extension=mongodb  1
;extension=odbc
extension=openssl
;extension=pdo_firebird
extension=pdo_mysql
```

Figure 8.8: php.ini file—adding MongoDB extension

Step 3—start WAMP server

You should start the WAMP server by typing "**wamp**" on the search area of the taskbar. Opening the WAMP server will launch the WAMP server on your Windows machine, as shown in *figure 8.9*:

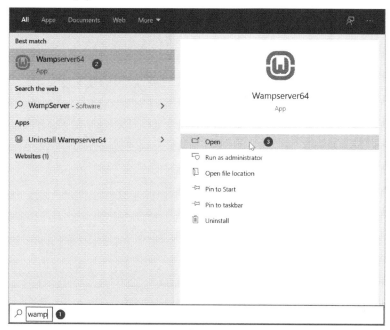

Figure 8.9: *Launching WAMP server*

1. Once the WAMP server has been successfully started, you will see the WAMP server icon (in green) in the Task Bar tray. When you run the WAMP server, it usually takes a few seconds to start all the services such as Apache, MySQL, and so on, and the icon changes from red to orange and finally to green. If the WAMP icon is green, it means that all the services have been successfully started, and now you can use the WAMP server, as shown in *figure 8.10*:

Figure 8.10: *WAMP server—all services have been started successfully*

Step 4—check MongoDB server windows service

Whenever you install MongoDB on Windows Machine by using MongoDB installer, by default, MongoDB service is installed, and by using this, we are able to run MongoDB server without any commands. This service should be running on our Windows machine so that we are able to use MongoDB Server and connect using any MongoDB client or using some programming language like PHP. In order to check that the MongoDB service is running correctly on our Windows machine, please follow these steps:

1. In the search section of your taskbar, type "**services**" and open it, as shown in *figure 8.11*:

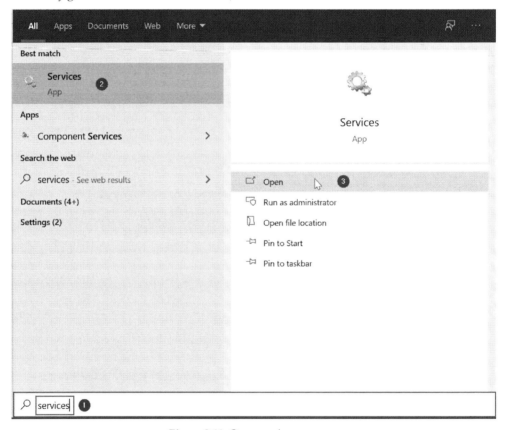

Figure 8.11: Open services manager

2. This will open Windows services manager. You will see all the services that are installed on your Windows machine. Navigate to MongoDB. Navigate to MongoDB server (MongoDB). Click this service and start it, if in case it is not yet started (you may leave this step if it is already started), as shown in *figure 8.12*:

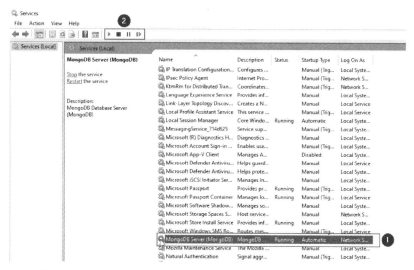

Figure 8.12: Starting MongoDB service from Windows service manager

Step 5—running localhost

Once the WAMP server has started on your machine, you can start working with the local server, which has Apache and PHP installed. As we have the required environment ready, we can run localhost.

1. To run localhost, just open your favorite browser like Google Chrome and type: **http://localhost/** and then press *Enter*. This will open up a new page, and you will be shown the WAMP server default page on your localhost. Here, you will get all the information about the version of the WAMP server and server configurations, which have a list of various software running in the background along with their version details such as Apache Web Server and PHP, as shown in *figure 8.13*:

Figure 8.13: WAMP server—localhost

If you are able to see this page, then this means that most of the things are ready to start the application development part of this chapter. Let us now start with the development before we start with the actual code. Let us do a few more steps.

Step 6—start creating a skeleton for your application

Follow these instructions to create the project folders:

It is also recommended that you should create a folder under your WAMP www folder for this purpose and save your files under that folder. The path could be somewhat like this: **D:\wamp64\www\bpb-catalog-app-backend**, as shown in *figure 8.14*:

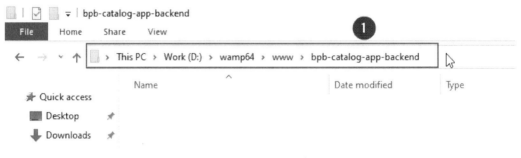

Figure 8.14: Start creating a skeleton for your application

1. Now, under the following path: **D:\wamp64\www\bpb-catalog-app-backend** create three more sub-folders named as follows and as shown in *figure 8.15*:

    - images

    - css

    - js

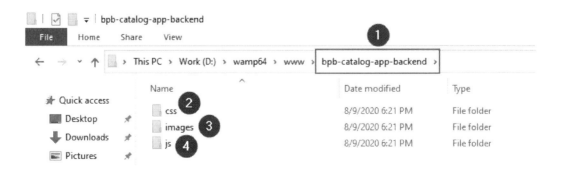

Figure 8.15: Start creating a skeleton for your application—subfolders

Step 7—create a MongoDB database for your application

Follow these instructions to create the MongoDB database for this application:

1. In the search section of your taskbar, type "**Compass**" and open it. This will open the MongoDB Compass client in your machine, as shown in *figure 8.16*:

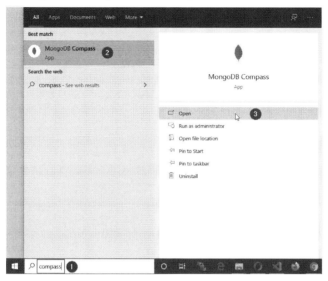

Figure 8.16: Create MongoDB database for your application—launch Compass

2. After the MongoDB Compass is launched, we need to first connect to MongoDB Server. For this, you can either connect using MongoDB URL String or by filling the individual fields like we are using in our example. Type "**localhost**" for hostname and "27017" for the port. Keep all other settings as it is and then click the **Connect** button to connect to the MongoDB server, as shown in *figure 8.17*:

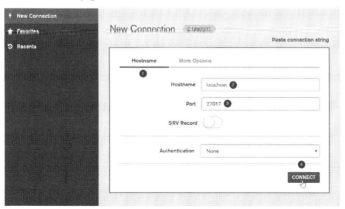

Figure 8.17: Create MongoDB database for your application—connect to MongoDB server using Compass

3.   As we need to create a new database for our application, click the "**CREATE DATABASE**" button to create a new database, as shown in *figure 8.18*:

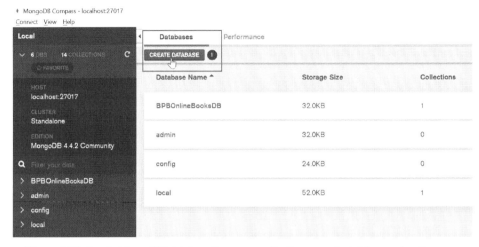

Figure 8.18: *Create MongoDB database for your application—create database using Compass*

4.   This will open a new popup window in which you need to enter the name of the database and also the name of the collection. Enter "**Database Name**" as "**BPBCatalogDB**" and "**Collection Name**" as "**BPBCatalogCollection**" and then click the "**CREATE DATABASE**" button to create a new database along with the collection. Once this is done, we will have a new database as well as a new collection ready to be used in our application, as shown in *figure 8.19*:

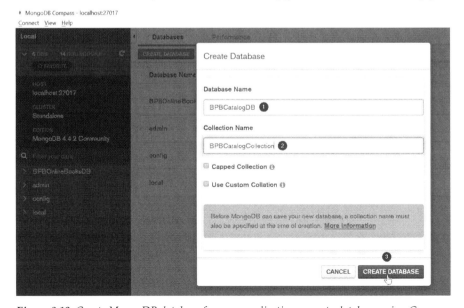

Figure 8.19: *Create MongoDB database for your application—create database using Compass*

Developing our application

As we are now ready with the right environment and skeleton of our application, along with the new database and collection that we are going to use in this application, let us start with the coding part.

Note that as we are using PHP and writing PHP code, it will be recommended to use some code editor or **Integrated Development Environment (IDE)** like Microsoft Visual Studio Code or any Code Editor of your choice. You can download and install Microsoft Visual Studio Code from this link: **https://code.visualstudio.com**. Microsoft Visual Studio Code is open-source and free software and is available for almost all operating systems.

Step 1—installing MongoDB PHP Library in our project folder using composer

As in the previous section of this chapter, we have installed composer; now let us install the MongoDB PHP library to our project folder so that we can use this library in our project and code.

1. Open a command prompt and then navigate to your project folder, which is: "**D:\wamp64\www\bpb-catalog-app-backend**" in our case. In the command prompt, type the following command:

   ```
   composer require mongodb/mongodb
   ```

   This will install the MongoDB PHP library into your project folder, as shown in *figure 8.20*:

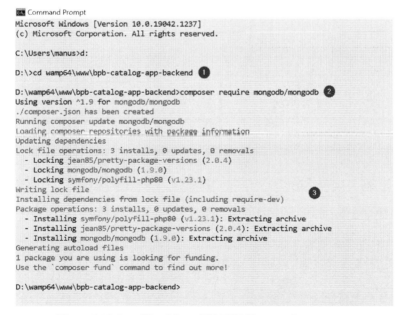

Figure 8.20: Installing MongoDB PHP library using composer

2. Once the composer has installed the MongoDB PHP library into your project folder, you can see that it has installed the MongoDB PHP library code and has created a "**vendor**" folder and two other files, "**composer.json**" and "**composer.lock**" (as shown in *figure 8.21*). You may browse the "**vendor**" folder and check the contents.

Figure 8.21: Installing MongoDB PHP library using composer —folder and files created by the composer during installation

Step 1—creating a MongoDB connection file

In our example, we have used the "**$mongoDBClientConnection**" variable, which is assigned as an object for the "**MongoClient()**" class. We have saved this file as "**mongodb-connection.php**" under this path: **D:\wamp64\www\bpb-catalog-app-backend** and the following is the code for the same, as shown in *figure 8.22*:

Code 1

```php
<?php
require 'vendor/autoload.php';
// Composer Autoloader which will include MongoDB PHP Library Files in the Project

$mongoDBClientConnection = new MongoDB\Client("mongodb://localhost:27017");
//Connecting to MongoDB Server
?>
```

Figure 8.22: Creating a MongoDB connection file – Microsoft Visual Studio Code

Step 2—creating an HTML structure and dividing it into parts

Before we can code the various sections, let us create a basic structure for our app. We will do it by writing some HTML and then dividing this HTML into a few parts and calling these parts of HTML with the help of PHP (including them using PHP). We will divide this code into two separate PHP files and name them as follows, as shown in *figure 8.23*:

- **header.php**
- **footer.php**

We are going to save these files in our project folder, which is: **D:\wamp64\www\bpb-catalog-app-backend**

Code 1—our basic HTML structure

```html
<!doctype html>

<html lang="en">
<head>
 <meta charset="utf-8">

 <title>BPB - Backend Catalog Application in PHP and MongoDB</title>
 <meta name="description" content="Backend Catalog of a Publication House">
 <meta name="author" content="BPB Publications">

 <link rel="stylesheet" href="css/styles.css">
</head>

<body>

 <script src="js/scripts.js"></script>
</body>

</html>
```

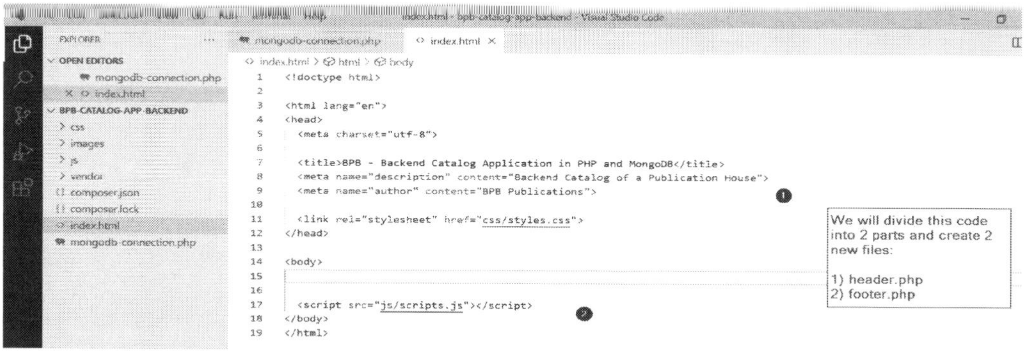

Figure 8.23: Working with PHP files using Microsoft Visual Studio Code

Code 2—our header.php file

```
<!doctype html>

<html lang="en">
<head>
  <meta charset="utf-8">

  <title>BPB - Backend Catalog Application in PHP and MongoDB</title>
    <meta name="description" content="Backend  Catalog  of  a  Publica-
tion House">
  <meta name="author" content="BPB Publications">

  <link rel="stylesheet" href="css/styles.css">
</head>

<body>
```

Code 3—our footer.php file

```
  <script src="js/scripts.js"></script>

</body>

</html>
```

Step 3—adding MongoDB connection and publishing house logo to our application

In this step, we are going to add Mongo DB connection (using PHP require method) and logo (using image using HTML **<img />** tag) in **header.php**. For this, open your **header.php** file and add the new code at the end of this file (we already have a **mongodb-connection.php** file which we have already created in our previous steps, and we also have one logo image in our project "**images**" directory named as "**bpb_logo.png**" which we are going to use here). Following is the updated code for **header.php**:

Code 1—our header.php file (updated)

```
<?php

require("mongodb-connection.php");

?>
```

```
<!doctype html>

<html lang="en">

<head>

  <meta charset="utf-8">


  <title>BPB - Backend Catalog Application in PHP and MongoDB</title>

    <meta name="description" content="Backend  Catalog  of  a  Publica-
tion House">

  <meta name="author" content="BPB Publications">


  <link rel="stylesheet" href="css/styles.css">

</head>


<body>


  <div class="top-section">

  <div class="logo"><img src="images/bpb-logo.png" alt="BPB Logo" title="B-
PB Logo"/></div>

    <div class="title-text"><h1>Backend Catalog of a Publication House</
h1></div>

  </div>

  <hr />
```

Step 4—creating application main file (index.php)

In this step, we will create a new file named "**index.php**", and which will be our main dashboard file (or template). We will include "**header.php**" and "**footer. php**" in this file, and we will save this file in the same location of our project folder, which is: **D:\wamp64\www\bpb-catalog-app-backend**

Code 1—our index.php file

```
<?php

include("header.php");
```

```
?>


<div class="content">

 <h2>Application Dashboard</h2>

</div>


<?php

include("footer.php");

?>
```

Step 5—testing the application for first run

In this step, we are going to simply open the application using the browser. For this type, your project URL on the browser, which is: **http://localhost/bpb-catalog-app-backend/** in our case. If everything is working fine till now and you have followed all the previous instructions, then a new page will open in the browser displaying all the code that we have done till now without any errors, as shown in *figure 8.24*:

Backend Catalog of a Publication House

Application Dashboard

Figure 8.24: *Testing the application for first run*

Step 6—adding CSS and JavaScript to our project

In this step, we are going to add some CSS and JavaScript to our project. If you have noticed in the "**header.php**" and "**footer.php**" files of our project, we already have a reference of one CSS file named "**styles.css**" in the "**header.php**" file and "**scripts.js**" in the "**footer.php**" file. Now let us create these two files under their respective folders. We will create the following new files under our project directory:

- **styles.css**: Under the "**css**" directory of our project and the path would be something similar to this: **D:\wamp64\www\bpb-catalog-app-backend\ css**

- **scripts.js**: Under the "**js**" directory of our project and the path would be something similar to this: **D:\wamp64\www\bpb-catalog-app-backend\js**

We would be writing some code for CSS, in which we would be using Flexbox, which is a modern and flexible (as the name suggests) layout model for CSS, and it is supported by all the modern browsers these days. We would be doing some alignments in the top section of the application where we would be aligning logo and top text in one line using CSS Flexbox, and the following is the code for the same:

Code 1—our styles.css file

```css
.top-section{
  display: flex;
  flex-direction: row;
  margin-left:20px;
  margin-right:20px;
}

.title-text{
  padding-left:50px;
}

.content{
  margin-left:20px;
  margin-right:20px;
}
```

Let us also add some JavaScript in the **scripts.js** file. Here we would only be testing if our JavaScript file is loading properly, and to verify this, we will print one message on the browser console. Following is the code for the same:

Code 2—our scripts.js file

```js
console.log("*******BPB Publications*******");

console.log("If you can see this in your Console that means The JavaScript File has been loaded Properly");
```

After you have created these two files, go back to your browser and refresh your page. Also, now open the console of your browser (you can open the console by right-clicking anywhere in the browser page and clicking **Inspect Element**. This will open the **Developer Tools,** where you can find the **Console** option).

If everything is working fine, then, in this case, you will see the screen with the new changes done by CSS on the top section as well as the console message printed using JavaScript, as shown in *figure 8.25*:

Application Dashboard

Figure 8.25: Application dashboard after adding CSS and JS code

As we are almost done with the initial setup and configuration of our application, let us now start creating the CRUD functionalities for our backend application. We have divided this application into the following parts and then will code each of them separately to develop a final application:

- Backend catalog dashboard

- Add new book functionality

- Listing of catalog

- Edit and update functionality

- Delete functionality

Backend catalog dashboard

In this part, we will be creating our catalog dashboard. We have already created an index file for this purpose in the previous section of this chapter. Now let us add some more functionalities in this section.

A typical application dashboard should be simple to use and should have all the functionalities which are user-friendly so that users can easily navigate and perform various operations. Let us keep this in mind and make it simple by following some steps.

Step 1 – Adding "Add New Book" button in our dashboard

We have added a few codes in "**index.php**", and our CSS File "**styles.css**" (which is in the "**css**" folder of our Project Directory), and the following is the new code for these two files that we have added to it:

Code 1—our index.php file

```php
<?php
include("header.php");
?>


 <div class="content">

  <h2>Application Dashboard</h2>

    <div class="addnewbook-container"><button type="button" name="addnew-book" id="addnewbook" class="addnewbook-btn" onclick="location.href='add-new-book.php'">Add New Book</button></div>

 </div>


<?php
include("footer.php");
?>
```

Code 2—our styles.css file

```css
/* Top Section */

.top-section{
 display: flex;
 flex-direction: row;
 margin-left:20px;
 margin-right:20px;
}

.title-text{
```

```
padding-left:50px;
}

/* Content Section */

.content{
margin-left:20px;
margin-right:20px;
}

/* Dashboard */

.addnewbook-container{
text-align:right;
}

.addnewbook-btn{
display: inline-block;
padding: 15px 30px;
background-color:#002b80;
border: none;
color: white;
font-size: 14px;
font-weight: bold;
cursor:pointer;
text-align: center;
text-decoration: none;
}
```

After the new changes done in these two files, you will see that a new button will appear in your dashboard, as shown in *figure 8.26*:

Figure 8.26: *Application dashboard after adding "Add New Book" button*

As a button has appeared in the dashboard, this button should now be used to perform some action. If some user clicks on this, there are two different ways to create this functionality:

1. Clicking this button will take you to a new page where there would be an HTML form in which the user can add details of a book.

2. Clicking this button will open up a popup dialog where there would be an HTML form in which the user can add details of a book.

In Case 2, we would stay on the same page without leaving this dashboard page, and it is a more user-friendly approach and better in terms of **User Experience** (**UX**).

But if we go with our second approach (which might seem to be a bit tricky for some readers), we need some libraries like jQuery and jQuery UI to achieve this, and we have to use AJAX too.

You might be familiar with jQuery, which is one of the most popular client-side JavaScript libraries. jQuery has many features such as **Document Object Model** (**DOM**) manipulations, event handling, CSS effects, animations, and much more. Many Web-based scripts and programs use jQuery as their base.

The second approach could be difficult for the readers who have less experience in jQuery. But if you want to try the second approach, you can do this with the help of jQuery. For this, you would be using jQuery and jQuery UI libraries and including them in your code. You would be using the jQuery UI Dialog Widget. If you want more details about this Widget, you can visit **https://jqueryui.com/dialog/**. Once you visit this link, you will get all the information from the official jQuery UI website, as shown in *figure 8.27*:

Figure 8.27: *jQuery UI widgets*

But we are not going with the second approach for this chapter as it could be more complex for some users. We would go with our first approach, which is simpler than the second approach. Also, the main target of this chapter is to make you aware of using MongoDB with PHP. So we are going to keep it simple for now.

Adding new book functionality

In this part, we will be creating new functionality to add a book. For this functionality, we need to create a new PHP file that will have an HTML form presented to the users so that users can fill in the details of the book. After the user fills in all the details of the book, press the Submit button of the form, and these details are stored in our MongoDB collection.

Let us now develop this functionality by following some steps:

Step 1—creating add new book functionality file (add-new-book.php)

In this step, we will create a new file named "**add-new-book.php**", which would be our main file (or template) to add new books. We will include "**header.php**" and "**footer.php**" in this file, and we will save this file in the same location of our project folder, which is: **D:\wamp64\www\bpb-catalog-app-backend** and following is the code for the same:

Code 1—our add-new-book.php file

```php
<?php
include("header.php");
?>

 <div class="content">
  <h2>Add New Book</h2>
 </div>

<?php
include("footer.php");
?>
```

Now add HTML form in this file so that the user can enter the book details, and the following is the code for the same:

Code 2—our add-new-book.php file (updated)

```php
<?php
include("header.php");
?>

 <div class="content">
  <h2>Add New Book</h2>

  <div class="addnewbook-form-container">

    <form action="add-new-book.php" onsubmit="return
addNewBookFormValidation()" method="post">
    <label for="book-title">Book Title:</label><br />
  <input type="text" id="book-title" name="book-title" placeholder="Please
Enter Book Title"><br />
    <label for="book-author-name">Book Author:</label><br />
      <input type="text" id="book-author-name" name="book-author-name"
placeholder="Please Enter Book Author Name"><br />
    <label for="book-isbn-number">Book ISBN Number:</label><br />
      <input type="text" id="book-isbn-number" name="book-isbn-number"
placeholder="Please Enter Book ISBN Number"><br />
    <label for="book-publication-year">Book Publication Year:</label><br
/>
    <input type="text" id="book-publication-year" name="book-publication-
year" placeholder="Please Enter Book Publication Year"><br />
    <input type="submit" value="Submit">
    </form>

  </div>

 </div>


<?php
include("footer.php");
?>
```

In this step, we are going to simply open the new application file that we have created just now using the browser. For this type, your project URL on the browser along with the file name, which is: **http://localhost/bpb-catalog-app-backend/add-new-book.php** in our case. If everything is working fine till now and you have followed all the previous instructions, then a new page will open in the browser displaying all the code that we have done till now without any errors, as shown in *figure 8.28*:

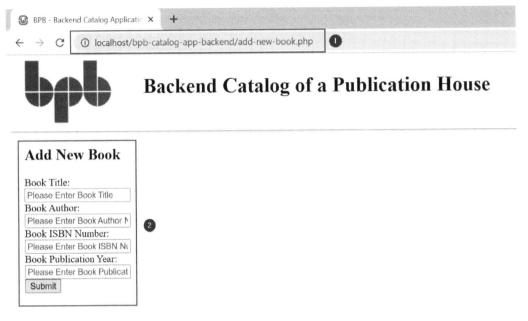

Figure 8.28: Application Add New Book page

Step 2—adding CSS and JavaScript to our form

In this step, we are going to add some CSS and JavaScript to our form so that it will look better. We can also add some validations so that if the user submits the form with blank values, then it will show some alerts, and the following is the code for the same:

Code 1—our styles.css file (appended code)

```
/* Add New Book */

.addnewbook-form-container{

 max-width:700px;

}

.addnewbook-form-container input[type=text] {
```

```css
  width: 100%;
  display: inline-block;
  padding: 10px 15px;
  margin: 10px 0;
  border: 1px solid #ff99ff;
  border-radius: none;
  box-sizing: border-box;
}


.addnewbook-form-container input[type=text]:hover {
  border: 1px solid #ff99ff;
  border-radius: none;
}


.addnewbook-form-container input[type=submit] {
  width: 100%;
  padding: 10px 15px;
  margin: 10px 0;
  background-color: #4d004d;
  color: white;
  border: none;
  border-radius: none;
  cursor: pointer;
}


.addnewbook-form-container input[type=submit]:hover {
  background-color: #73264d;
  cursor: pointer;
}
```

After applying this CSS, the add new book page will look better, as shown in *figure 8.29*:

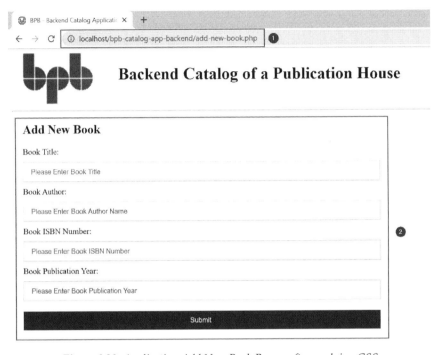

Figure 8.29: Application Add New Book Page—after applying CSS

Code 2—our scripts.js file (updated code)

```
console.log("*******BPB Publications*******");

console.log("If you can see this in your Console that means The JavaScript File has been loaded Properly");

function addNewBookFormValidation() {

  var booktitle = document.getElementById("book-title").value;

  var bookauthorname = document.getElementById("book-author-name").value;

  var bookisbnnumber = document.getElementById("book-isbn-number").value;

    var bookpublicationyear = document.getElementById("book-publication-year").value;

  if (booktitle == "" || bookauthorname == "" || bookisbnnumber == "" || bookpublicationyear == "") {

    alert("Please fill out all the Fields Correctly, Some Fields are left Blank");
```

```
    return false;
  }
}
```

After applying this JavaScript validation in the add new book page form, an alert box will start working as expected if the user tries to fill the form without entering the values in the form, as shown in *figure 8.30*:

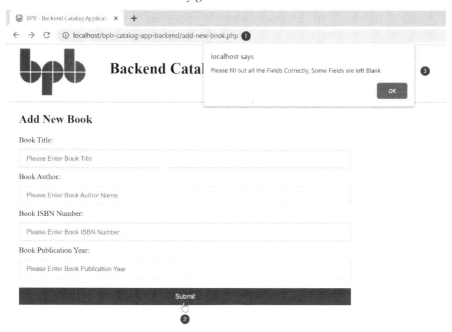

Figure 8.30: *Application Add New Book Page—after applying JS*

Let us now add two more fields in this form. The first one is for the "**Book Price**" and the second one is for the "**Book Cover Image**" and also update our **styles.css** and **scripts.css** file accordingly.

Step 3—Adding two more fields "Book Price" and "Book Cover Image"

As we are almost done with the form part, let us add two more fields in this form related to Book Price and Book Cover Image, and then we are ready for the next steps:

Code 1—our add-new-book.php file (updated code)

```
<form action="add-new-book.
```

```
php" onsubmit="return addNewBookFormValidation()" method="post" enctype="-
```

```
multipart/form-data">

    <div class="form-content-container">

      <div class="form-content-left">

        <h3>Basic Info</h3>
        <label for="book-title">Book Title:</label><br />
            <input type="text" id="book-title" name="book-title" placehold-
er="Please Enter Book Title"><br />
        <label for="book-author-name">Book Author:</label><br />
                <input type="text" id="book-author-name" name="book-au-
thor-name" placeholder="Please Enter Book Author Name"><br />
        <label for="book-isbn-number">Book ISBN Number:</label><br />
            <input type="text" id="book-isbn-number" name="book-isbn-num-
ber" placeholder="Please Enter Book ISBN Number"><br />
            <label for="book-publication-year">Book Publication Year:</la-
bel><br />
            <input type="text" id="book-publication-year" name="book-publica-
tion-year" placeholder="Please Enter Book Publication Year"><br />
        <input type="submit" value="Submit" name="submit-form-button">

      </div>

      <div class="form-content-right">
        <h3>Additional Info</h3>
        <label for="book-price">Book Price:</label><br />
            <input type="text" id="book-price" name="book-price" placehold-
er="Please Enter Book Price"><br />
            <label for="book-cover-image">Book Cover Image (Optional):</la-
bel><br />
        <input type="file" id="book-cover-image" name="book-cover-image">

      </div>

    </div>

    </form>
```

Code 2—our styles.css file (appended code)

```css
.addnewbook-form-container input[type=submit]:hover {

 background-color: #73264d;

 cursor: pointer;

}


.addnewbook-form-container .form-content-container{

 display: flex;

 flex-direction: row;

}


.addnewbook-form-container .form-content-container .form-content-left{

 width:70%;

 margin-right:10px;

}


.addnewbook-form-container .form-content-container .form-content-right{

 width:30%;

 margin-left:10px;

}
```

Code 3—our scripts.js file (updated code)

```javascript
console.log("*******BPB Publications*******");

console.log("If you can see this in your Console that means The JavaScript File has been loaded Properly");


function addNewBookFormValidation() {


  var booktitle = document.getElementById("book-title").value;

  var bookauthorname = document.getElementById("book-author-name").value;

  var bookisbnnumber = document.getElementById("book-isbn-number").value;

     var bookpublicationyear = document.getElementById("book-publication-year").value;

  var bookprice = document.getElementById("book-price").value;
```

```
if (booktitle == "" || bookauthorname == "" || bookisbnnumber == "" || book-
publicationyear == "" || bookprice == "") {
  alert("Please fill out all the Fields Correct-
ly, Some Fields are left Blank");
  return false;
  }
}
```

After applying updates in all three files, there would be a change in the look and feel of the form, as shown in *figure 8.31*:

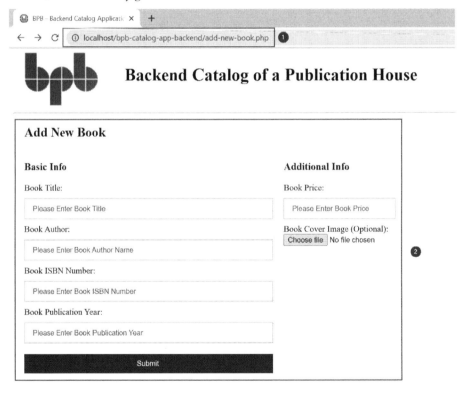

Figure 8.31: *Application Add New Book page—adding new fields*

As we are done with the form part, let us now start with the form submitting part and storing the values entered from the form in our MongoDB Collection:

Step 4—submitting the form values to MongoDB

In this step, we are going to write some HTML, CSS, and PHP code, which will take all the values submitted from the form and use MongoDB driver extension; it will then interact with the MongoDB server and submit these forms values to the MongoDB collection. We have also added one extra HTML text area field (optional) in our form and added the code in PHP so that if the user enters a book description, then it would be added to our MongoDB database. Also, we have added the code to upload the book cover image file to the "**images**" folder if the user selects any book cover image during the form submission.

Code 1—our add-new-book.php file (updated PHP code)

```php
<?php
include("header.php");

// Form Submit and MongoDB Collection Related Code

if(isset($_POST['submit-form-button'])){ // If the Form is Submitted

  // Collecting all the Data Submiited by the Form Post Method and As-
signing it to PHP Variables
  $booktitle = $_POST['book-title'];

  $bookauthorname = $_POST['book-author-name'];

  $bookisbnnumber = $_POST['book-isbn-number'];

  $bookpublicationyear = $_POST['book-publication-year'];

  $bookprice = $_POST['book-price'];

  // If the User doesn't Enter any Book Descrip-
tion then add this text "Book Description is Not Available" to Document
  $bookdescription = ($_POST['book-description'] == '') ? 'Book Descrip-
tion is Not Available' : $_POST['book-description'];

  // $mongoDBClientConnection is defined in our mongodb-connection.
php File which we have included in our header.php
  // $mongoDBClientConnection->BPBCatalogDB->BPBCatalogCollec-
tion = "Connection String"->"Database Name"->"Collection Name"
  $mongoDBCollection = $mongoDBClientConnection->BPBCatalogDB->BPBCata-
logCollection;

  //Create a Array with the field-value Pairs
  $documentArray =['title' => $booktitle, 'authorname' => $bookauthor-
```

```
name, 'isbnnumber' => $bookisbnnumber, 'publicationyear' => $bookpublica-
tionyear, 'price' => $bookprice, 'description' => $bookdescription];


// Using insertOne Method to insert the Document in a Collec-
tion based on key-value Pairs
$result = $mongoDBCollection->insertOne($documentArray);


// If the Book Cover Image File is Selected and Uploaded
if(isset($_FILES['book-cover-image'])){

// File Details

$upload_dir = 'images/';
$file_name = $_FILES['book-cover-image']['name'];
$file_ext_arr = explode('.', $file_name);
$file_ext = strtolower(end($file_ext_arr));
$file_tmp_name =$_FILES['book-cover-image']['tmp_name'];
$new_file_name = $result->getInsertedId().'.'.$file_ext;
$upload_file_with_path = $upload_dir.$new_file_name;

$book_cover_upload_status = false;

if(move_uploaded_file($file_tmp_name, $upload_file_with_path)) {
  $book_cover_upload_status = true;

  // Now Update the Current Document with the name of the Book Cov-
er Image File
  // $mongoDBCollection->updateOne - First Parameter is the Que-
ry String or Filter Criteria to Match the Document and Second Parame-
ter are field-value pairs which has to be updated
    $updateResult = $mongoDBCollection->updateOne(
      [ '_id' => $result->getInsertedId() ],
      [ '$set' => [ 'coverimage' => $new_file_name ]]
    );

  }else{
```

```php
    $book_cover_upload_status = false;
  }

  }

?>
  <div class="form-submitted">Form is Submitted!<br />Document is Success-
fully Inserted with ID = <?php echo $result->getInsertedId(); ?><br />
  <?php
    if($book_cover_upload_status == true) {
    echo "Book Cover Image File has been successfully Uploaded <br />";
    } else {
    echo "Error While Uploading the Book Cover File <br />»;
    }
  ?>
</div>
  <br />
  <div class="addnewbookagain-container"><button type="button" name="add-
newbookagain" id="addnewbookagain" class="addnewbookagain-btn" on-
click="location.href='add-new-book.php'">Add New Book Again</button></
div>
  <?php
  }
  ?>
```

Code 2—our add-new-book.php file (updated HTML code)

```php
<div class="content">
  <h2>Add New Book</h2>
  <div class="gotodashboard-container"><button type="button" name="got-
odashboard" id="gotodashboard" class="gotodashboard-btn" onclick="loca-
tion.href='index.php'">Go To Dashboard</button></div>
  <?php
  if(!isset($_POST['submit-form-button'])){ // If the Form is Not Sub-
```

mitted, Then Show the Form, else if the form is Submitted then Don't Show the Form

```
?>

<div class="addnewbook-form-container">

    <form action="add-new-book.php" onsubmit="return addNewBookFormValida-
tion()" method="post" enctype="multipart/form-data">

    <div class="form-content-container">

      <div class="form-content-left">

        <h3>Basic Info</h3>
        <label for="book-title">Book Title:</label><br />
        <input type="text" id="book-title" name="book-
title" placeholder="Please Enter Book Title"><br />
        <label for="book-author-name">Book Author:</label><br />
        <input type="text" id="book-author-name" name="book-author-
name" placeholder="Please Enter Book Author Name"><br />
        <label for="book-isbn-number">Book ISBN Number:</label><br />
        <input type="text" id="book-isbn-number" name="book-isbn-
number" placeholder="Please Enter Book ISBN Number"><br />
        <label for="book-publication-year">Book Publication Year:</
label><br />
        <input type="text" id="book-publication-year" name="book-
publication-year" placeholder="Please Enter Book Publication Year"><br />
        <input type="submit" value="Submit" name="submit-form-button">

      </div>

      <div class="form-content-right">

        <h3>Additional Info</h3>
        <label for="book-price">Book Price:</label><br />
        <input type="text" id="book-price" name="book-
price" placeholder="Please Enter Book Price"><br />
        <label for="book-price">Book Description (Optional):</
```

```
label><br />

        <textarea id="book-description" name="book-
description" placeholder="Please Enter Book Description"></
textarea><br />

        <label for="book-cover-image">Book Cover Image (Optional):</
label><br />

        <input type="file" id="book-cover-image" name="book-cover-image">

      </div>

    </div>

    </form>

  </div>

  <?php
  }
  ?>

 </div>

<?php
include("footer.php");
?>
```

Code 2—our styles.css file (appended CSS code)

```
/* Add New Book Additional Styles */

.gotodashboard-container{
 text-align:right;
}

.gotodashboard-btn{
 display: inline-block;
 padding: 15px 30px;
 background-color:#002b80;
```

```css
 border: none;

 color: white;

 font-size: 14px;

 font-weight: bold;

 cursor:pointer;

 text-align: center;

 text-decoration: none;

}

.form-submitted{

 display: inline-block;

 padding: 15px 30px;

 background-color:#00802b;

 border: #004d1a;

 color: white;

}

.addnewbookagain-container{

 margin-top:20px;

}

.addnewbookagain-btn{

 display: inline-block;

 padding: 15px 30px;

 background-color:#4d004d;

 border: none;

 color: white;

 font-size: 14px;

 font-weight: bold;

 cursor:pointer;

 text-align: center;

 text-decoration: none;

}
```

```
.addnewbookagain-btn:hover{

 background-color: #73264d;

 cursor: pointer;

}

.addnewbook-form-container textarea {

 width: 100%;

 height:150px;

 display: inline-block;

 padding: 10px 15px;

 margin: 10px 0;

 border: 1px solid #ff99ff;

 border-radius: none;

 box-sizing: border-box;

}
```

Once we have added this code, we can now refresh the "**Add New Book**" page (**add-new-book.php**) using our browser and add some new records, as shown in *figure 8.32*:

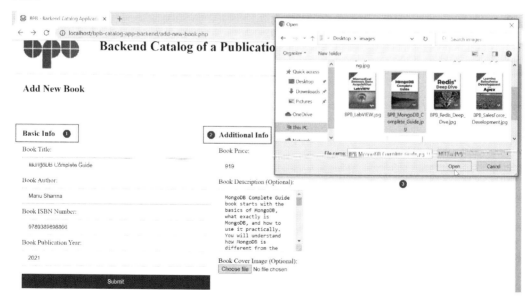

Figure 8.32*: Application Add New Book page—submitting a form*

After you add this record and the record will be entered successfully in the MongoDB database, it will show you the success message on your screen. You can also add new books by clicking the button "**Add New Books Again**", as shown in *figure 8.33*:

Figure 8.33: Application Add New Book page—form is successfully submitted

Now, after adding new books by submitting the book details by form, if we check the MongoDB collection with MongoDB Compass, we can easily see the new MongoDB documents in our MongoDB collection, as shown in *figure 8.34*:

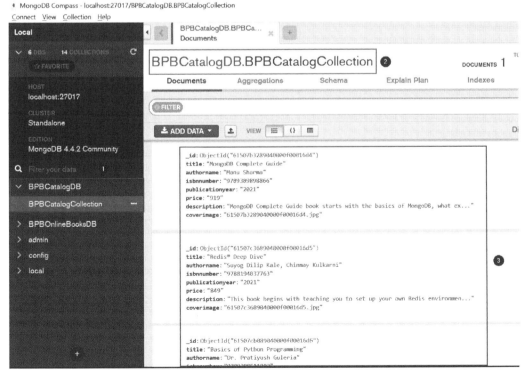

Figure 8.34: Application Add New Book page—verifying form submitted values from MongoDB Compass

Also, we can check that all the book cover images have been successfully uploaded to our Project "**images**" folder, as shown in *figure 8.35*:

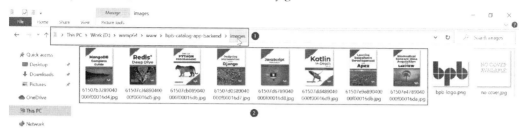

Figure 8.35: Application Add New Book page — book cover image files have been successfully uploaded

Listing of catalog functionality

In this part, we will be creating new functionality to list all the books that have been entered by the "**Add New Book**" functionality in our previous section. For this functionality, we need to use our existing "**index.php**" file in which we will have a simple HTML layout presented to the users so that users can view the details of the book, and there would be a delete button to delete any book along with the book details which are stored to our MongoDB Collection.

Let us now develop this functionality by following some steps.

Step 1—creating list books functionality in our dashboard with our index file (index.php)

The following are the code updates for **index.php** that is located in the "**root**", as well as **styles.css** that is located in the "**css**" folder of our project.

Code 1—finding all the documents from MongoDB collection (updated index.php file)

```php
<?php

include("header.php");

// List Book Functionality


 // $mongoDBClientConnection is defined in our mongodb-connection.
php File which we have included in our header.php

 // $mongoDBClientConnection->BPBCatalogDB-
>BPBCatalogCollection = "Connection String"->"Database Name"-
>"Collection Name"
```

```
$mongoDBCollection = $mongoDBClientConnection->BPBCatalogDB-
>BPBCatalogCollection;

// Using $mongoDBCollection-
>find() Method to find all the Documents in the Collection

$documents = $mongoDBCollection->find();

?>
```

Code 2—displaying the list of all the documents from MongoDB collection by using PHP foreach() construct (updated index.php file—HTML part)

```
<div class="content">

  <h2>Application Dashboard</h2>

    <div class="addnewbook-container"><button type="button" name="addnew-
book" id="addnewbook" class="addnewbook-btn" onclick="location.href='add-
new-book.php'">Add New Book</button></div>

  <br />

  <div class="row-container">

   <div class="row">

    <div class="col-container headings">

      <div class="col">

          Book ID

          </div>

          <div class="col">

          Book Title

          </div>

          <div class="col">

          Delete

     </div>

    </div>

   </div>
```

```php
<?php
// Fetch Documents from the Collection
// Iteration using PHP foreach() Construct
foreach ($documents as $document) {
?>

<div class="row">
 <div class="col-container">
  <div class="col">
  <?php echo $document['_id']; ?>
  </div>
  <div class="col">
  <?php echo $document['title']; ?>
  </div>
  <div class="col">
  <a class="delete-book-link" onclick="return confirm('Please confirm deletion');" href="delete-book.php?id=<?php echo $document['_id']; ?>">Delete</a>
  </div>
 </div>
</div>

<?php
}
?>

</div>

</div>
<?php
include("footer.php");
?>
```

Code 3—our updated styles.css file (appended code)

```css
/* Dashboard – List Books */

.row-container{
 max-width:1000px;
 margin-bottom:40px;
}

.col-container{
 display: flex;
}

.col-container.headings{
font-size:20px;
font-weight:bold;
}

.row{
 margin-top:5px;
 margin-bottom:5px;
 border-bottom: 1px solid #ff99ff;
}

.col{
 width:300px;
}

.delete-book-link{
 display: inline-block;
 padding: 15px 30px;
 background-color:#4d004d;
 border: none;
 color: white;
 font-size: 14px;
```

```
font-weight: bold;

cursor:pointer;

text-align: center;

text-decoration: none;

}
```

Once we have added this code, we can now refresh the dashboard page (**index. php**) using our browser. We can see that our project dashboard is now listing all the books, which we have entered into the MongoDB database using the "**Add New Book**" functionality in our previous section, as shown in *figure 8.36*:

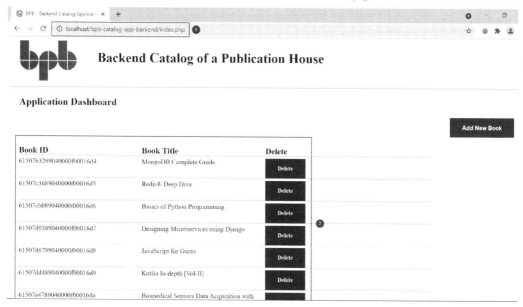

Figure 8.36: *List books functionality in our dashboard*

Deleting functionality

In this part, we will be creating new functionality to delete a book, which is shown by the "**Listing of Catalog**" functionality in our previous section. For this functionality, we need to create a new "**delete-book.php**" file in which we will only write PHP code that will delete the document from MongoDB collection based on the id which is passed from our "**index.php**" delete link. Have a look at the following code again, which we have already used in our dashboard catalog listing in "**index.php**"

Code 1—delete code (index.php—no change)

```
<a class="delete-book-link" onclick="return confirm('Please confirm dele-
tion');" href="delete-book.php?id=<?php echo $document['_id']; ?>">De-
lete</a>
```

Let us now develop the delete functionality by following some steps:

Step 1—creating delete book functionality file (delete-book.php)

In this step, we will create a new file named "**delete-book.php**", which would be our main file (or template) to delete existing books. We will include "**header. php**" and "**footer.php**" in this file, and we will save this file in the same location of our project folder, which is: **D:\wamp64\www\bpb-catalog-app-backend** and following is the code for the same:

Code 1—delete book functionality (delete-book.php)

```php
<?php

include("header.php");

// $mongoDBClientConnection is defined in our mongodb-connection.
php File which we have included in our header.php

// $mongoDBClientConnection->BPBCatalogDB-
>BPBCatalogCollection = "Connection String"->"Database Name"-
>"Collection Name"

$mongoDBCollection = $mongoDBClientConnection->BPBCatalogDB-
>BPBCatalogCollection;

// Get Document ID from PHP $_GET Method

$documentid = new MongoDB\BSON\ObjectID($_GET['id']);

$deleteResult = $mongoDBCollection->deleteOne(['_id' => $documentid]);

//If Delete is Sucessful then Forwarded to the Dashboard (index.php)

if($deleteResult->getDeletedCount()==1){

    header("Location: index.php?delete=true");

    exit();

}

include("footer.php");

?>
```

Code 2—delete book functionality (index.php— small update for displaying an alert after the book is deleted successfully)

```
<div class="content">

  <h2>Application Dashboard</h2>

  <?php
  // If the Book is Sucessfully Deleted then show the Alert Box
  if(isset($_GET['delete'])){
  ?>
  <script>
   alert("The Book Record is Deleted from the Database");
  </script>
  <?php
  }
  ?>

  <div class="addnewbook-container"><button type="button" name="addnew-
book" id="addnewbook" class="addnewbook-btn" onclick="location.href='add-
new-book.php'">Add New Book</button></div>
```

Once we have added this code, we can now refresh the dashboard page (**index.php**) using our browser, and then we can click on the "*Delete*" button to check the delete book functionality, as shown in *figure 8.37*:

Figure 8.37: *Delete book functionality in our dashboard*

We have seen how we can create a backend with CRUD features using PHP and MongoDB along with frontend programming languages such as HTML, CSS, and JavaScript. You should feel free to make changes in the code and create various other functionalities.

Edit and update functionality

As this is a practical chapter and we have learned so many things in this chapter, try to code this edit and update functionality with the skills that you have learned from this chapter. You can take references from the MongoDB PHP library. The official URLs are listed as follows:

- MongoDB official home page for PHP library: **https://docs.mongodb.com/php-library/current/**

- PHP official home page for MongoDB PHP library: **https://www.php.net/ manual/en/mongodb.tutorial.library.php**

Conclusion

In this chapter, we have covered the practical step-by-step development of CRUD-based backend applications using PHP and MongoDB along with frontend languages such as HTML, CSS, and JavaScript. Finally, we have learned how we can create a dashboard for our application and various other related functionalities required for the overall development of the catalog management system for a publication house. In the upcoming chapter, we will be covering new applications, which are related to APIs using Node.js and Express.js; we will learn how we can use MongoDB data with API calls; these APIs will further be used in our upcoming advanced chapter of mobile application development.

Questions

1. What is Composer?

2. What is the PHP MongoDB library?

3. Explain the process of using the MongoDB PHP library with your PHP-based project.

## CHAPTER 9

MongoDB Step by Step Practical Application Development Using JavaScript (Node.js with Express.js)

REST API development—creating RESTful Web services of a publication house

Many of you could be familiar with the term *"API"* some of you could have already been using them in your applications. What exactly is an API? and how we can develop and use these in our applications? This chapter covers the same, and in this chapter, we will learn how to practically develop REST-based APIs using Node.js, Express.js, and MongoDB. All the sections have been explained in a step-by-step practical manner so that by the end of this chapter, you will feel more confident in Node.js, Express.js, and MongoDB Web services and API development.

Structure

In this chapter, we will discuss the following topics:

- An overview of our RESTful web services developed using Node.js and MongoDB
- Requirements
- Brief introduction to API

- Brief introduction to RESTful APIs

- Pre-development steps

- Developing our APIs

- Using REST API to fetch data from MongoDB collection based on MongoDB document ID (REST GET method)

- Using REST API to insert data into MongoDB collection (REST POST method)

- Using REST API to update data into MongoDB document based on MongoDB document ID (REST PUT method) and giving thumbs up for a book

- Using REST API to update data into MongoDB document based on MongoDB document ID (REST PUT method) and giving thumbs down for a book

Objectives

After studying this chapter, the reader will be able to understand how we can develop RESTful Web services developed using Node.js and MongoDB and what are the basic requirements before one can start learning and coding them. In this chapter, the reader will learn about API and RESTful APIs and will also understand what are the pre-development steps required to set up the right environment for API development. This chapter covers how one can develop APIs and how one can use the REST method to fetch data from MongoDB collection based on MongoDB document ID (REST GET method), REST method to add data into MongoDB collection (REST POST method), and also understand how one can use REST method to update data into MongoDB document based on MongoDB document ID (REST PUT method).

RESTful Web services using Node.js and MongoDB—an overview

In this chapter, we are going to develop REST APIs using Node.js and MongoDB. We will be creating a RESTful web service in which we will be able to create a few APIs using some HTTP methods.

This API (RESTful Web services) will have the following features:

- Ability to list (read) all the books in the catalog

- Ability to add (insert) new book entry

- Ability to modify (update) the details of existing book entry

- Ability to delete the existing book-entry (code yourself)

In order to create this interface, we would be writing some codes using the following:

- **Node.js**: To connect to MongoDB server using the Node.js and do server-side operations and interact with MongoDB.

- **Express.js**: Express.js is the application framework for Node.js and is used widely for developing web applications and API.

Requirements

The reader should have the basic knowledge and understanding of the following:

- Node.js

- Express.js (recommended, installation, and a brief introduction is given in this chapter)

- JavaScript

- API (recommended and a brief introduction is given in this chapter)

- RESTful APIs (recommended and a brief introduction is given in this chapter)

Introduction to API

API is an acronym for **Application Programming Interface,** and it is used to communicate between different devices or applications running on these devices. It allows different applications to talk and communicate with each other. Every API call has a defined method and data format that we need to follow in order to implement these API calls.

There are two main API types:

- **Simple Object Access Protocol (SOAP)**: This was originally developed by Microsoft, and it has been used for many years. It uses XML.

- **Representational State Transfer (REST)**: This is more flexible, easy to implement, and popular than SOAP these days among developers worldwide.

In this chapter, we will be using REST-based APIs.

RESTful APIs

RESTful APIs are based on the REST protocols, and these API uses the REST methods to communicate between the devices and applications.

There are mainly four major parts of REST-based APIs as follows:

- **Root endpoint and paths**: These are basically the route to the API access. It is just like a URL, for example, **https://api.bpbonline.com/getALLBPBBooks**. Here, **https://api.bpbonline.com** is the API root endpoint, and getALLBPBBooks is the path to access the particular API

- **Method**: These are some methods like GET (to get the resource from the server), POST (to create a new resource on the server), PUT (to update an existing resource on the server), DELETE (to delete an existing resource on the server), and so on.

- **Headers**: They are used to provide information to both client and server and can be used in various scenarios.

- **Body**: It contains the data that needs to be sent to the server. It is useful whenever we want to use API to send some data which needs to be added. For example, in the case of adding some book with the API call, we need to send the details of the book like *"Title"* or *"Year of Publication"*.

What our final application will look like?

As we will complete all the sections of this chapter, our final App will look as shown in *figure 9.1* and *figure 9.2*.

Application running from the command prompt

Following is the screenshot of the API app, which is serving the requests on localhost and port 3,000, waiting for the incoming requests from the other clients such as Postman.

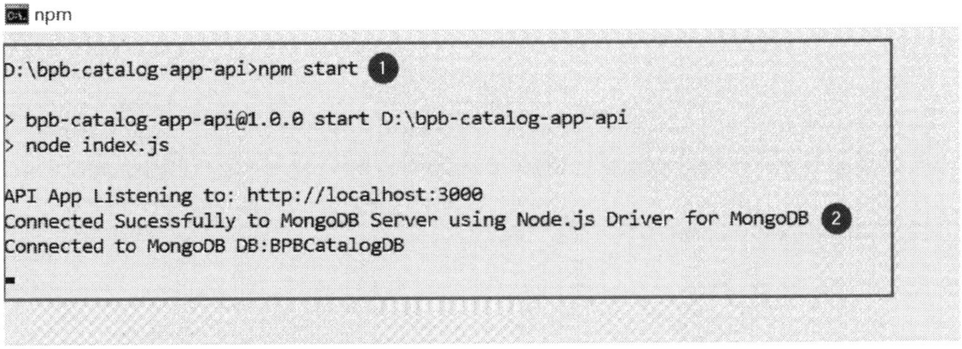

Figure 9.1: *Application command line interface—preview*

API calls using Postman application

Following is the screenshot of the Postman software client, which shows how the API calls are made.

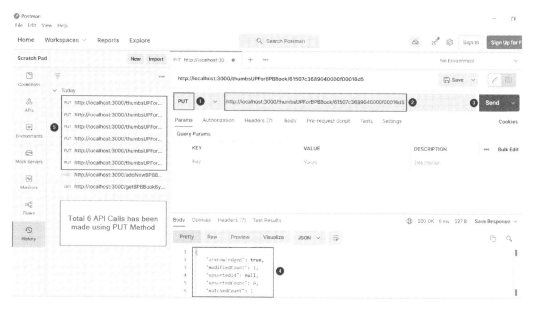

Figure 9.2: Calling APIs using Postman application—preview

Let us divide our application into the following sections so that we can then combine all these sections having all the features of this backend catalog application. The following are the sections that we would be working on:

- Adding REST API endpoint to fetch data from MongoDB collection based on MongoDB document ID (REST GET method)

- Adding REST API endpoint to add data into MongoDB Collection (REST POST method)

- Adding REST API endpoint to update data into MongoDB Document based on MongoDB Document ID (REST PUT method)—giving Thumbs Up for a book

- Adding REST API Endpoint to update data into MongoDB Document based on MongoDB Document ID (REST PUT method)—giving Thumbs Down for a book

Let us start now with the real development part. To start with, let us first get ready with the real environment so that what we will code will reflect on the system.

Pre-development steps

In our previous chapter [*Chapter 4, Starting up Programming with MongoDB and JavaScript (Node.js)*], where we have given the introduction about getting started with MongoDB and JavaScript (Node.js), we have already covered how to install the Node.js and NPM (Node Package Manager). Follow these steps before we start to code:

Step 1—check Node.js and NPM on your system

You should first verify that Node.js and **Node Package Manager (NPM)**. In order to verify these two softwares on your Windows Machine, open the command prompt by typing "**cmd**" from the search bar located in the taskbar, as shown in *figure 9.3*:

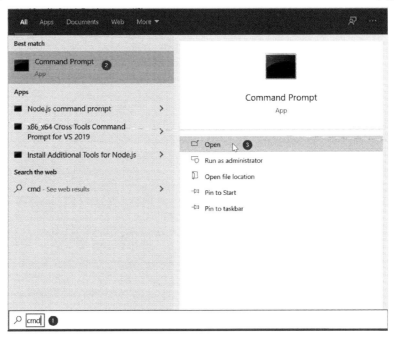

Figure 9.3: Open command prompt

1. Type the following two commands one by one to verify Node.js and NPM installation in the command prompt, as shown in *figure 9.4*:

```
node --version
```

```
npm --version
```

■ Command Prompt

```
Microsoft Windows [Version 10.0.19042.1237]
(c) Microsoft Corporation. All rights reserved.

C:\Users\manus>node --version  ❶
v14.17.5

C:\Users\manus>npm --version  ❷
6.14.14

C:\Users\manus>
```

1) Checking Node.js Version

2) Checking NPM Version

Figure 9.4: Command prompt—verifying Node.js and NPM version on Windows

As you can see, both Node.js and NPM have been correctly installed on your Windows Machine.

Step 2—creating a project folder in your system

Choose any location on your machine and create a new folder or directory named as "**bpb-catalog-app-api**". The location could be similar to **D:\bpb-catalog-app-api**, as shown in *figure 9.5*:

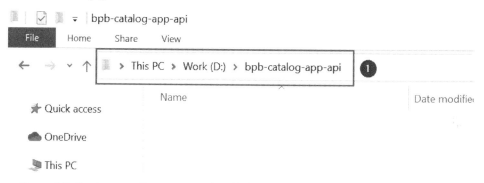

Figure 9.5: Create a new directory named as "bpb-catalog-app-api" on your Windows Machine

Step 3—NPM init

NPM init is a command-based interface used to set up new or existing NPM based packages; when we type "**npm init**" command in our Project Directory, which is: **D:\bpb-catalog-app-api** and it will ask us a few details such as *"Package Name"*,

"Package Version", *"Author"*, and so on. After we enter all these details, it will create a *"`package.json`"* file automatically, as shown in *figure 9.6*:

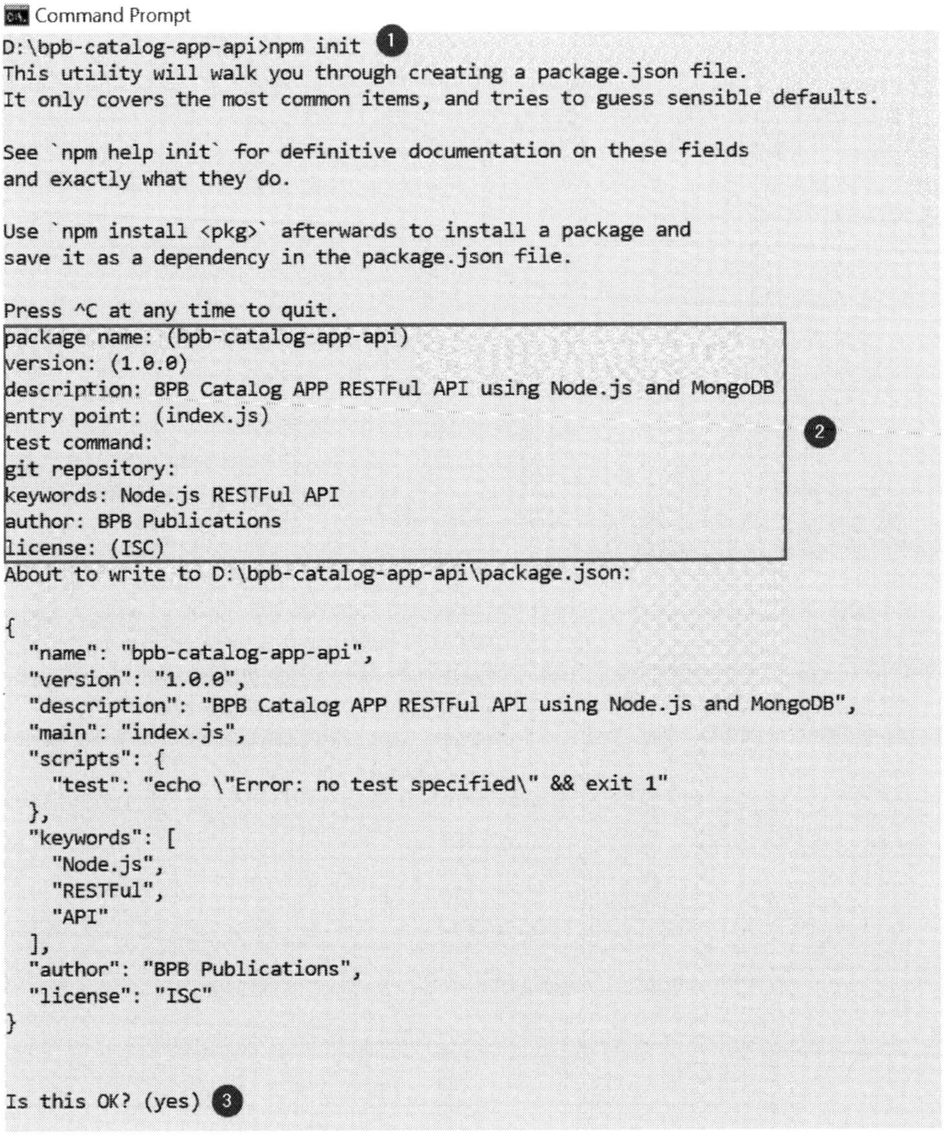

```
Command Prompt
D:\bpb-catalog-app-api>npm init  1
This utility will walk you through creating a package.json file.
It only covers the most common items, and tries to guess sensible defaults.

See `npm help init` for definitive documentation on these fields
and exactly what they do.

Use `npm install <pkg>` afterwards to install a package and
save it as a dependency in the package.json file.

Press ^C at any time to quit.
package name: (bpb-catalog-app-api)
version: (1.0.0)
description: BPB Catalog APP RESTFul API using Node.js and MongoDB
entry point: (index.js)
test command:
git repository:                                                          2
keywords: Node.js RESTFul API
author: BPB Publications
license: (ISC)
About to write to D:\bpb-catalog-app-api\package.json:

{
  "name": "bpb-catalog-app-api",
  "version": "1.0.0",
  "description": "BPB Catalog APP RESTFul API using Node.js and MongoDB",
  "main": "index.js",
  "scripts": {
    "test": "echo \"Error: no test specified\" && exit 1"
  },
  "keywords": [
    "Node.js",
    "RESTFul",
    "API"
  ],
  "author": "BPB Publications",
  "license": "ISC"
}

Is this OK? (yes)  3
```

Figure 9.6: Command prompt—npm init

After *"`npm init`"* is executed, it will create a new file, *"`package.json`"* in case we are running it the first time under the folder where it was run. We can verify this by opening this file in some IDE like Visual Studio code, as shown in *figure 9.7*:

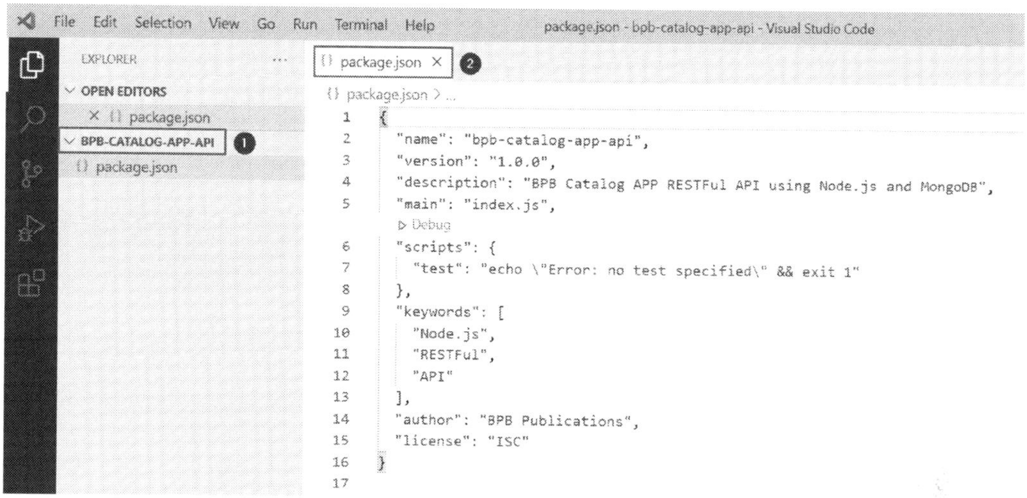

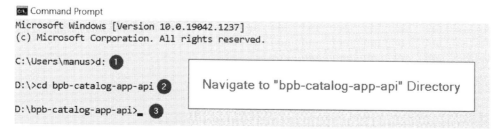

Figure 9.7: Visual Studio code—npm init

Step 4—installing the Express.js using NPM

Before we learn how to install and use Express.js, let us understand what Express. js is.

About Express.js:

Express.js is a major backend framework for Node.js, and it is very widely used. Express.js is a modular-based framework, and it is very helpful in Web application development, as well as API development using Node.js.

Express.js provides an easy way to create routes, and based on these routes, the calls are diverted to the various sections of the application that are related to the particular calls. Thus, it is very easy to write the code related to the routes, and it is very developer-friendly.

As we have now learned about Express.js, let us now install it using NPM. To install Express.js with NPM, follow these steps:

1. Open up your command prompt and navigate to this directory "**bpb-catalog-app-api**", as shown in *figure 9.8*:

Figure 9.8: Navigating to "bpb-catalog-app-api" directory

2. Open your favorite browser, such as Google Chrome, and in the address bar, type: **https://expressjs.com** and press *Enter*. This will open the *"Express.js"* home page. Here you will see all the details about Express.js, including the command to install it in your project, as shown in *figure 9.9*:

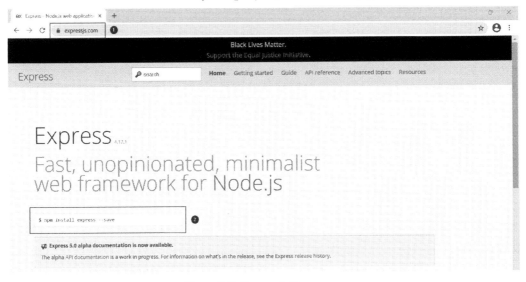

Figure 9.9: Express.js Home page

3. Now run any one of the following commands mentioned. This will install Express.js for Node.js to our directory, where we are now going to create our Node.js application along with MongoDB (as shown in *figure 9.10*).

```
npm install express
```

   OR

```
npm i express
```

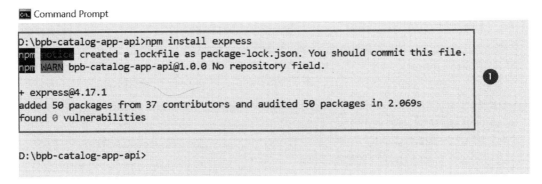

Figure 9.10: Installing Express.js

Step 4 –running Express.js using NPM

1. Create a new file **index.js** in the project directory, which is: **D:\bpb-catalog-app-api** in our case. Following is the new code for this file that we have added in it:

Code 1—our index.js file

```
const express = require('express'); // Express Module

const app = express();

const port = 3000; // Port, You can Change this Port to anything you wou
ld like For example 8000, For this Book we will Keep this as 3000 for No
de.js > Express.js Based API Examples

app.get('/', (req, res) => {

  res.send('Welcome to BPB Publications RESTful API') // This is the De-
fault API Message

});

app.listen(port, () => {

  console.log("API App Listening to: http://localhost:" + port); // Con-
nection Listing to Port 3000

});
```

2. Open **package.json** file in your project folder and add start script under **scripts** section. Following is the code for the same (as shown in *figure 9.11*).

Code 1—update package.json file

```
"scripts": {

  "start": "node index.js",

  "test": "echo \"Error: no test specified\" && exit 1"

},
```

Figure 9.11: Updating "package.json" file and adding the start script

3. Open the command prompt and then navigate to your project folder and run the following command (as shown in *figure 9.12*).

    ```
    npm start
    ```

    The preceding command will check the "**package.json**" file for the start option under scripts, and as we have given the value as "**node index.js**", here, Node.js will execute the index.js. So, this is the better way of running Node.js applications. As and when projects grow in size, we can have various options available under "scripts", and we can use npm to execute them. This is also really helpful when we have various versions of the applications, such as the development version or production version.

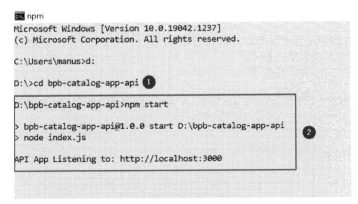

Figure 9.12: Running "npm start" in command prompt

4. Now, open your favorite browser, such as Google Chrome, and type: **http://localhost:3000/** and press *Enter*. This will open our API route or endpoint "/", which is defined in **index.js,** and show us the message "**Welcome to BPB Publications RESTful API**", as shown in *figure 9.13*:

Figure 9.13: Opening default API route (endpoint) in browser

Step 5—installing the MongoDB Driver for Node.js using NPM

1. If you are still on Step 4, then you need to stop the Node Script, which is already running. For this, press *"Ctrl + C"* to stop the Node Script, which is already running (the system may prompt you that if you want to "Terminate this Job". Press *"Y"* to terminate it), and then you can continue to Point 3.

2. If you have already done that and is returning back, then open up your command prompt and navigate to this directory "**bpb-catalog-app-api**"

3. Now, run any one of the following commands that have been mentioned in the MongoDB driver home page of the NPM website at: **https://www.npmjs.com/package/mongodb**. This will install the MongoDB driver for Node.js to our directory, where we are now going to create our Node.js application along with MongoDB (as shown in *figure 9.14*).

```
npm i mongodb
```

OR

```
npm install mongodb
```

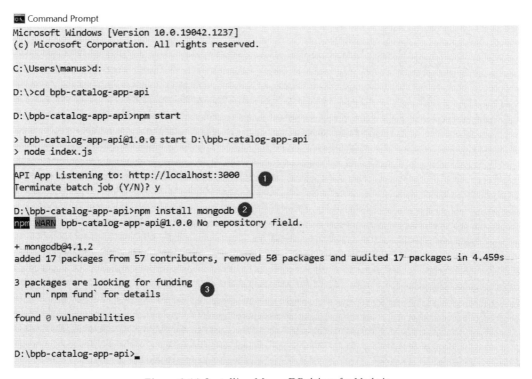

Figure 9.14: *Installing MongoDB driver for Node.js*

If you open your "**bpb-catalog-app-api**" folder (or directory), you will find that a folder named as "**node_modules**" has been created automatically by the preceding steps while we have installed NPM modules, and along with this process, a file named as "**package-lock.json**" has also been created. Basically, whenever you install any node module in Node.js, it will create a folder named as "**node_modules**", where it will download and copy all the node modules, which are required by a specific module (here, we have installed Express.js and MongoDB Driver for Node.js) or we can say those Node.js modules on which the NPM modules like Express.js or MongoDB driver is dependent plus its own files, as shown in *figure 9.15*:

Figure 9.15: *"node_modules" Folder and "package-lock.json"*
File is automatically created by the NPM installation process

You may also open the "**node_modules**" folder and could see the other modules, which are downloaded by the installation process, as shown in *figure 9.16*:

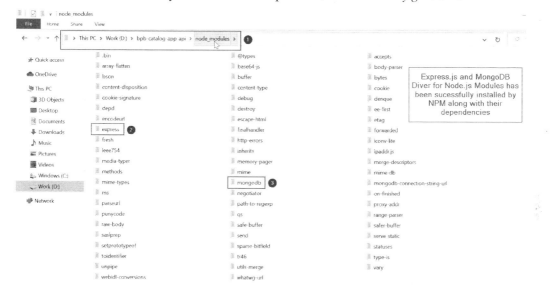

Figure 9.16: Express.js and MongoDB driver has been installed along with the other dependencies

The "**package-lock.json**" is a file where the module and its dependencies are displayed in JSON tree format. For more information about "**package-lock.json**", you can visit this URL: **https://docs.npmjs.com/configuring-npm/package-lock-json.html**

As we are done with the setup of our environment with Express.js and MongoDB Driver, now we can start with the programming part.

Developing our APIs

As we are now ready with the right environment and the skeleton of our application, along with the new database and collection that we are going to use in this API development, let us start with the coding part.

Note that as we are using Node.js and writing Node.js code. It is recommended to use some Code Editor or **Integrated Development Environment** (**IDE**) like Microsoft Visual Studio Code or any code editor of your choice. You can download and install Microsoft Visual Studio Code from this link: **https://code.visualstudio.com**. Microsoft Visual Studio Code is open-source and free software and is available for almost all operating systems.

Step 1—connecting to MongoDB (updating index.js)

In our example, we have used "**MongoDBClient**" constant, which is assigned as an object for "**MongoClient**" class. Then, we have called the connect method using this object which will help to connect to MongoDB. We have done changes in our "**index.js**" under this path: **D:\bpb-catalog-app-api**, and the following is the code for the same (as shown in *figure 9.17*).

Code 1

```
const express = require('express'); // Express Module

const app = express();

const port = 3000; // Port, You can Change this Port to anything you wou
ld like For example 8000, For this Book we will Keep this as 3000 for No
de.js > Express.js Based API Examples

const MongoDBClient = require('mongodb').MongoClient; // MongoDB Driver

const MongoDBObjectId = require("mongodb").ObjectId; // Create a new Ob
jectID instance, used for Converting String to MongoDB Objec-
tID Type and opposite

app.use(express.json());

app.use(express.urlencoded({ extended: true }));

app.get('/', (req, res) => {
  res.send('Welcome to BPB Publications RESTful API') // This is the De-
fault API Message
});

app.listen(port, () => { // Here Our Application will try to cre-
ate a Host using Express.js and Listen to the requests on Port Spec-
fied, In our Case it is "3000"

  // MongoDB Connection URL String

  const url = 'mongodb://localhost:27017';

  // Connecting to MongoDB Server using connect Method

  MongoDBClient.
connect(url, { useUnifiedTopology: true }, function(err, client) {

    if(err){
```

```
        console.
log("Some Error While Connecting to MongoDB Server" + err);
    }else{
        console.log("Connected Sucessfully to MongoDB Server using Node.
js Driver for MongoDB");

        // Select DB
        dbname = "BPBCatalogDB";
        db = client.db(dbname);

        // Get the "BPBCatalogCollection" Collection
        collection = db.collection('BPBCatalogCollection');
        console.log("Connected to MongoDB DB:" + dbname)

    }
  });

  console.log("API App Listening to: http://
localhost:" + port); // Connection Listing to Port 3000
});
```

Following is the screenshot for the same in Microsoft Visual Studio Code:

Figure 9.17: Creating a MongoDB connection file—Microsoft Visual Studio Code

You can see that MongoDB connection related code is put inside the code block where the application is creating the host on a port 3,000, Also note that we are using the same MongoDB database and collection that we have used in the previous chapter [*Chapter 8, MongoDB Step by Step Practical Application Development Using PHP*] in which we have created a CRUD backend application using PHP and MongoDB.

Step 2—adding REST API endpoint to fetch data from MongoDB collection (REST GET method)

In our example, we have used Express.js "**app.get()**" method in which we have declared our route or API endpoint as "**getAllBPBBooks**". We have done changes in our "**index.js**" under this path: **D:\bpb-catalog-app-api**, and the following is the code for the same.

Code 1 (index.js updated)

```
app.get('/', (req, res) => {

  res.send('Welcome to BPB Publications RESTful API') // This is the De-
fault API Message

});


// API Endpoint "getAllBPBBooks" using GET Request

app.get("/getAllBPBBooks", (request, response) => {

  collection.find().toArray((error, result) => { // Featching the Collec-
tion Data using "toArray"

      if(error) { // If any Error

          return response.status(500).send(error);

      }else{

          response.send(result); // Send Response Back to the Client

      }

  });

});
```

Now, after updating the code, we need to restart our Node.js application if it has not been restarted yet. In order to do this, go to the command prompt where your Node.js App is currently running and then press "*Ctrl + C*" and then "*Y*" when you are prompted to terminate the task. After this, you should again type "**npm start**", and press *Enter* to run this Node.js API application again on your machine, as shown in *figure 9.18*:

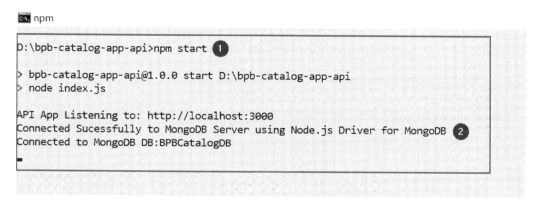

Figure 9.18: Restarting our application

In our example, we have created an API that uses the GET method. We can use the browser to fetch this data, as shown in *figure 9.19*:

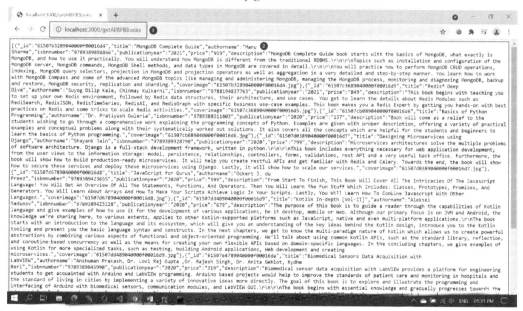

Figure 9.19: Calling our API from browser

But as we can use any of the RESTful methods such as POST, PUT, or DELETE, in this case, we need some better way to perform API calls during our development. In this case, we can use some better applications, which will serve our purpose during the API development. There are many ways to do it, including "curl", powerful command-line software to transfer the data to or from the server. Let us use some GUI-based apps. For this chapter, we would be using "Postman".

Step 3—download and install Postman

1. Postman is a software application that is helpful for API development, and it is one of the widely used applications among developers. Visit: **https://www.postman.com/downloads/** and click the **Download the App** button, as shown in *figure 9.20*:

Figure 9.20: *Postman Home page*

2. You can download the Postman installer and run it. Just follow the instructions. The installation would be similar to the other software installers that you run on your Windows Machine (in case you are using other operating systems such as Linux or Mac OS, then please follow the related instructions for installing on these operating systems) After you have successfully installed Postman on your machine, open it and launch it. This will open the application on your machine.

After the Postman application is launched, choose the GET method. Enter the API Endpoint as **http://localhost:3000/getAllBPBBooks** under the "**Enter Request URL**" and then click "**Send**" button. After you click "**Send**" button, it will take a few seconds to call the API and get the records from the API, as shown in *figure 9.21*:

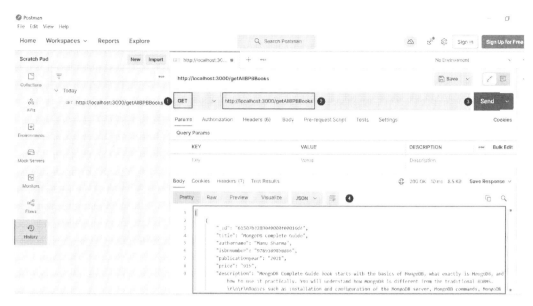

Figure 9.21: Postman application—calling our API using GET method

Step 4—adding REST API endpoint to fetch data from MongoDB collection based on MongoDB Document ID (REST GET method)

In our example, we have used Express.js "**app.get()**" method in which we have declared our route or API endpoint as "**getBPBBookById**". We have done changes in our "**index.js**" under this path: **D:\bpb-catalog-app-api**. We have added this code just after the previous code where we have created our API route or endpoint for "**getAllBPBBooks**", and the following is the code for the same:

Code 1 (index.js updated)

```
// API Endpoint "getBPBBookById" using GET Request
app.get("/getBPBBookById/:bookid", (request, response) => {
 collection.findOne({ "_id": new MongoDBObjectId(request.params.bookid)}, (error, result) => {// Here we are not using "toArray" because it is a single document and also we are using MongoDB findOne() Method instead of find()
   if(error) { // If any Error
     return response.status(500).send(error);
   }else{
     response.send(result); // Send Response Back to the Client
   }
 });
});
```

In our example, we have created an API that uses the GET method. We can use the browser to fetch this data based on Book ID. We can now use the Postman application to fetch this data using the GET method (as shown in *figure 9.22*).

Now, after updating the code, we need to restart our Node.js application. In order to do this, press "*Ctrl + C*" and then "*Y*" when you are prompted to terminate the task. After this, you should again type "**npm start**", and press *Enter* to run this Node.js API application again on your machine.

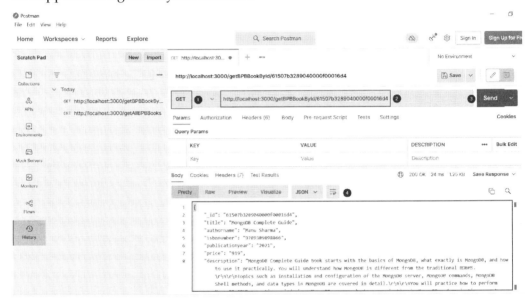

Figure 9.22: Postman application—calling our API using GET method and book ID

Step 5—adding REST API endpoint to add data into MongoDB collection (REST POST method)

In our example, we have used Express.js "**app.post()**" method in which we have declared our route or API endpoint as "**addNewBPBBook**". We have done changes in our "**index.js**" under this path: **D:\bpb-catalog-app-api**. We have added this code just after the previous code where we have created our API route or endpoint for "**getBPBBookByID**", and the following is the code for the same.

Code 1 (index.js updated)

```
// API Endpoint "addNewBPBBook" using POST Request

app.post("/addNewBPBBook", (request, response) => {

  collection.insertOne(request.body, (error, re-
sult) => { // Here we are using "request.body" parameter which will tak
e the values from the body of the POST request made by the CLient while
```

```
this API is called

    if(error) { // If any Error

        return response.status(500).send(error);

    }else{

        response.send(result); // Send Response Back to the Client

    }

  });

});
```

In our example, we have created an API that uses the POST method. We can now use the Postman application to send this data using the POST method. We also need to provide the body to this API before we call this API. So, select "**Body**" under Postman params and then insert JSON with key and body. You can take the following example. (as shown in *figure 9.23*).

Now, after updating the code, we need to restart our Node.js application. In order to do this, go to the Command Prompt where your Node.js App is currently running and then press "*Ctrl + C*" and then "*Y*" when you are prompted to terminate the task. After this, you should again type "**npm start**", and press *Enter* to run this Node.js API application again on your machine.

Code 2 (JSON body params to be used in Postman)

```
{

    "title": "Practical Robotics in C++",

    "authorname": "Lloyd Brombach",

    "isbnnumber": "9789389423464",

    "publicationyear": "2021",

    "price": "1040",

    "description": "Practical Robotics in C++ teaches the complete spectrum
of Robotics, right from the setting up a computer for a robot controller
to putting power to the wheel motors. The book brings you the workshop
knowledge of the electronics, hardware, and software for building a mobile
robot platform. You will learn how to use sensors to detect obstacles, how
to train your robot to build itself a map and plan an obstacle-avoiding
path, and how to structure your code for modularity and interchangeability
with other robot projects. Throughout the book, you can experience the
demonstrations of  complete coding of robotics with the use of simple and
```

clear C++ programming. In addition, you will explore how to leverage the Raspberry Pi GPIO hardware interface pins and existing libraries to make an incredibly capable machine on the most affordable computer platform ever."

}

Figure 9.23: *Postman application—calling our API using POST method and with body params*

After we press "**Send**" button from the Postman application, the API request will be sent along with the body, and a new document is inserted into our MongoDB collection. We can also see in the Postman that we receive a response back with the status: "**200 OK**" along with the response body, as shown in *figure 9.24*:

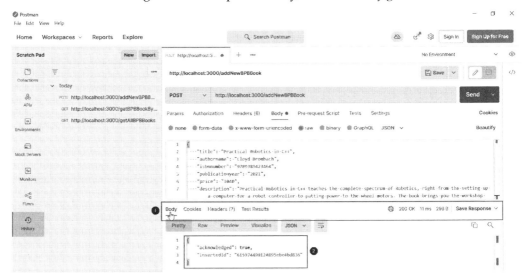

Figure 9.24: *Postman application—response body*

We can also verify this using any MongoDB client such as MongoDB Compass (official GUI-based client application for MongoDB). Just launch MongoDB Compass on your computer and then navigate to our Application MongoDB Collection, which is "**BPBCatalogCollection**" in our case. You can see that the new MongoDB document has been successfully inserted by our API, as shown in *figure 9.25*:

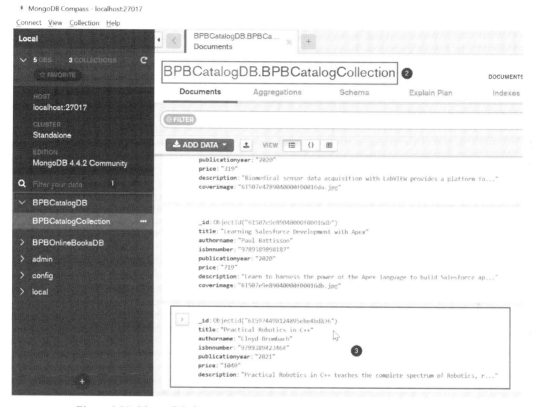

Figure 9.25: *MongoDB Compass—verifying the new document added by our API*

Step 5—adding REST API Endpoint to update data into MongoDB document based on MongoDB Document ID (REST PUT method)—giving thumbs up for a book

In our example, we have used Express.js "**app.put()**" method in which we have declared our route or API Endpoint as "**thumbsUPForBPBBook**". We have done changes in our "**index.js**" under this path: **D:\bpb-catalog-app-api**. We have added this code just after the previous code where we have created our API route or endpoint for "**addNewBPBBook**", and the following is the code for the same.

Code 1 (index.js updated)

```
// API Endpoint "thumbsUPForBPBBook" using PUT Request

app.put("/thumbsUPForBPBBook/:bookid", (request, response) => {

    collection.findOne({ "_id": new MongoDBObjectId(request.params.book-
id)},(error, result) => { // We are Fetching Book Record from our Col-
lection

  if(error) { // If any Error

      return response.status(500).send(error);

  }else{

      if(isNaN(result.thumbsUPCounter)){ // If there is no existing val-
ue for "thumbsUPCounter" in the MongoDB Document

      var thumbsUPCounterValue = 1; // Just assign a new Value to 1

      }else{

          var thumbsUPCounterValue = result.thumbsUPCount-
er + 1; // We are taking the existing "thumbsUPCount-
er" value from our Database and then Incrementing the Thums UP
Counter value "thumbsUPCounterValue" to 1

      }

      collection.updateOne({ "_id": new MongoDBObjectId(request.params.
bookid)}, { $set: {thumbsUPCounter:thumbsUPCounterValue} }, (error, re-
sult) => { // We are using MongoDB updateOne() Method to Update the in-
cremented "thumbsUPCounter" value back to the database

          if(error) { // If any Error

              return response.status(500).send(error);

          }else{

              response.send(result); // Send Response Back to the Client

          }

      });

  }

  });

});
```

In our example, we have created an API that uses the PUT method. We can now use the Postman application to update MongoDB documents using the PUT method.

Now, after updating the code, we need to restart our Node.js application. In order to do this, go to the Command Prompt where your Node.js App is currently running and then press "*Ctrl + C*" and then "*Y*" when you are prompted to terminate the task. After this, you should again type "**npm start**", and press *Enter* to run this Node.js API application again on your machine.

After we press "**Send**" button from the Postman application, the API request will call the endpoint and will update the MongoDB document based on the document ID provided and increase the value of Thumbs Up counter "**thumbsUPCounter**" to 1 every time this API is called. We can also see in the Postman that we receive a response back with the status: "**200 OK**" along with the response body. In our example, we have made six calls to this API, which includes four calls using one book ID and two calls using another book ID, as shown in *figure 9.26*:

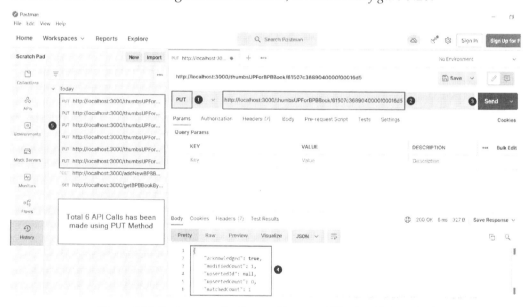

Figure 9.26: Postman application—calling our API using PUT method

We can also verify this using the MongoDB Compass. Just launch MongoDB Compass on your computer and then navigate to our application MongoDB collection, which is "**BPBCatalogCollection**" in our case. You can see that MongoDB documents have been successfully updated by our API calls. In case MongoDB Compass has been already opened in your machine, then just click the refresh button on the top left corner to refresh the MongoDB collection documents data, as shown in *figure 9.27*:

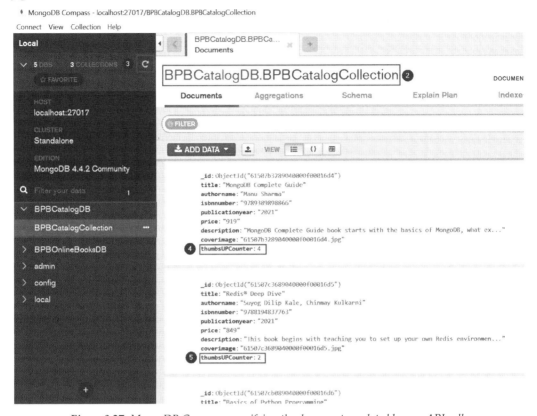

Figure 9.27: *MongoDB Compass—verifying the documents updated by our API calls*

Step 5—adding REST API Endpoint to update data into MongoDB document based on MongoDB Document ID (REST PUT method)—giving Thumbs Down for a book

Before we add this functionality to our API application, let us create a dummy book as we never want to give thumbs down to any good books that we have in our database. For this, we have to use our existing API "**addNewBPBBook**" and pass the JSON in the body params before calling this API using the POST method, as shown in *figure 9.28*:

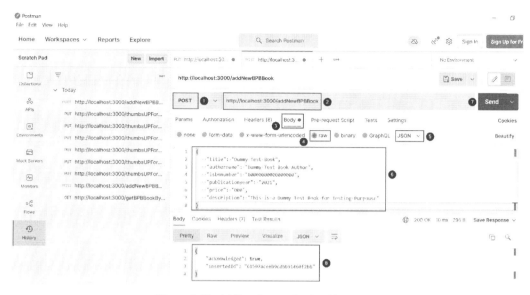

Figure 9.28: Adding dummy book with our API

In our example, we have used Express.js "**app.put()**" method in which we have declared our route or API endpoint as "**thumbsDOWNForBPBBook**". We have done changes in our "**index.js**" under this path: **D:\bpb-catalog-app-api**. We have added this code just after the previous code where we have created our API route or endpoint for "**thumbsUpForBPBBook**", and the following is the code for the same.

Code 1 (index.js updated)

```
// API Endpoint "thumbsDOWNForBPBBook" using PUT Request

app.put("/thumbsDOWNForBPBBook/:bookid", (request, response) => {

  collection.findOne({ "_id": new MongoDBObjectId(request.params.book-
id)},(error, result) => { // We are Fetching Book Record from our Col-
lection

  if(error) { // If any Error

     return response.status(500).send(error);

  }else{


     if(isNaN(result.thumbsDOWNCounter)){ // If there is no existing val-
ue for "thumbsDOWNCounter" in the MongoDB Document

       var thumbsDOWNCounterValue = 1; // Just assign a new Value to 1

     }else{
```

```
      var thumbsDOWNCounterValue = result.thumbsDOWN-
Counter + 1; // We are taking the existing "thumbsDOWNCounter" val-
ue from our Database and then Incrementing the Thums UP Counter value-
 "thumbsDOWNCounterValue" to 1

    }

    collection.updateOne({ "_id": new MongoDBObjectId(request.params.
bookid)}, { $set: {thumbsDOWNCounter:thumbsDOWNCounterValue} }, (er-
ror, result) => { // We are using MongoDB updateOne() Method to Up-
date the incremented "thumbsDOWNCounter" value back to the database

        if(error) { // If any Error

            return response.status(500).send(error);

        }else{

            response.send(result); // Send Response Back to the Client

        }

    });


  }


  });
});
```

In our example, we have created an API that uses the PUT method. We can now use the Postman application to update MongoDB documents using the PUT method.

Now, after updating the code, we need to restart our Node.js application. In order to do this, go to the Command Prompt where your Node.js App is currently running and then press *"Ctrl + C"* and then *"Y"* when you are prompted to terminate the task. After this, you should again type *"**npm start**"*, and press *Enter* to run this Node.js API application again on your machine.

After we press "**Send**" button from the Postman application, the API request will call the endpoint and will update the MongoDB document based on the Document ID provided and increase the value of Thumbs DOWN Counter "**thumbsDOWNCounter**" to 1 every time this API is called. We can also see in the Postman that we receive a response back with the status: "**200 OK**" along with the response body. In our example, we have made two calls to this API using our Dummy book ID that we created before, as shown in *figure 9.29:*

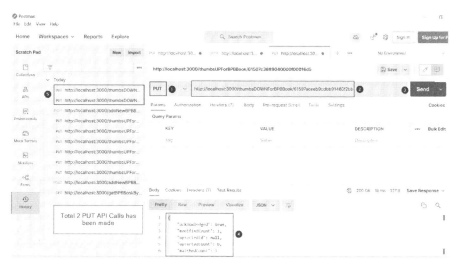

Figure 9.29: *Postman application—calling our API using PUT method*

We can also verify this using the MongoDB Compass; just launch MongoDB Compass in your computer and then navigate to our Application MongoDB Collection, which is "**BPBCatalogCollection**" in our case. You can see that MongoDB documents have been successfully updated by our API Calls. In case MongoDB Compass has been already opened in your machine, then just click the refresh button on the top left corner to refresh the MongoDB Collection documents data, as shown in *figure 9.30*:

Figure 9.30: *MongoDB Compass—verifying the documents updated by our API calls*

Adding REST API endpoint to delete MongoDB document based on MongoDB document ID (REST DELETE method)

As this is a practical chapter and we have learned so many things in this chapter, try to code this delete API functionality with the skills you have learned from this chapter. You can take references from the Node.js MongoDB driver and Express.js Official documentation home page as listed:

- Node.js MongoDB driver official repository home page at GitHub: **https://github.com/mongodb/node-mongodb-native**

- Express.js Official Guide: **https://expressjs.com/en/guide/routing.html**

Conclusion

In this chapter, we have learnt how to develop REST-based APIs using practical step-by-step development. We have also learnt how we can use Node.js, Express.js, and MongoDB driver to develop these APIs. Later, we have also learnt about the REST-based methods and various other related functionalities required for the overall development of APIs for a Publication House. In the upcoming chapter, we will cover the practical step-by-step development of a mobile app developed using React Native and MongoDB. We will learn how to create a mobile app for a publication house and will start with the overview of our mobile app development using React Native, Expo, Expo CLI, Node.js, Express.js, and MongoDB, along with the API's, which we have created in this chapter.

Questions

1. What is an API?

2. What is REST-based API?

3. What are the two main API types?

4. What is Express.js?

5. What are the different types of REST methods? Name a few of them.

6. What is the Postman application, and why it is useful for API development?

CHAPTER 10

MongoDB Step by Step Practical Mobile App Development Using React Native

Have you ever thought about how dynamic mobile apps works? Some of you might have some questions in your mind about how these mobile applications render data from the database and show them to the mobile users in their apps? Interesting? Let us learn how to create a dynamic data-driven mobile app. This chapter covers the practical step-by-step development of a mobile app developed using React Native and MongoDB. We will learn how to create a mobile app for a publication house and will start with the overview of our mobile app development using React Native, Expo, Expo CLI, Node.js, Express.js, and MongoDB. We will learn how to add the *"Thumbs Up"* and *"Thumbs Down"* functionality and how to store their counts in the MongoDB Database using the API calls. In this chapter, all the sections have been covered step by step and detailed manner.

Structure

In this chapter, we will discuss the following topics:

- An overview of our mobile app developed using React Native and MongoDB
- Requirements
- Connecting to MongoDB via API
- Starting with React Native mobile app development

- API Fetch part—networking

- Working on book list section

- Introduction to CORS

- Installing and adding CORS Module in our Node.js (Express.js) API app

- Enabling CORS in Node.js (Express.js) app routes

- Adding book pictures in the book list section of our mobile app

- Adding "Thumbs Up" and "Thumbs Down" in the book list section of our mobile app

- Adding database functionality to "Thumbs Up" and "Thumbs Down" of our mobile app

- Running the React Native mobile app on an Android device/emulator

Objectives

After studying this chapter, the reader will be able to understand an overview of our mobile app developed using React Native and MongoDB. We will start with React Native mobile app development and learn about the API Fetch Part—networking in React Native, and we will also be working on the Book List section. We will understand what CORS is and learn about installing and adding CORS Module in our Node.js (Express.js) API app. We will also be enabling CORS in Node.js (Express.js) app Routes so that the CORS-related issues will get resolved during the API calls made by the React Native mobile app. We will work on adding Book Pictures in the Book List section of our mobile app, "Thumbs Up" and "Thumbs Down" in the Book List section of our mobile app, and in the last part of this book, we will add Database Functionality to "Thumbs Up" and "Thumbs Down" of our mobile app and then run the React Native mobile app on Android device/emulator.

An overview of our mobile app developed using React Native and MongoDB

In this chapter, we are going to develop a mobile app using React Native and MongoDB.

We will be using RESTful Web from our Node.js (Express.js) API app.

This React Native mobile app will have the following features:

- Ability to list (read) all the books in the catalog and show their information and book picture

- Ability to give (insert) new "thumbs up" and "thumbs down" to a book

So, in order to create this mobile app, we will be writing and modifying some codes using the following:

- **React Native**—to build the cross-platform mobile app
- Expo and Expo CLI—use expo and expo tools helpful in creating the mobile app
- Node.js—to connect to MongoDB server using the Node.js and to do server-side operations and interacting with MongoDB
- Express.js—Express.js is the application framework for Node.js and is used widely for developing Web applications and API

Requirements

Readers should have the basic knowledge and understanding of the following (recommended and brief introduction of all these is provided in the previous chapters of the book):

- React Native
- Expo and Expo CLI
- Android Studio
- Node.js
- JavaScript
- API

 RESTful APIs

Example 1—connecting to MongoDB via API

Before we start connecting to MongoDB with the API. Let us make sure that the Node.js application that we have created in the previous chapter of this book is started [*Chapter 9, MongoDB Step by Step Practical Application Development Using JavaScript (Node.js with Express.js)*], so that we can use it.

In *Chapter 9, MongoDB Step by Step Practical Application Development Using JavaScript (Node.js with Express.js)*, we have also discussed the Postman and created APIs to read and write to MongoDB collection. Let's now first start the Node.js application.

We need to follow these steps:

1. To start the Node.js API application, you need to open the command prompt and navigate to the correct directory that is related to the API development

part using Node.js and Express.js, which is "**D:\bpb-catalog-app-api**" in our case, as shown in *figure 10.1*:

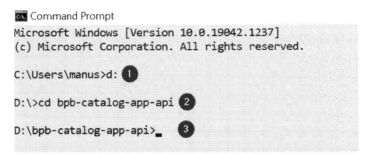

Figure 10.1: Command prompt and navigate to the Node.js and Express.js API project folder

2. The next step is to start this application using the "**npm start**" as we have learned earlier. Once this application is started, you will see the console messages that the application has been connected to the MongoDB database, and we can use this application and the APIs to be further used in our react native mobile app, which we are further enhancing in this chapter, as shown in the *figure 10.2*:

```
npm

D:\bpb-catalog-app-api>npm start  1

> bpb-catalog-app-api@1.0.0 start D:\bpb-catalog-app-api
> node index.js

API App Listening to: http://localhost:3000
Connected Sucessfully to MongoDB Server using Node.js Driver for MongoDB  2
Connected to MongoDB DB:BPBCatalogDB
```

Figure 10.2: Starting the API App using "npm start"

3. The next step is to write a code in our React Native mobile app so that we can be able to connect our mobile app to MongoDB Server using the API call and then fetch some dynamic data into our mobile app. To achieve this, we need to further do some code in our React Native App that we have started in *Chapter 5, Starting up Programming with MongoDB and React Native* of this book).

For this, we need to open our React Native mobile app folder in some code editor like Microsoft Visual Studio Code or any editor of your choice, and then we need to open **App.js** in the code editor. In our case, the location of the React Native mobile app folder is as follows:

"**D:\bpb-catalog-mobile-app**"

Please refer to the following code; we have now used two React.js Hooks in the **App.js** file.

> **Note:** Hooks are the latest introduction in React.js; they are helpful in writing the codes without the use of Class. You can think of these as special functions which are useful for doing some special things in React.js

Here, we have used the following two hooks:

- **useEffect**: This hook is used for some side effects tasks such as data fetching, manually changing the DOM in React.js Components, and so on.

- **useState**: This hook lets us use React State to the function components.

Code 1

The following code is the *"import section"* of our script where we are importing React and React Native libraries.

```
import { StatusBar } from 'expo-status-bar';

import React from 'react';

import { StyleSheet, Text, View, Image } from 'react-native'; // Imported the Image Component

import { useEffect, useState } from 'react'; // import the useEffect and useState React.js Hooks
```

We have a new code now in our default **App()** function where we have used the **fetch()** API, which is a React Native API for network-related stuff; we have used it to make API call. We have used the same API endpoint "**http://localhost:3000/ getAllBPBBooks**" which we have created in our last chapter [*Chapter 9, MongoDB Step by Step Practical Application Development Using JavaScript (Node.js with Express.js)*] as well, it also contains all the other codes of this app (which are Stylesheet, Header Section, Book List Section and the Return Part of this App) and following is the code for the same:

Code 2

Our application is divided into sections for better readability, and comments in the code will make you better understand these sections.

```
export default function App() {

// API Fetch Part - Networking

// Style Sheets
```

```
// Header Section

// Books List Section

// Return Part of the App


}
```

The default function **App()** will contain all the sections of our mobile app.

Code 3—API fetch part—networking

The following code is the API Fetch Part of React Native; using the Fetch API; we can access the API endpoint and get the data from the MongoDB database.

```
// API Fetch Part - Networking

const [isLoading, setLoading] = useState(true);

const [data, setData] = useState([]); // setData Function and useState
Hook is helpful in using the React State of the function Components

useEffect(() => {

  fetch('http://localhost:3000/getAllBPBBooks') // Our API Call using
Fetch API "API Developed in Node.js and Express.js Chapter of this Book"

    .then((response) => response.json()) // Response from the API Server

    .then((json) => setData(json)) // Using setData Function response is
sent back and then it is stored in "data"

    .catch((error) => console.error(error)) // Error if any is caught
and logged

    .finally(() => setLoading(false)); // Finally the task is done

}, []);
```

The other two sections of the code remain the same (with a few little updated codes for styling and layout) as of the previous chapter of this book, where we have started learning on how to create a mobile app using React Native. These are related to the Style Sheet, App Header section, and the code of the same is as follows:

Code 3—style sheets

Following are the style sheets that are used in our app to make it look nice. In React Native, we are using the **StyleSheet.create()** method to create the style sheets for our mobile application.

```
// Style Sheets
const styles = StyleSheet.create({
  container: {
    flex: 1,
    backgroundColor: '#fff',
    alignItems: 'center',
    justifyContent: 'flex-start', /* Flex Start */
    maxWidth:300,
    marginLeft:'auto',
    marginRight:'auto',
  },
  logo: {
    flex: 1,
    backgroundColor: '#fff',
    alignItems: 'center',
    justifyContent: 'center',
    width:250,
    height: 150,
    marginTop:20,
    marginBottom:20
  },
  heading: {
    fontSize:15,
    fontWeight:'bold'
  },
  booklistview: {
    borderWidth:2,
    borderColor:'blue',
    marginTop:20
  }
});
```

Code 4—header section

In the header section of our app, we are creating one variable which we will be going to use later in the return part of the app, and in this section, we are using a **\<View\>**, **\< image\>**, **\<Text\>**, and **\<StatusBar\>** components or React Native.

```
// Header Section

const appHeaderSection = (

  <View>

  <Image source={require('./images/bpb-logo.png')} style={styles.logo} />

  <Text style={styles.heading} >Welcome to BPB Online Mobile App</Text>

  <StatusBar style="auto" />

  </View>

);
```

We have added one more section in which we will display the data of the books that we have in our MongoDB Server using the API call, and the following is the code for the same:

Code 5—book list section

In the following code, we are using the **map()** function to create a list from the Book Data, which we fetched from the Fetch API of react-native.

```
// Header Section

const appHeaderSection = (

  <View>

  <Image source={require('./images/bpb-logo.png')} style={styles.logo} />

  <Text style={styles.heading} >Welcome to BPB Online Mobile App</Text>

  <StatusBar style="auto" />

  </View>

);

// Books List Section

// We are using the "data" which was fetched using the fetch API and then
we are iterating the same with the help of "map" to present the list of
books

const appBookdListSection = (
```

```
<View style={styles.booklistview}>

  <ul>

  {data.map((book, index) =>

    <Text key={book._id}>

      <li style={{paddingRight:'10px'}}><b>{book.title}</b> <i>[By:
{book.authorname}]</i></li>

    </Text>

  )}

  </ul>

</View>

);
```

We have just added "**appBookdListSection**" in the *"Return Part of the App"*. This part of the default **App()** function will return the actual application to us after all the process is done.

Code 6—return part of the app

In the last part of the code, we are using a **<View>,** which will show the header section and the book list section of the app and following is the code for the same:

```
return (

 <View style={styles.container}>

 {appHeaderSection}

 {appBookdListSection}

 </View>

 );


} // Default App Function Ends Here
```

Let us now run this code using Expo CLI (keeping in mind that our Node.js and Express.js API application is still running).

Now, navigate to your React Native app from the command prompt; the location of our React Native app in our case is: "**D:\bpb-catalog-mobile-app\bpb-mobile-app**" from the command prompt and run the following command:

npm start

After you enter this command, Expo CLI will try to run the React Native app, and after some time, it will try to open the Expo developer tools in the default browser of your machine automatically.

Once the Expo developer tool is loaded in your browser, click the link which says "**Run in web browser**", as shown in *figure 10.3*:

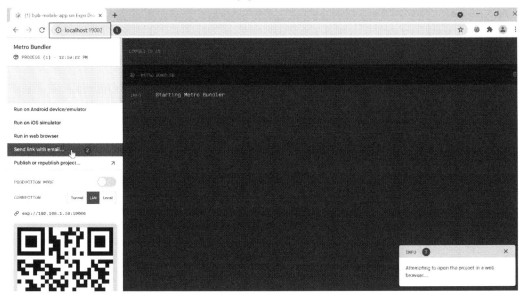

Figure 10.3: *Starting the Metro Bundler (Expo Dev Tools) using the EXPO CLI—"expo start" Command*

Once you click the link "**Run in web browser**", the Metro Bundler will try to build our app, and when it finishes building our app, it will try to open our app in the default browser in a separate tab of the browser, as shown in *figure 10.4*:

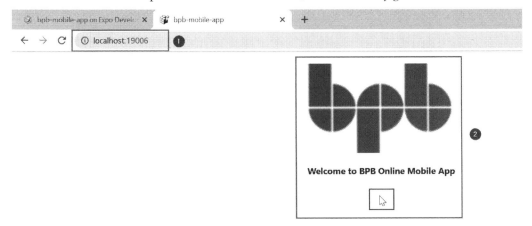

Figure 10.4: *Expo Dev tools—open our app in Web browser*

Now many of us would be thinking that why our book section, which we have coded in our example, is not shown in the app as it would have been called by the Fetch API and displayed as a list.

The reason for this could be found in the *"Console"* of our browser; let us open our *"Console"* to troubleshoot this issue. To open the console, first, click the browser menu (Google Chrome in our case), then click the *"**More tools**"* option. It will open another menu under which you will see the *"**Developer tools**"*. Click the **Developer tools** from where we can further navigate to console, as shown in *figure 10.5*:

Figure 10.5: *Open our app in Web browser—book section not showing—open developer tools*

The **console** will be open along with the **Developer tools,** and you can see the console logs, as shown in *figure 10.6*:

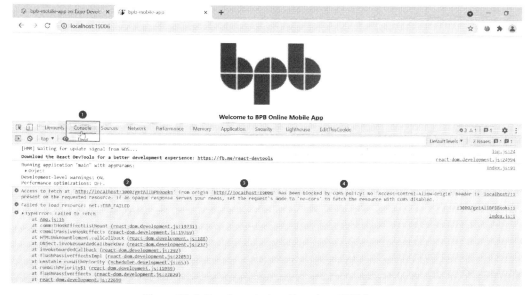

Figure 10.6: *Developer tools—Console—CORS error*

If we check in our console we get the following message:

```
Access to fetch at 'http://localhost:3000/getAllBPBBooks' from origin
'http://localhost:19006' has been blocked by CORS policy: No 'Access-
Control-Allow-Origin' header is present on the requested resource. If an
opaque response serves your needs, set the request's mode to 'no-cors' to
fetch the resource with CORS disabled.
```

So, we can see that something is blocked here, and because of this reason, our React Native app is unable to fetch the book's data using the API call.

So, what exactly is happening here?

Let us understand this first before rectifying this issue. If you see, the following things are happening here:

- Our React Native API call is requested from **http://localhost:19006**

- Our React Native API request is blocked from **http://localhost:3000/getAllBPBBooks**

- The CORS policy: No 'Access-Control-Allow-Origin' is the reason for this blockage

CORS

CORS is the acronym for Cross-Origin Request Sharing, and it is a protocol or mechanism to restrict the access of resources that originates from other domains.

In our example, you can see that the React Native app, which is running on Port 19006, is requesting the "Book Data" from the Node.js and Express.js API App, which is running on a different domain (Port 3000). So, the CORS policy has been applied to this request, and the request is failed.

Resolving the issue

To resolve this issue, we can do any one of the following things:

1. Add "**Access-Control-Allow-Origin**" header on the requested resource

2. Use some Node.js modules, which will help to resolve this issue

3. Set the request's mode to "**no-cors**" to fetch the resource with CORS disabled.

It is better to use some Node.js and Express.js official methods to resolve this issue. In Node.js, there is a package named "**cors**", which is a middleware to enable CORS with Express.js routes. Let us install and enable this on our Node.js and Express.js application so that the API calls which are requested from our React Native App will be served without a CORS issue.

Please open your browser and open this link: **https://www.npmjs.com/package/ cors**. You will see all the details related to the "**cors**" package for Node.js and how we can use it with Express.js, as shown in *figure 10.7*:

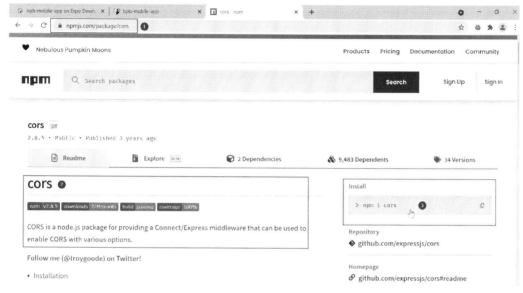

Figure 10.7: *NPM—"cors" Package for Node.js—Home Page*

Now, we need to first install and use this "**cors**" package in our Node.js and Express. js-based application.

Remember this and it is important that the CORS related changes that we are going to do now, including the installation of the Node.js "**cors**" package, will be done in the following application directory (and not in our current React Native app directory):

`D:\bpb-catalog-app-api`

So, you need to navigate to the current directory and do the required changes.

Let us start doing changes now, but before we do any code change, we need to first stop our Node.js and Express.js app, which is already running. To do this, open your command prompt where your Node.js and Express.js-based applications are running, and then to stop these, press *"Ctrl + C"*. Once you press this key, you will be asked that would you like to "Terminate batch job". Press *"Y"* and then enter. Doing this will stop your Node.js and Express.js application, as shown in *figure 10.8*:

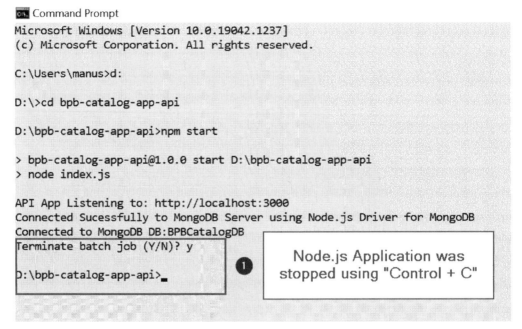

Figure 10.8: Command prompt—stopping our Node.js API app

Now, we can install our Node.js "**cors**" package using NPM to this remain in the same command prompt where you have just stopped your Node.js and Express.js-based application and then run the following command to install "**cors**" using NPM, as shown in *figure 10.9*:

```
npm install cors
```

OR

```
npm i cors
```

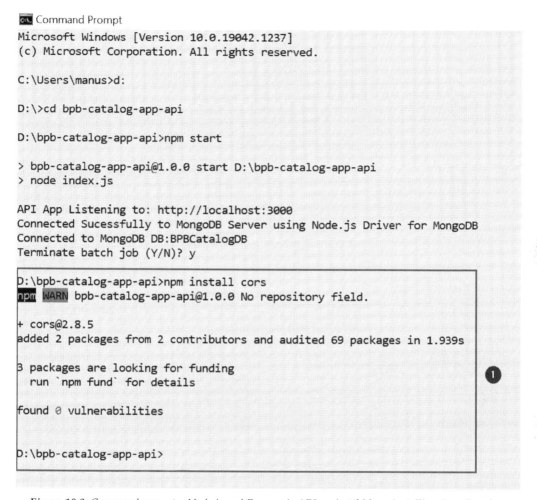

```
Command Prompt
Microsoft Windows [Version 10.0.19042.1237]
(c) Microsoft Corporation. All rights reserved.

C:\Users\manus>d:

D:\>cd bpb-catalog-app-api

D:\bpb-catalog-app-api>npm start

> bpb-catalog-app-api@1.0.0 start D:\bpb-catalog-app-api
> node index.js

API App Listening to: http://localhost:3000
Connected Sucessfully to MongoDB Server using Node.js Driver for MongoDB
Connected to MongoDB DB:BPBCatalogDB
Terminate batch job (Y/N)? y
```

```
D:\bpb-catalog-app-api>npm install cors
npm WARN bpb-catalog-app-api@1.0.0 No repository field.

+ cors@2.8.5
added 2 packages from 2 contributors and audited 69 packages in 1.939s

3 packages are looking for funding
  run `npm fund` for details

found 0 vulnerabilities

D:\bpb-catalog-app-api>
```

Figure 10.9: Command prompt—Node.js and Express.js API project folder—installing "cors" package

Now, as the "**cors**" package is installed successfully, we can do some modifications in our "**index.js**" file of our Node.js and Express.js-based application, and the location for the same is "

The following are the changes that we are going to do:

Change 1 in index.js—adding CORS module using require

```
var cors = require('cors') // CORS Module
```

We have added this single line of code after Express Module:

```
const express = require('express'); // Express Module

var cors = require('cors') // CORS Module

const app = express();

const port = 3000; // Port, You can Change this Port to anything you would
like For example 8000, For this Book, we will Keep this as 3000 for Node.
js > Express.js Based API Examples


const MongoDBClient = require('mongodb').MongoClient; // MongoDB Driver

const MongoDBObjectId = require("mongodb").ObjectId; // Create a new
ObjectID instance, used for Converting String to MongoDB ObjectID Type
and opposite


app.use(express.json());

app.use(express.urlencoded({ extended: true }));
```

Change 2 in index.js—enabling CORS in "getAllBPBBooks" route

```
// API Endpoint "getAllBPBBooks" using GET Request

app.get("/getAllBPBBooks", cors(), (request, response) => {
```

We have added **cors()** function in the get based method of our Express.js Route
(**getAllBPBBooks**):

```
app.use(express.json());

app.use(express.urlencoded({ extended: true }));


app.get('/', (req, res) => {

  res.send('Welcome to BPB Publications RESTful API') // This is the
Default API Message

});


// API Endpoint "getAllBPBBooks" using GET Request

// Now CORS Enabled
```

```
app.get("/getAllBPBBooks", cors(), (request, response) => {

  collection.find().toArray((error, result) => { // Fetching the
Collection Data using "toArray"

      if(error) { // If any Error

          return response.status(500).send(error);

      }else{

          response.send(result); // Send Response Back to the Client

      }

  });

});
```

Figure 10.10: Microsoft Visual Studio Code—opening "index.js" file

So, we have done only two lines of code changes or updates, and now you will see that our CORS issue will be resolved for this API call when fetch is called in our React Native app.

Before we can resume working on our react Native app, we have to start this Node. js and Express.js-based application. To do this, run the following command in the same command prompt where we recently installed the "**cors**" package for Node.js using NPM, as shown in *figure 10.11*:

```
▇ npm
Microsoft Windows [Version 10.0.19042.1237]
(c) Microsoft Corporation. All rights reserved.

C:\Users\manus>d:

D:\>cd bpb-catalog-app-api

D:\bpb-catalog-app-api>npm start

> bpb-catalog-app-api@1.0.0 start D:\bpb-catalog-app-api
> node index.js

API App Listening to: http://localhost:3000
Connected Sucessfully to MongoDB Server using Node.js Driver for MongoDB
Connected to MongoDB DB:BPBCatalogDB
Terminate batch job (Y/N)? y

D:\bpb-catalog-app-api>npm install cors
npm WARN bpb-catalog-app-api@1.0.0 No repository field.

+ cors@2.8.5
added 2 packages from 2 contributors and audited 69 packages in 1.939s

3 packages are looking for funding
  run `npm fund` for details

found 0 vulnerabilities

D:\bpb-catalog-app-api>npm start

> bpb-catalog-app-api@1.0.0 start D:\bpb-catalog-app-api
> node index.js

API App Listening to: http://localhost:3000                    ❶
Connected Sucessfully to MongoDB Server using Node.js Driver for MongoDB
Connected to MongoDB DB:BPBCatalogDB
▇
```

Figure 10.11: Command prompt—restarting the API app

After you make these updates in your Node.js and Express.js and start your application, you can refresh your browser where your React Native app is running. Once you refresh the browser window, you will see that the CORS issue is resolved, and you will be able to see the Book List section of your React Native App, as shown in *figure 10.12*:

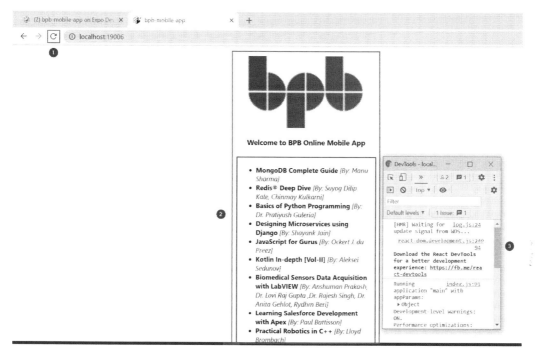

Figure 10.12: Refreshing the mobile app browser Window—book section appears

As we have seen how we can connect React Native mobile app with MongoDB and how we can show the MongoDB Data in mobile apps using React Native, let us add some more functionalities in our app with some more examples.

Example 2—adding book pictures in the book list section of our mobile app

We have done some updates to our code and added the following code for fetching images from the localhost.

Code 1 (updated App.js file) —CSS section (added some more CSS and changed the class names to "camelCase")

```
// Style Sheets
const styles = StyleSheet.create({
  bookContainer: {
    flex: 1,
    backgroundColor: '#fff',
```

```
    alignItems: 'center',
    justifyContent: 'center',
    marginLeft:'auto',
    marginRight:'auto',
    borderWidth:2,
    borderColor:'darkblue',
    padding:10
  },
  logo: {
    backgroundColor: '#fff',
    alignItems: 'center',
    justifyContent: 'center',
    width:150,
    height: 100,
    marginTop:5,
    marginBottom:5,
    marginLeft:'auto',
    marginRight:'auto'
  },
  heading: {
    fontSize:17,
    fontWeight:'bold',
    marginTop:5,
    marginBottom:5,
    marginLeft:'auto',
    marginRight:'auto',
    marginBottom:20
  },
  appBookdListSection:{
    marginBottom:400
  },
```

```
bookCover: {
 width:280,
 height: 350,
 marginTop:20,
 marginBottom:20
},
bookListTitle: {
 fontSize:25,
 fontWeight:'bold',
 maxWidth:280,
 marginLeft:'auto',
 marginRight:'auto'
},
bookListAuthor: {
 fontSize:20,
 fontWeight:'bold',
 fontStyle:'italic',
 maxWidth:280,
 marginLeft:'auto',
 marginRight:'auto'
},

/* Item Separator CSS */

itemSeparator:{
 height: 0.5,
 width: '100%',
 backgroundColor:'darkblue',
 borderWidth:2,
 borderBottomColor:'darkmagenta',
 marginTop:20,
```

```
    marginBottom:20,

    maxWidth:280,

    marginLeft:'auto',

    marginRight:'auto'

  }

});
```

Code 2 (updated App.js File) —update in book list section and use of react native "FlatList" component instead of ".map" method

As we are expanding our application and want to show images of the book, we are going to use React Native's **FlatList** component as it is useful in displaying the structured data in the scrollable list and also renders only that data to the screen, which is shown on the screen and will not render all the data. **FlatList** has many other features, such as separator support and scroll loading.

For more information about the React Native **FlatList** component, you can refer to the official documentation at: **https://reactnative.dev/docs/flatlist**

Following is the updated code for the **App.js** file:

Importing the React Native "FlatList" and "SafeAreaView":

```
import { StatusBar } from 'expo-status-bar';

import { StyleSheet, Text, View, Image } from 'react-native'; //
Imported the Image Component

//import React from 'react';

import React, { useEffect, useState } from 'react'; // Import the
useEffect and useState React.js Hooks

import { SafeAreaView, FlatList } from 'react-native'; // Import React
Native FlatList and SafeAreaView
```

Code change in header section—update in image path, calling logo image from app backend:

```
// Header Section

const appHeaderSection = (

  <View>
```

```
  <Image  source={{uri:'http://localhost/bpb-catalog-app-backend/images/
bpb-logo.png'}} style={styles.logo} />

 <Text style={styles.heading} >Welcome to BPB Online Mobile App</Text>

 <StatusBar style="auto" />

 </View>

);
```

Code change in book list section:

```
// Books List Section
// We are using the "data" which was fetched using the fetch API and
then we are using the React Native Flatlist Component to render the Book-
related data.

const ItemView = ({item}) => {

  return (

    // Single Comes here which will be repetitive for the FlatListItems

    <View style={styles.bookContainer}>

      <Text style={styles.bookListTitle}>

        {item.title}

      </Text>

      <Text style={styles.bookListAuthor}>

        {item.authorname}

      </Text>

    <View><Image source={{uri:'http://localhost/bpb-catalog-app-backend/
images/'+item.coverimage}} style={styles.bookCover}/>

      </Vicw>

    </View>

  );

};

const ItemSeparatorView = () => {

  return (

    //Item Separator

    <View style={styles.itemSeparator} />
```

```
   );
};

const appBookdListSection = (
    <View style={styles.appBookdListSection}>
      <FlatList
        data={data}
        //data defined in constructor
        ItemSeparatorComponent={ItemSeparatorView}
        //Item Separator View
        renderItem={ItemView}
        keyExtractor={(item, index) => index.toString()}
      />
    </View>
);
```

In the preceding code, we have also used the image component and fetched all the book cover images dynamically using the data, which is fetched using the Fetch API call. Here, if you see, the source of the image is coming from our localhost PHP backend application.

Example: '**http://localhost/bpb-catalog-app-backend/images/**'+book. coverimage

Where "**book.coverimage**" is the file name of the cover image for the book. These book data have been entered by us while we have created our backend application using PHP and MongoDB.

If you remember that in our previous chapter [*Chapter 8, MongoDB Step by Step Practical Application Development Using PHP*] of this book, we have created the "*Backend for Publication House*" using PHP, MongoDB, and WAMP Server.

We need to now run that backend application, too, before we can run and test our React Native app so that images can be fetched using our backend app URL, as discussed earlier.

Please start the WAMP server first and check if your backend application is working fine. For this, follow these steps:

1. Type "**WAMP**" on the "*Search Bar*" in the *Task Bar* of your Windows and open it, as shown in *figure 10.13*:

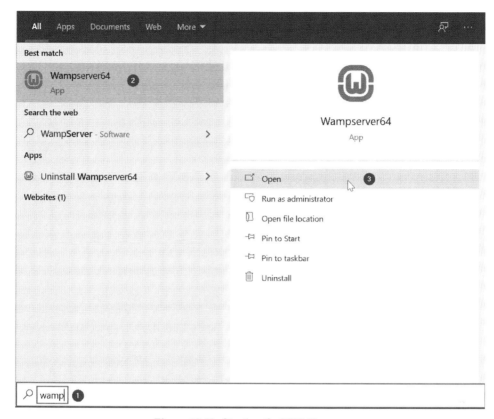

Figure 10.13: Starting the WAMP server

2. Once the WAMP server has started all the services, you can see the WAMP server icon in green color under your *"Windows System Tray"*, as shown in *figure 10.14*:

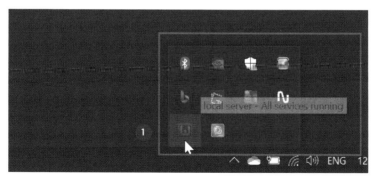

Figure 10.14: Windows system tray—WAMP started

3. Now verify if our PHP and MongoDB Based application is running fine by typing: **http://localhost/bpb-catalog-app-backend/** in your browser

address bar, and you should see your PHP and MongoDB-based backend application running smoothly, as shown in *figure 10.15*:

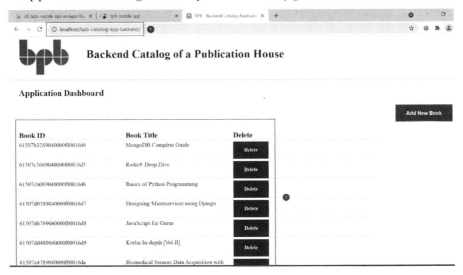

Figure 10.15: PHP and MongoDB based backend catalogue application

Now, we can refresh our browser to check our React Native mobile app. The interesting thing to note here is that once you do changes in your React Native app, the Expo will automatically refresh your code, and you can see the instant changes in the browser whatsoever you are doing it in your code. So the changes would be reflected automatically. But as we have started the WAMP server to serve the book images for this app, let us refresh our React Native app in the browser, and we can see the changes reflected as the result of our new code, as shown in *figure 10.16*:

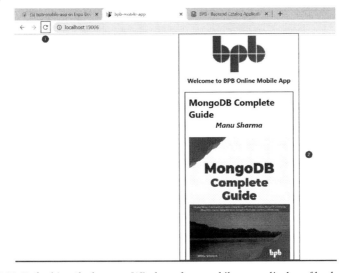

Figure 10.16: Refreshing the browser Window of our mobile app—display of book cover images

We can scroll and see that all the books have been listed correctly by our React Native-based mobile app, as shown in *figure 10.17*:

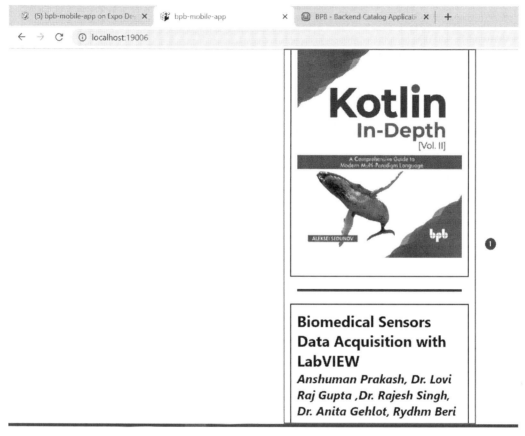

Figure 10.17: *Refreshing the browser Window of our mobile app*
—display of book cover images—scrolling to view more books

So, we have seen how we can add dynamic images to our mobile app, which are fetched from the PHP-based backend application that we have created earlier. Now, let us add some more functionality to our app with some more interesting examples.

Example 3—adding "Thumbs Up" and "Thumbs Down" in the book list section of our mobile app

In the last examples, we have added the books list and book image and have used the Fetch API to show the list of the books. Now, let us add some more functionality in this app so that we can give the "Thumbs Up" or "Thumbs Down" to a book.

We need some good icons for this purpose which can be clickable and for this reason, we have to add an NPM Package for this which is named "*Expo Vector Icons*".

To install it first, visit the official NPM page of this package. Open this URL in your browser window: **https://www.npmjs.com/package/@expo/vector-icons**, as shown in *figure 10.18*:

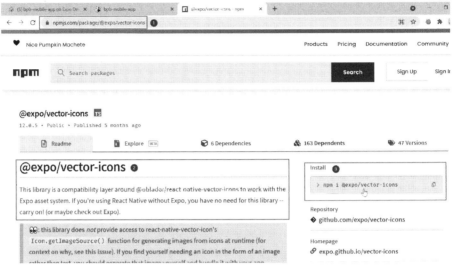

Figure 10.18: *NPM—Expo Vector Icons— Home Page*

Now, we need to install this package in our React Native mobile app. Before we can install this package, we need to first stop our app, which is running using the Expo CLI from the command prompt. To stop the app, go to the command prompt from where we have run our React Native app using Expo CLI and then type "*Ctrl + C*". This will stop our app, as shown in *figure 10.19*:

Figure 10.19: *Stopping our mobile app*

Now, we need to install the "**Expo Vector Icons**" package in our React Native app. To do this, type the following command (as shown in *figure 10.20*):

```
npm i @expo/vector-icons
```

OR

```
npm install @expo/vector-icons
```

We have done some updates to our code and added the following code for fetching images from the localhost.

Figure 10.20: *React Native mobile app folder*
—Installing "Expo Vector Icons" Package using npm install command

As we have now installed the required "*Expo Vector Icons*", we can now use the same in our app. We can start our app again using the following command:

```
npm start
```

So, we have done the following updates in our code to implement the "Thumbs Up" and "Thumbs Down" functionality.

Code 1 (updated App.js file)—import FontAwesome from Vector Icons

```
import { StatusBar } from 'expo-status-bar';

import { StyleSheet, Text, View, Image } from 'react-native'; // Imported
the Image Component
```

```
//import React from 'react';

import React, { useEffect, useState } from 'react'; // Import the useEffect
and useState React.js Hooks

import { SafeAreaView, FlatList } from 'react-native'; // Import React
Native FlatList and SafeAreaView

import { FontAwesome } from '@expo/vector-icons'; // Import Font Awesome
```

Code 2 (updated App.js File)—CSS section (added some more CSS for "Thumbs Up" and "Thumbs Down")

```
/* Item Separator CSS */

  itemSeparator:{

    height: 0.5,

    width: '100%',

    backgroundColor:'darkblue',

    borderWidth:2,

    borderBottomColor:'darkmagenta',

    marginTop:20,

    marginBottom:20,

    maxWidth:280,

    marginLeft:'auto',

    marginRight:'auto'

  },

  /* New CSS for "Thumbs Up" and "Thumbs Down" */

  thumbsUP: {

    width:200,

    marginBottom:5,

  },

  thumbsDOWN: {

    width:200,

    marginTop:5,
```

```
        marginBottom:5
    }

  });
```

Code 3 (updated App.js file)—added "Thumbs Up" and "Thumbs Down" button components and functions

```
// Header Section
const appHeaderSection = (
  <View>
    <Image source={{uri:'http://localhost/bpb-catalog-app-backend/images/
bpb-logo.png'}} style={styles.logo} />
    <Text style={styles.heading} >Welcome to BPB Online Mobile App</Text>
    <StatusBar style="auto" />
  </View>
);

// Thumbs Up Button
const thumbsUP = (
  <FontAwesome.Button name="thumbs-up" onPress={() => doThumbsUP()}>
    Thumbs Up
  </FontAwesome.Button>
);

// Thumbs Down Button
const thumbsDOWN = (
  <FontAwesome.Button name="thumbs-down" onPress={() => doThumbsDOWN()}>
    Thumbs Down
  </FontAwesome.Button>
);

const doThumbsUP = () => {
  console.log('Thumbs Up Pressed');
```

```
}

const doThumbsDOWN = () => {

  console.log('Thumbs Down Pressed');

}
```

Code 4 (updated App.js file)—book list section (added "Thumbs Up" and "Thumbs Down" button components)

Here, we have added the "Thumbs Up" and "Thumbs Down" buttons in all the books listed under the book section of the app.

```
// Books List Section

// We are using the "data" which was fetched using the fetch API and
then we are using the React Native Flatlist Component to render the Book-
related data.

const ItemView = ({item}) => {

  return (

    // Single Comes here which will be repetitive for the FlatListItems

    <View style={styles.bookContainer}>

      <Text style={styles.bookListTitle}>

        {item.title}

      </Text>

      <Text style={styles.bookListAuthor}>

        {item.authorname}

      </Text>

      <View><Image source={{uri:'http://localhost/bpb-catalog-app-backend/
images/'+item.coverimage}} style={styles.bookCover}/>

      </View>

      <View style={styles.thumbsUP}>

      {thumbsUP}

      </View>

      <View style={styles.thumbsDOWN}>

      {thumbsDOWN}
```

```
      </View>
    </View>
  );
};
```

So, if you see the button components, you will see that the event *"onPress"* is in both of the buttons that we have created. When the user presses these buttons, their respective functions will be called, and the logs will be shown in the console, as shown in *figure 10.21*:

Figure 10.21: *Dev Tools > Console > Console logs*

Example 4—adding database functionality to "Thumbs Up" and "Thumbs Down" of our mobile app

In the last example, we have added functionality for "Thumbs Up" and "Thumbs Down" to a book. This functionality will be incomplete if we cannot store "Thumbs Up" and "Thumbs Down" counts to the MongoDB database. To have this functionality, we have to use two more APIs from our Node.js (Express.js) API app.

We already have two existing API methods for this purpose that we can use here. But, we need to first stop our Node.js API App as explained previously in this chapter and then enable "CORS" in these API methods.

We can now do some modifications in our "**index.js**" file of our Node.js, and Express.js-based application, and the location for the same is: "

The following are the changes that we are going to do:

Change 1 in index.js—enabling CORS in "thumbsUPForBPBBook" route

```
// API Endpoint "thumbsUPForBPBBook" using PUT Request

app.put("/thumbsUPForBPBBook/:bookid", cors(), (request, response) => {
```

We have added **cors()** function in the get based method of our Express.js Route (**thumbsUPForBPBBook**):

```
// API Endpoint "thumbsUPForBPBBook" using PUT Request

app.put("/thumbsUPForBPBBook/:bookid", cors(), (request, response) => {

    collection.findOne({  "_id":  new  MongoDBObjectId(request.params.
bookid)},(error, result) => { // We are Fetching Book Record from our
Collection
  if(error) { // If any Error
      return response.status(500).send(error);
  }else{

    if(isNaN(result.thumbsUPCounter)){ // If there is no existing value
for "thumbsUPCounter" in the MongoDB Document
    var thumbsUPCounterValue = 1; // Just assign a new Value to 1
    }else{
        var thumbsUPCounterValue = result.thumbsUPCounter + 1; // We are
taking the existing "thumbsUPCounter" value from our Database and then
Incrementing the Thumbs UP Counter value "thumbsUPCounterValue" to 1
    }
      collection.updateOne({  "_id":  new  MongoDBObjectId(request.params.
bookid)}, {  $set:  {thumbsUPCounter:thumbsUPCounterValue}  }, (error,
result) => { // We are using MongoDB updateOne() Method to Update the
incremented "thumbsUPCounter" value back to the database
        if(error) { // If any Error
            return response.status(500).send(error);
        }else{
            response.send(result); // Send Response Back to the Client
```

```
      }
    });

  }

  });
});
```

Change 2 in index.js—enabling CORS in "thumbsDOWNForBPBBook" route

```
// API Endpoint "thumbsDOWNForBPBBook" using PUT Request
```

```
app.put("/thumbsDOWNForBPBBook/:bookid", cors(), (request, response) => {
```

We have added **cors()** function in the get based method of our Express.js route (**thumbsDOWNForBPBBook**):

```
// API Endpoint "thumbsDOWNForBPBBook" using PUT Request
```

```
app.put("/thumbsDOWNForBPBBook/:bookid", cors(), (request, response) => {


    collection.findOne({  "_id":   new   MongoDBObjectId(request.params.
bookid)},(error, result) => { // We are Fetching Book Record from our
Collection
  if(error) { // If any Error

    return response.status(500).send(error);

  }else{


    if(isNaN(result.thumbsDOWNCounter)){ // If there is no existing value
for "thumbsDOWNCounter" in the MongoDB Document

    var thumbsDOWNCounterValue = 1; // Just assign a new Value to 1

    }else{

    var thumbsDOWNCounterValue = result.thumbsDOWNCounter + 1; // We are
taking the existing "thumbsDOWNCounter" value from our Database and then
Incrementing the Thumbs UP Counter value "thumbsDOWNCounterValue" to 1

    }

    collection.updateOne({  "_id": new MongoDBObjectId(request.params.
bookid)}, { $set: {thumbsDOWNCounter:thumbsDOWNCounterValue} }, (error,
```

```
result) => { // We are using MongoDB updateOne() Method to Update the
incremented "thumbsDOWNCounter" value back to the database

        if(error) { // If any Error

            return response.status(500).send(error);

        }else{

            response.send(result); // Send Response Back to the Client

        }

    });

  }

 });

});
```

Sometimes, enabling "cors" on a particular route might still give you CORS related issues as follows:

Access to fetch at 'http://localhost:3000/ thumbsUPForBPBBook/615974498124895ebe4bd836' from origin 'http:// localhost:19006' has been blocked by CORS policy: Response to preflight request doesn't pass access control check: No 'Access-Control-Allow- Origin' header is present on the requested resource. If an opaque response serves your needs, set the request's mode to 'no-cors' to fetch the resource with CORS disabled.

It is generally recommended to enable CORS on a route that is required to serve the requests from other apps, but if you still face the issues as described previously, you may enable the whole app for CORS. For this, you need to put the following code in our Node.js App as shown:

```
app.use(cors()) // Enable Whole App for CORS
```

You can include the preceding code in the top section of your Node.js app as follows:

```
const express = require('express'); // Express Module
```

```
var cors = require('cors') // CORS Module
```

```
const app = express();
```

```
const port = 3000; // Port, You can Change this Port to anything you would
like For example 8000, For this Book, we will Keep this as 3000 for Node.
js > Express.js Based API Examples
```

```
const MongoDBClient = require('mongodb').MongoClient; // MongoDB Driver
```

```
const MongoDBObjectId = require("mongodb").ObjectId; // Create a new
ObjectID instance, used for Converting String to MongoDB ObjectID Type
and opposite
```

```
app.use(express.json());
```

```
app.use(express.urlencoded({ extended: true }));
```

```
app.use(cors()) // Enable Whole App for CORS
```

As we have now done these updates in our Node.js API app, we should stop and start our app again using "*Ctrl + C*" to stop and the "**npm start**" command to start our Node.js app from the command prompt as explained in the previous section of this chapter.

After our API app has been started successfully. Now, in our React Native app, we need to add these API calls inside the "doThumbsUP" and "doThumbsDOWN" methods, respectively, and below are the updated codes for the same.

Code 3 (updated App.js file)—updated "Thumbs Up" and "Thumbs Down" button components, functions, and book list section

Following is the major change in the code as we have now passed the book ID (**item._id**) in the book section while creating the buttons, and this is further passed to the other method for "**onPress**" event method calls.

```
// Thumbs Up Button

const thumbsUP = (id) => {

  return (

  <FontAwesome.Button name="thumbs-up" onPress={() => doThumbsUP(id)}>

    Thumbs Up

  </FontAwesome.Button>

  )

};
```

```
// Thumbs Down Button

const thumbsDOWN = (id) => {

  return (

  <FontAwesome.Button name="thumbs-down" onPress={() =>
doThumbsDOWN(id)}>
```

```
    Thumbs Down

  </FontAwesome.Button>

  )

};

const doThumbsUP = (id) => {

  console.log('Thumbs Up Pressed');

  console.log(id);

  fetch('http://localhost:3000/thumbsUPForBPBBook/'+id, {

    method: 'PUT'

  }) // Our API Call using Fetch API "API Developed in Node.js and
Express.js Chapter of this Book"

}

const doThumbsDOWN = (id) => {

  console.log('Thumbs Down Pressed');

  console.log(id);

  fetch('http://localhost:3000/thumbsDOWNForBPBBook/'+id, {

    method: 'PUT'

  }) // Our API Call using Fetch API "API Developed in Node.js and
Express.js Chapter of this Book"

}

// Books List Section
// We are using the "data" which was fetched using the fetch API and then we
are using the React Native Flatlist Component to render the Book-related data.

const ItemView = ({item}) => {

  return (

    // Single Comes here which will be repetitive for the FlatListItems

    <View style={styles.bookContainer}>

      <Text style={styles.bookListTitle}>

        {item.title}

      </Text>

      <Text style={styles.bookListAuthor}>

        {item.authorname}
```

```
    </Text>
    <View><Image source={{uri:'http://localhost/bpb-catalog-app-
backend/images/'+item.coverimage}} style={styles.bookCover}/>
    </View>
    <View style={styles.thumbsUP}>
    {thumbsUP(item._id)}
    </View>
    <View style={styles.thumbsDOWN}>
    {thumbsDOWN(item._id)}
    </View>
  </View>
  );
};
```

We can verify this change and check if the "**onPress**" event method calls are now updating the values of the "**thumbsUPCounter**" as well as "**thumbsUPCounter**" of the book records (documents in the MongoDB database). For this, you need to open MongoDB Compass and check the status of these counters ("**thumbsUPCounter**" as well as "**thumbsUPCounter**" document fields in our collection "**BPBCatalogCollection**" which is under the database "**BPBCatalogDB**"), as shown in *figure 10.22*:

Figure 10.22*: MongoDB Compass — checking the "ThumbsUPCounter" and "ThumbsDOWNCounter"*

As you can see, the "**onPress**" event method calls are now updating the values of the "**thumbsUPCounter**" as well as "**thumbsUPCounter**" of the book records (documents in the MongoDB database).

Now it is time to open this app in Android Emulator so that we are sure that it will work perfectly fine on mobile. But, before we can do that, we need to change all the references of "**http://localhost**" to the IP address of our machine.

Let us see how we can check the IP address of our Windows machine. To do this, follow these steps:

1. On the system tray of your Windows Task Bar, select **WiFi Network** and then click on the **Properties** of the network to which you are connected, as shown in *figure 10.23*:

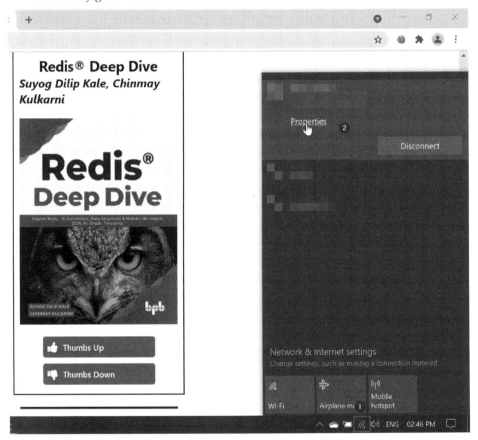

Figure 10.23: Windows system tray > WiFi Network > Your Connected Network > Properties

2. Once you click the **Properties** of your network, it will open up a new window. You need to scroll down and check for your Local IP Address. You should use "**IPv4 address**", as shown in *figure 10.24*:

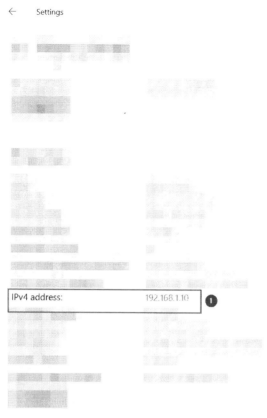

Figure 10.24: *Windows system tray > WiFi Network >*
Your Connected Network > Properties > IPv4 address

In our case, the IP Address is "**192.168.1.10**".

Now, in order to view your application correctly under Android device/emulator, you need to change all the references of the "**http://localhost**" in **App.js** to "**http://192.168.1.10**". Following are the code snippets that need to be changed in **App.js**.

Changes in App.js

```
// API Fetch Part - Networking

const [isLoading, setLoading] = useState(true);

const [data, setData] = useState([]); // setData Function and useState
Hook is helpful in using the React State of the function Components

useEffect(() => {

  fetch('http://192.168.1.10:3000/getAllBPBBooks') // Our API Call
```

```
using Fetch API "API Developed in Node.js and Express.js Chapter of this Book"
      .then((response) => response.json()) // Response from the API
Server
      .then((json) => setData(json)) // Using setData Function response
is sent back and then it is stored in "data"
      .catch((error) => console.error(error)) // Error if any is caught
and logged
      .finally(() => setLoading(false)); // Finally the task is done
  }, []);

// Header Section
const appHeaderSection = (
  <View>
  <Image source={{uri:'http://192.168.1.10/bpb-catalog-app-backend/
images/bpb-logo.png'}} style={styles.logo} />
  <Text style={styles.heading} >Welcome to BPB Online Mobile App</Text>
  <StatusBar style="auto" />
  </View>
);

const doThumbsUP = (id) => {
  console.log('Thumbs Up Pressed');
  console.log(id);
  fetch('http://192.168.1.10:3000/thumbsUPForBPBBook/'+id, {
    method: 'PUT'
  }) // Our API Call using Fetch API "API Developed in Node.js and
Express.js Chapter of this Book"
}

const doThumbsDOWN = (id) => {
  console.log('Thumbs Down Pressed');
  console.log(id);
  fetch('http://192.168.1.10:3000/thumbsDOWNForBPBBook/'+id, {
    method: 'PUT'
  }) // Our API Call using Fetch API "API Developed in Node.js and
Express.js Chapter of this Book"
```

```
}

// Books List Section
// We are using the "data" which was fetched using the fetch API and then we
are using the React Native Flatlist Component to render the Book-related data.

const ItemView = ({item}) => {
  return (
    // Single Comes here which will be repetitive for the FlatListItems
    <View style={styles.bookContainer}>
      <Text style={styles.bookListTitle}>
        {item.title}
      </Text>
      <Text style={styles.bookListAuthor}>
        {item.authorname}
      </Text>
      <View><Image source={{uri:'http://192.168.1.10/bpb-catalog-app-
backend/images/'+item.coverimage}} style={styles.bookCover}/>
      </View>
      <View style={styles.thumbsUP}>
      {thumbsUP(item._id)}
      </View>
      <View style={styles.thumbsDOWN}>
      {thumbsDOWN(item._id)}
      </View>
    </View>
  );
};
```

To open the app in Android Emulator, you can then go to the Expo Dev Tools page in your browser and click the link, which says "**Run on Android device/ emulator**". Once you click this link, the Expo Dev Tools will try to launch the app in the Emulator with the help of Metro Bundler. But in case it does not work, you can first open Android Studio and then open AVD Manager and then run the **Android Virtual Device (AVD)**. This step has been explained in our previous chapter [*Chapter 5, Starting up Programming with MongoDB and React Native*], where we have started the App Development using React Native. You can follow the same instructions, as shown in *figure 10.25*:

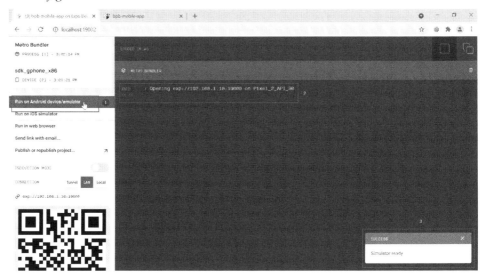

Figure 10.25: *Expo dev tools > run on android device/emulator*

After you click the "**Launch this AVD in Emulator**", it will open the Android Virtual Device. After that, you can again click the link, which says "**Run on Android device/emulator**". This will launch our app in Android Emulator, as shown in *figure 10.26*:

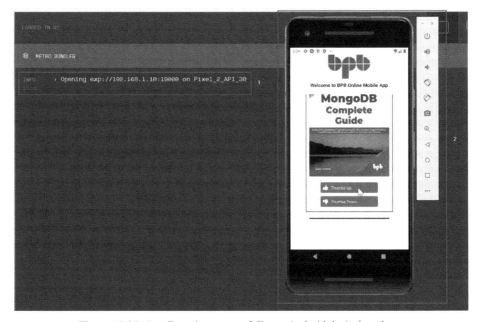

Figure 10.26: *App Running successfully on Android device/emulator*

You can also press the "Thumbs Up" and "Thumbs Down" buttons and check the Books Records (MongoDB Documents) for the counter updates using MongoDB Compass, as explained in the previous step.

Conclusion

In this chapter, we have covered the practical step-by-step development of a mobile app developed using React Native and MongoDB, and we have learned how to create a mobile app for a publication house. This chapter explains all the sections in step by step practical manner, and after reading this chapter, you must have felt more confident in React Native and MongoDB mobile app development. In the upcoming chapter, we will cover the practical step-by-step development of a frontend application developed using Python and MongoDB. We will learn how to create a website for a publication house where we start with the overview of our frontend development using Python, Django, and MongoDB.

Questions

1. What is CORS?

2. How can we solve the issue of CORS for Node.js applications using the Express.js framework?

3. Explain the React Native's Fetch API?

4. Write a few words on React Native FlatList component.

CHAPTER 11
MongoDB Step by Step Practical Frontend Development Using Python

Frontend development—creating a website of a publication house

This chapter covers the practical step-by-step development of the frontend application developed using Python and MongoDB. In this chapter, we will learn how to create a website for a publication house. This chapter starts with an overview of our frontend development using Python, Django, PyMongo, and MongoDB. We will start this chapter with basic requirements. Later in this chapter, we will learn how we can build the various functionalities of the frontend application like displaying the book catalog list and displaying the book cover images, a total number of "Thumbs Up" and "Thumbs Down" for that particular book using the Python and its Django framework with the help of Python's official MongoDB driver. In this chapter, all the sections have been explained in a step-by-step practical manner so that by the end of this chapter, you feel more confident in dynamic Python application development with MongoDB.

Structure

In this chapter, we will discuss the following topics:

- An overview of our frontend application developed using Python and MongoDB

- Installing Python's Django framework on Windows operating system

- Building our frontend application
  - o Step 1—Install Django using PIP
  - o Step 2—Creating a default Django project
  - o Step 3—Creating a new Django app
  - o Step 4—Updating the Django app and Django project files
  - o Step 5—Using PyMongo in Django to connect to MongoDB
  - o Step 6—Adding CSS and static files in our Django app
  - o Step 7—Designing our frontend with CSS Flex (Flexible Box Layout)
  - o Step 8—Adding book pictures to our frontend app
    - ▪ Step 8.1—Start WAMP server
    - ▪ Step 8.2—Running localhost
    - ▪ Step 8.3—Coding part
  - o Step 9—Adding more details functionality to our frontend app
  - o Step 10—Fixing underscore attribute issue for Django using the Django template tags
  - o Step 11—Creating the More Details page
  - o Step 12—Designing the More Details page
  - o Step 13—Making "Thumbs Up" and "Thumbs Down" looks nicer

Objectives

After studying this chapter, you will learn how to develop the frontend application using Python, Django, PyMongo, and MongoDB. This chapter starts with the basic requirements, and then in the latter part of this chapter, readers will learn how they can build the various functionalities of the frontend application like displaying the book catalog list and displaying the book cover images, total number of "Thumbs Up" and "Thumbs Down" for that particular book using the Python and its Django framework with the help of Python's official MongoDB driver.

An overview of our frontend application developed using Python and MongoDB

In this chapter, we are going to develop a frontend application using Python and MongoDB.

We are going to use Python's Django framework and Python's official MongoDB driver, "PyMongo" which we have already worked on in *Chapter 6, Starting up Programming with MongoDB and Python*.

This Python frontend application will have the following features:

- Ability to list (read) all the books in the catalog and show their information and book picture

- Ability to show the total number of "Thumbs Up" and "Thumbs Down" counts related to the particular book

So, in order to create this frontend application, we would be writing and modifying some codes using the following:

- Python and Python's Django framework—to build the frontend application

- PyMongo driver for MongoDB—to connect with Mongo DB

Requirements

The reader should have the basic knowledge and understanding of the following:

- Python (recommended; a brief introduction is given in *Chapter 6, Starting up Programming with MongoDB and Python* of this book).

Installing Python's Django framework on Windows operating system

Let us install the Django framework on Windows operating system by following the step-by-step installation method.

Installation steps

Let us start with the installation of Python on our machine; the following are the steps that are required to be performed to install Django.

Step 1—Install Django using PIP

1. Open the Django official website download page—**https://www.
djangoproject.com/download/** in your favorite browser, as shown in
figure 11.1:

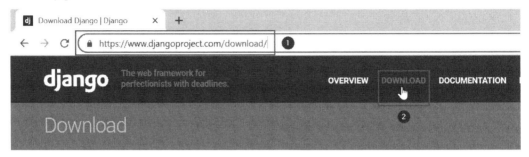

How to get Django

Django is available open-source under the BSD license. We recommend using the latest
version of Python 3. The last version to support Python 2.7 is Django 1.11 LTS. See the
FAQ for the Python versions supported by each version of Django. Here's how to get it:

Option 1: Get the latest official version

The latest official version is 3.2.8 (LTS). Read the 3.2.8 release notes, then install it with
pip:

```
pip install Django==3.2.8
```

Figure 11.1: Django official website download page

2. In order to install the Django framework, we need to first create our project
folder that is "**bpb-catalog-app-frontend**" in our case, the location of this
folder is "**D:\bpb-catalog-app-frontend**", as shown in *figure 11.2*:

Figure 11.2: Creating a project folder: "bpb-catalog-app-frontend"

3. Now first, open the Command Prompt and navigate to the project folder, the path of which is "**D:\bpb-catalog-app-frontend**" in our case, as shown in *figure 11.3*:

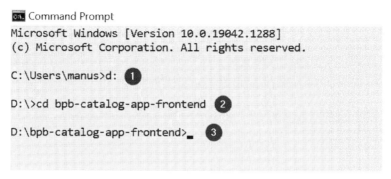

Figure 11.3: *Command prompt — navigating to our Project Folder: "bpb-catalog-app-frontend"*

4. Now in the Command Prompt, then navigate to the project directory, which is "**D:\bpb-catalog-app-frontend**" in our case and type the following command and press *Enter* to install the Django framework for Python (as shown in *figure 11.4*):

```
pip install Django
```

```
C:\Windows\System32\cmd.exe
Microsoft Windows [Version 10.0.19042.1288]
(c) Microsoft Corporation. All rights reserved.

D:\bpb-catalog-app-frontend>pip install Django  ①
Collecting Django
  Using cached Django-3.2.8-py3-none-any.whl (7.9 MB)
Collecting asgiref<4,>=3.3.2
  Using cached asgiref-3.4.1-py3-none-any.whl (25 kB)
Collecting sqlparse>=0.2.2
  Using cached sqlparse-0.4.2-py3-none-any.whl (42 kB)
Collecting pytz
  Using cached pytz-2021.3-py2.py3-none-any.whl (503 kB)
Installing collected packages: sqlparse, pytz, asgiref, Django
Successfully installed Django-3.2.8 asgiref-3.4.1 pytz-2021.3 sqlparse-0.4.2  ②
WARNING: You are using pip version 21.2.3; however, version 21.3.1 is available.
You should consider upgrading via the 'C:\Users\manus\AppData\Local\Programs\Python\Python310\python.exe -m pip install --upgrade pip' command.

D:\bpb-catalog-app-frontend>
```

Figure 11.4: *Installing Django*

5. Now in the same Command Prompt, type the following command to verify if Django has been installed successfully (as shown in *figure 11.5*):

```
python -m django --version
```

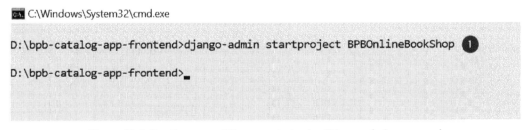

Figure 11.5: Installing Django

Step 2—Creating a default Django project

1. Open the Command Prompt, then navigate to the project directory that is "**D:\bpb-catalog-app-frontend**" in our case and type the following command and press *Enter* to create the new Django project (as shown in *figure 11.6*):

```
jango-admin startproject BPBOnlineBookShop
```

C:\Windows\System32\cmd.exe

```
D:\bpb-catalog-app-frontend>django-admin startproject BPBOnlineBookShop  ❶

D:\bpb-catalog-app-frontend>_
```

Figure 11.6: Creating a new Django project using Django admin command

2. If you look into your main project folder, which is "**D:\bpb-catalog-app-frontend**", you will now see that there is a new Django project folder created by the command given in point 1 of this step with the name same as the Django project name "**BPBOnlineBookShop**" given as the parameter to the command. You will see that under the folder "**BPBOnlineBookShop**", there is one subfolder with the same name plus one file, "**manage.py**" that is a command-line utility to communicate with the Django project, all these have been automatically created by the Django Admin command "**django-admin**". So this is the starting point of creating our Django application, as shown in *figure 11.7*:

Figure 11.7: New folder and files are created by the Django admin command

3. Now go to the command prompt and navigate to the Django project, the location of which is "**D:\bpb-catalog-app-frontend\BPBOnlineBookShop**" and then run the following command (as shown in *figure 11.8*):

```
python manage.py runserver
```

```
C:\Windows\System32\cmd.exe - python manage.py runserver

D:\bpb-catalog-app-frontend>cd BPBOnlineBookShop  1

D:\bpb-catalog-app-frontend\BPBOnlineBookShop>python manage.py runserver  2
Watching for file changes with StatReloader
Performing system checks...

System check identified no issues (0 silenced).
```

Figure 11.8: Starting our app with Django—run server command

4. Once you run the command mentioned in the above point, you will get the message that Python has started the development server in the local URL such as **http://127.0.0.1:8000** in our case, as shown in *figure 11.9*:

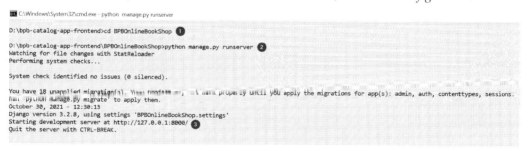

Figure 11.9: Starting our app with Django—run server command—development server started

5. Open your favorite browser, such as Google Chrome, and type the abovementioned URL: **http://127.0.0.1:8000** in the Address Bar and

press *Enter*. Once you do this, you will see the Django demo app loaded in your browser window, as shown in *figure 11.10*:

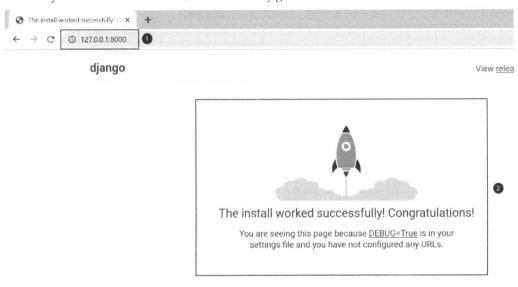

Figure 11.10: *Django demo app loaded in the browser*

Step 3—Creating a New Django app

In the previous step, we have created a default demo project in Django. Note that the Django project can have many apps; now it is time to create a new Django app so that we can connect it to MongoDB.

1. Open the Command Prompt, then navigate to the Django Project Directory, which is "**D:\bpb-catalog-app-frontend\BPBOnlineBookShop**" in our case and type the following command and press *Enter* to create the new Django app under the current Django project (as shown in *figure 11.11*):

    ```
    python manage.py startapp BPBOnlineBookShopMongoDBApp
    ```

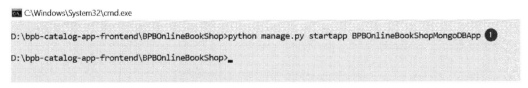

Figure 11.11: *Django—creating a new app*

2. If you look into your Django project folder, which is "**D:\bpb-catalog-app-frontend\BPBOnlineBookShop**" in our case, you will now see that there is a new Django app folder created by the command given in point 1 of this step with the name same as the Django app name" **BPBOnlineBookShopMongoDBApp**" given as the parameter to the command. You will see that under the folder "**BPBOnlineBookShopMongoDBApp**", there is one subfolder with the name "**migrations**", plus other python app-related files which has been created automatically by Django, as shown in *figure 11.12*:

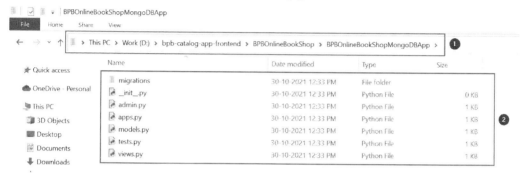

Figure 11.12: *Django—creating a new app*
—new app related files and folders created by Django command

The important thing that is related to Django app files in this scenario is that Django created the necessary files for our app, and the only thing now we need to do is to modify these files or add new files according to our requirements. Before we make our app dynamic with MongoDB, we have to do some adjustments to the existing files and create some new files. With the help of the next step, we will do some modifications in the current Django app, as well as Django project files, so that it would render us the HTML output as required to display by the app.

Step 4—Updating the Django app and Django project files

Let us first create a template that we would like to render on the home page of the Django project; as in the previous step of this chapter, we have seen that when we start our project and browse it using the browser, it opens up the default Django Home Page. As we are working on our custom app now, we want to show the app-specific page. So in order to achieve this, we will do some modifications and additions to the current Django app folder as well as the Django project folder. Following are the points for this step:

1. Open the current Django Project in any Code Editor or **Integrated Development Environment** (**IDE**) like Visual Studio Code, as shown in *figure 11.13*:

Figure 11.13: Opening a Django project in a Code Editor like Visual Studio Code

2. Now create a new folder named "**templates**" under the app folder, which is "**BPBOnlineBookShopMongoDBApp**" in our case, as shown in *figure 11.14*:

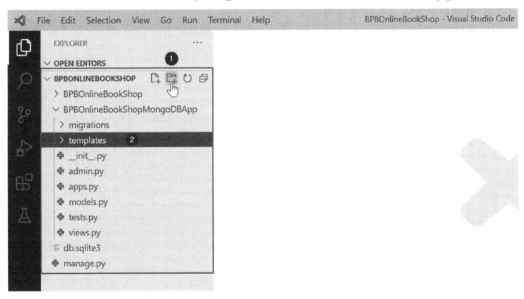

Figure 11.14: Creating a "templates" folder in our Django app

3. Now create a new folder named as same as our Django app name "**BPBOnlineBookShopMongoDBApp**" under the "**templates**" folder. This structure will be according to the Django naming convention, as shown in *figure 11.15*:

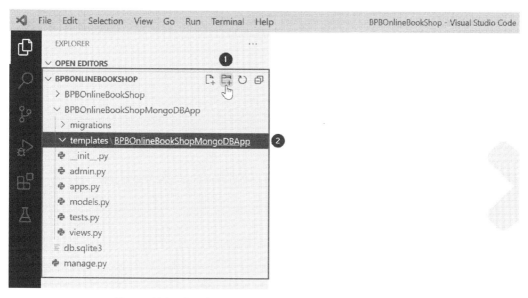

Figure 11.15: *Creating a "BPBOnlineBookShopMongoDBApp"*
subfolder under the "templates" folder in our Django App

4. Now create a new HTML Template file named "**bpbAppIndex.html**" under the current path, which is "**D:\bpb-catalog-app-frontend\ BPBOnlineBookShop\BPBOnlineBookShopMongoDBApp\templates\ BPBOnlineBookShopMongoDBApp**" in our case, as shown in *figure 11.16*:

Figure 11.16: *Creating a "bpbAppIndex.html" file under the*
"BPBOnlineBookShopMongoDBApp" folder in our Django app

5. Now add the following HTML in the "**bpbAppIndex.html**" file, as shown in *figure 11.17*:

```
<!DOCTYPE html>

<html lang="en">

<head>

    <title>Welcome to BPB Online Bookshop</title>

</head>

<body>

    <h1>BPB Online Bookshop<h1>

</body>

</html>
```

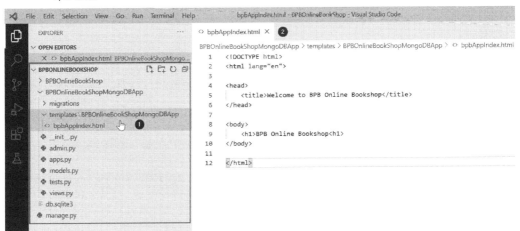

Figure 11.17: Adding HTML code in "bpbAppIndex.html" file

6. Modify the "**views.py**" file in our app and create a new function related to the rendering of the view, as shown in *figure 11.18*:

```
from django.shortcuts import render

# Create your views here.


def bpbAppIndex(request):
  return render(request, 'BPBOnlineBookShopMongoDBApp/bpbAppIndex.html')
```

Figure 11.18: Modifying "views.py" file in our Django app

7. We need to create a new file named **urls.py** in our app and connect this file to the existing **urls.py** file of the project folder. The newly created **urls.py** is similar to the **urls.py** which is located in our project folder. If we look into the default "**urls.py**" file located in our project directory, we can code some code from there to be pasted in the newly created "**urls.py**" file in our app. Following is the code that we will use in our app's **urls.py** file with a few changes. We have copied the following lines from the existing **urls.py** file in our project directory.

```
from django.urls import path


urlpatterns = [
  path('',),
]
```

8. Basically, the "**import**" statement and "**urlpatterns**" list, and we will do some changes in this file. The first thing is to include the views to be used in this file so that we can use the views that we created in our app, as shown in *figure 11.19*:

```
from django.urls import path

from . import views


urlpatterns = [
```

```
    path('', views.bpbAppIndex, name='BPB-Book-Shop-Home-Page'),
]
```

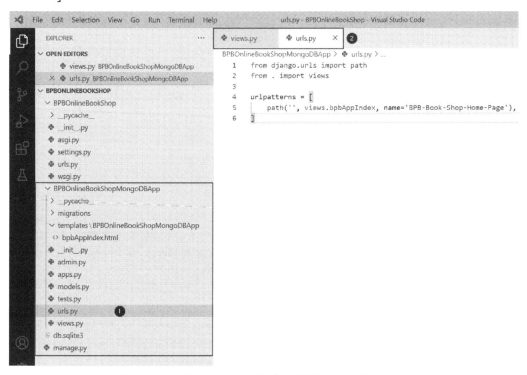

Figure 11.19: Creating a new "urls.py" file in our Django app

9. We have to finally map this "**urls.py**" file which is our app's directory, to the **urls.py** file of our project's directory. For this purpose, we need to open the **urls.py** file located in our project's directory and map both **urls.py** files using the "**urlpatterns**" list of the project's directory **urls.py;** the code is shown as follows:

First, we have to add the include function in the import sections of the "**django.urls**"

```
from django.urls import path,include
```

And then add the following line to the "**urlpatterns**":

```
path('', include('BPBOnlineBookShopMongoDBApp.urls'))
```

The final code in our project's "**urls.py**" file will look like this, as shown in *figure 11.20:*

```
from django.contrib import admin

from django.urls import path, include

urlpatterns = [

    path('admin/', admin.site.urls),

    path('', include('BPBOnlineBookShopMongoDBApp.urls'))

]
```

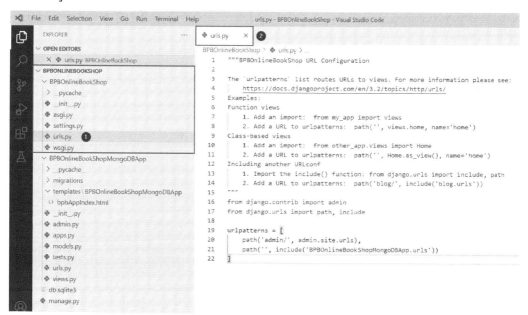

Figure 11.20: *Updating the "urls.py" file in our Django project*
—including the "urls.py" file from our Django app

10. The next step is the register our app in the "**settings.py**" file located in the project's directory. Open the "**settings.py**" file in the project's directory and register the app in the "Application definition" section under the "**INSTALLED_APPS**" list as follows:

    "**BPBOnlineBookShopMongoDBApp.apps.
    BpbonlinebookshopmongodbappConfig**",

    The above code contains the **<Name of our App>.apps.<Name of the Class defined in the apps.py file Located in the App's Folder>**

The name of the class file of our app is located under the "**apps.py**" file in our app directory, as shown in *figure 11.21*:

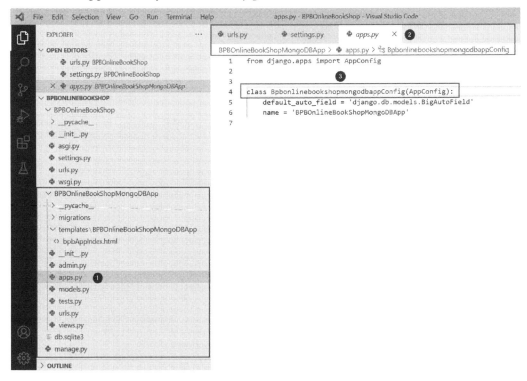

Figure 11.21*: "apps.py" file under our app folder — taking reference to the app class file*

11. We need to copy the class name from the "**apps.py**" file located in the app's folder to use while registering our app in the list of installed apps, as shown in *figure 11.22*:

The final code will look like the following:

```
# Application definition


INSTALLED_APPS = [
    'django.contrib.admin',
    'django.contrib.auth',
    'django.contrib.contenttypes',
    'django.contrib.sessions',
    'django.contrib.messages',
    'django.contrib.staticfiles',
```

```
'BPBOnlineBookShopMongoDBApp.apps.
BpbonlinebookshopmongodbappConfig',
]
```

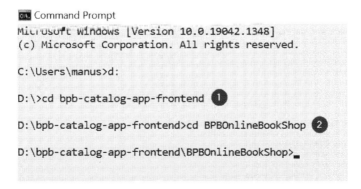

```
File  Edit  Selection  View  Go  Run  Terminal  Help              settings.py  BPBOnlineBookShop  Visual Studio Code

EXPLORER                              ...      ● urls.py        ● settings.py  ×     ● apps.py
∨ OPEN EDITORS                                 BPBOnlineBookShop  >  ● settings.py  >  ...
     ● urls.py  BPBOnlineBookShop           25   # SECURITY WARNING: don't run with debug turned on in production!
  ×  ● settings.py  BPBOnlineBookShop       26   DEBUG = True
     ● apps.py  BPBOnlineBookShopMongoDBApp 27
∨ BPBONLINEBOOKSHOP                         28   ALLOWED_HOSTS = []
  ∨ BPBOnlineBookShop                       29
     > __pycache__                          30
     ● __init__.py                          31   # Application definition
     ● asgi.py                              32
     ● settings.py  ❶                       33   INSTALLED_APPS = [
     ● urls.py                              34       'django.contrib.admin',
     ● wsgi.py                              35       'django.contrib.auth',
  ∨ BPBOnlineBookShopMongoDBApp             36       'django.contrib.contenttypes',
     > __pycache__                          37       'django.contrib.sessions',
     > migrations                           38       'django.contrib.messages',
     ∨ templates \ BPBOnlineBookShopMongoDBApp 39    'django.contrib.staticfiles',
      <> bpbAppIndex.html                   40       'BPBOnlineBookShopMongoDBApp.apps.BpbonlinebookshopmongodbappConfig',
     ● __init__.py                          41   ]
     ● admin.py                             42
     ● apps.py                              43   MIDDLEWARE = [
     ● models.py                            44       'django.middleware.security.SecurityMiddleware',
     ● tests.py                             45       'django.contrib.sessions.middleware.SessionMiddleware',
     ● urls.py                              46       'django.middleware.common.CommonMiddleware',
     ● views.py                             47       'django.middleware.csrf.CsrfViewMiddleware',
     ▪ db.sqlite3                           48       'django.contrib.auth.middleware.AuthenticationMiddleware',
     ● manage.py                            49       'django.contrib.messages.middleware.MessageMiddleware',
                                            50       'django.middleware.clickjacking.XFrameOptionsMiddleware',
                                            51   ]
                                            52
                                            53   ROOT_URLCONF = 'BPBOnlineBookShop.urls'
> OUTLINE                                   54
```

Figure 11.22*: Updating "settings.py" file in our Django project and
registering our new app under the list of installed apps*

12. Now we have actually created our app, and it is now ready to be run. To do this, we need to open the Command Prompt and navigate to our project folder, which is located at "**D:\bpb-catalog-app-frontend\ BPBOnlineBookShop**", as shown in *figure 11.23*:

```
Command Prompt
Microsoft Windows [Version 10.0.19042.1348]
(c) Microsoft Corporation. All rights reserved.

C:\Users\manus>d:

D:\>cd bpb-catalog-app-frontend  ❶

D:\bpb-catalog-app-frontend>cd BPBOnlineBookShop  ❷

D:\bpb-catalog-app-frontend\BPBOnlineBookShop>_
```

Figure 11.23*: Command Prompt—navigating to our project folder*

13. We can run the server using the following command, as shown in *figure 11.24*:

```
python manage.py runserver
```

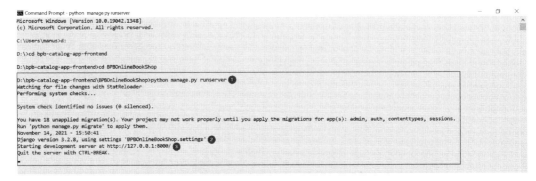

Figure 11.24: *Command Prompt—Django run server command—starting our app*

14. If we open **http://127.0.0.1:8000** in our browser, we will see our app will show the HTML which is rendered from the template view file for the home page path, as shown in *figure 11.25*:

Figure 11.25: *App home page is opened in browser—with new updates*

Step 5—Using PyMongo in Django to connect to MongoDB

Now we will use PyMongo in Django to connect our Django app with MongoDB.

1. The first step is to open the Django project's "**settings.py**" file and do the following modifications:

    Comment the existing database-related settings, and add a new database connection string.

```
# DATABASES = {
#     'default': {
#         'ENGINE': 'django.db.backends.sqlite3',
```

```
#              'NAME': BASE_DIR / 'db.sqlite3',
#      }
# }

DB_CONNECTION_STRING = 'mongodb://localhost:27017/'
```

Here, we are using the default localhost settings for MongoDB with the default port number to connect Django with MongoDB using PyMongo.

Note:

1. We are not using Django features fully in this chapter. This chapter gives you an overview of creating a Python app with MongoDB. You can integrate Django apps with MongoDB in many other ways, like using Django and other drivers with some more features.

2. More information can be found at:
   https://docs.djangoproject.com/en/3.2/ref/settings/#databases
   https://pypi.org/project/djongo/

3. In this chapter, we are using PyMongo, which we have already installed and used in *Chapter 6, Starting up Programming with MongoDB and Python* of this book. Please go through the instructions on how to install and use PyMongo with Python from *Chapter 6, Starting up Programming with MongoDB and Python* if you want to refresh the basics related to PyMongo.

2. Open the "**views.py**" file and add the following code:

```
import pymongo # Import PyMongo

from django.conf import settings # Import the Settings (We will use
DB_CONNECTION_STRING from the settings file)
```

The code and the comments above are self-explanatory.

3. Then in our existing view function "**bpbAppIndex**". We will add the code to fetch the data from the existing database "**BPBCatalogDB**" and collection "**BPBCatalogCollection**" using the following code:

```
# Create your views here.

def bpbAppIndex(request):

    # Connect to MongoDB Database from the Connection String
Defined in Django Project "settings.py"
    PyMongoclient = pymongo.MongoClient(settings.DB_CONNECTION_
STRING)
```

```
# Define the Database
dbname = PyMongoclient['BPBCatalogDB']

# Use Collection
collection_name = dbname["BPBCatalogCollection"]
```

Then, the next step is to fetch the data from the collection.

```
# Fetch All the Documents from Collection
BPBBooks = collection_name.find({})
```

The last step is to pass the MongoDB data object variable "**BPBBooks**" to the related template's output file "**BPBOnlineBookShopMongoDBApp/ bpbAppIndex.html**" using the JSON **Style** "**Key**": "**Value**" as an additional parameter to the "**render**" function.

```
# Pass the Data Object to the Template Output by passing as a
parameter using "Key" : "Value" Style
    return render(request, 'BPBOnlineBookShopMongoDBApp/
bpbAppIndex.html', {'BPBBooks' : BPBBooks})
```

The above data object will be used in the template file to show the values fetched from the database.

The overall "**views.py**" file will look like this, as shown in *figure 11.26*:

```
from django.shortcuts import render

import pymongo # Import PyMongo

from django.conf import settings # Import the Settings (We will
use DB_CONNECTION_STRING from the settings file)

# Create your views here.

def bpbAppIndex(request):

    # Connect to MongoDB Database from the Connection String
Defined in Django Project "settings.py"
    PyMongoclient = pymongo.MongoClient(settings.DB_CONNECTION_
STRING)

    # Define the Database
    dbname = PyMongoclient['BPBCatalogDB']

    # Use Collection
    collection_name = dbname["BPBCatalogCollection"]
```

```
# Fetch All the Documents from Collection
BPBBooks = collection_name.find({})

# Pass the Data Object to the Template Output by passing as a
parameter using "Key" : "Value" Style
return render(request, 'BPBOnlineBookShopMongoDBApp/
bpbAppIndex.html', {'BPBBooks' : BPBBooks})
```

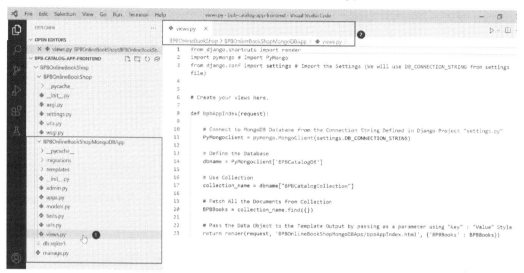

Figure 11.26: Our app's "views.py" updated file

4. In the related template output file "**BPBOnlineBookShopMongoDBApp/
   bpbAppIndex.html**", we will iterate the data object passed as a parameter
   from the "**render**" function in the "**views.py**" file to show the list of books
   title using the following code (as shown in *figure 11.27*):

```
<!DOCTYPE html>
<html lang="en">

<head>
    <title>Welcome to BPB Online Bookshop</title>
</head>

<body>
    <h1>BPB Online Bookshop</h1>
        <hr />
        <ul>
        {% for BPBBook in BPBBooks %}
```

```
        <li>{{BPBBook.title}}</li>
        {% endfor %}
        <ul>
    </body>

    </html>
```

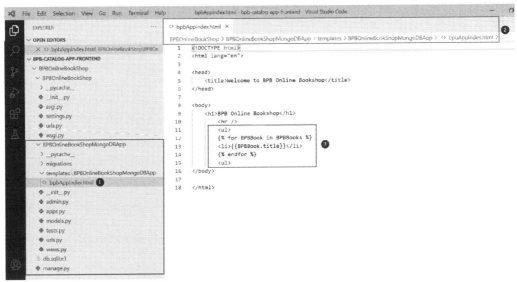

Figure 11.27: Our app's template view file — "bpbAppIndex.html" updated

5. We can now run the server using the following command (as shown in *figure 11.28*):

```
python manage.py runserver
```

C:\Windows\System32\cmd.exe - python manage.py runserver

```
D:\bpb-catalog-app-frontend\BPBOnlineBookShop>python manage.py runserver
Watching for file changes with StatReloader
Performing system checks...

System check identified no issues (0 silenced).
November 28, 2021 - 14:09:40
Django version 3.2.8, using settings 'BPBOnlineBookShop.settings'
Starting development server at http://127.0.0.1:8000/
Quit the server with CTRL-BREAK.
```

Figure 11.28: Django run server command — running our app

6. If we open our browser, we will see our app will show the HTML and the title of the books fetched from the MongoDB collection documents, as shown in *figure 11.29*:

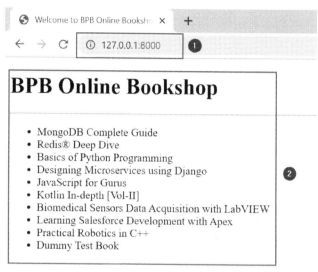

Figure 11.29: *Opening our app in the browser*
—new updates are loaded—list of books fetched from MongoDB collection

Step 6—Adding CSS and static files in our Django app

Now, we can add some CSS to our template and make it look nicer.

To do this, we need to create a new folder with the name "**static**" to hold CSS and other static files like static images and JavaScript files so that we can call them in our template.

This "**STATIC_URL**" is already defined in the "**settings.py**" file under the main project directory (as shown in *figure 11.30*).

For more details, you can refer to this URL: **https://docs.djangoproject.com/en/3.2/ howto/static-files/**

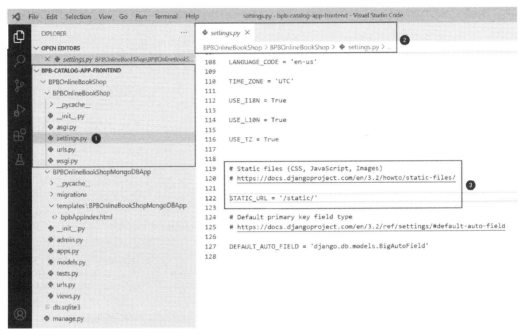

Figure 11.30: Django project—"settings.py" file—STATIC_URL path

You may change this to any other name. But for our case, we will keep it as it is and will create a new folder with the name "**static**" in our Django app.

We will be following the Django specific path for our static files, which is:

`my_app/static/my_app/example.jpg`

This is in our case:

`BPBOnlineBookShopMongoDBApp/static/ BPBOnlineBookShopMongoDBApp/example.jpg`

1. So first, we will create a "**static**" folder under our app directory, which is "**BPBOnlineBookShopMongoDBApp**" (as shown in *figure 11.31*)..

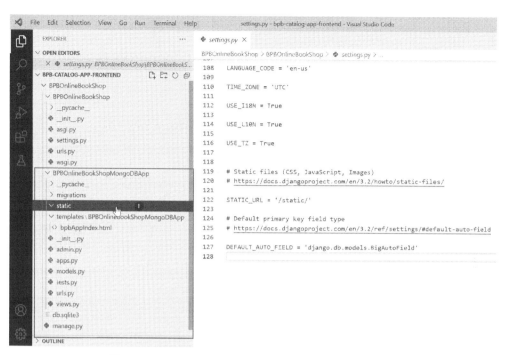

Figure 11.31: Our app — creating a new Folder named "static"

2. Then we will create another sub-directory with the same name as our app, which is "**BPBOnlineBookShopMongoDBApp**" under the newly created "**static**" directory, as shown in *figure 11.32*:

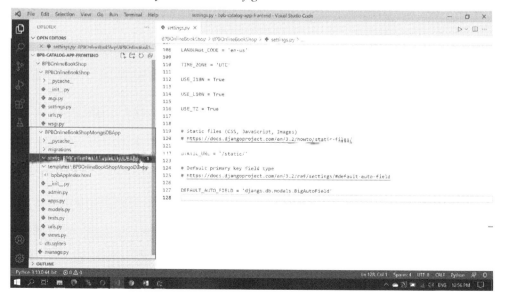

Figure 11.32: Our app — creating a new subfolder named
"BPBOnlineBookShopMongoDBApp" under the "static" folder

3. We will now test this by copying the "**BPB Publications**" logo file into this location or path, as shown in *figure 11.33*:

Figure 11.33*: Copying static files such as logos to a newly created folder under our "static" folder*

4. As now we have a static logo file present in the location, let us try to access this file from our template output file. For this, we will add the following code in our template file "**bpbAppIndex.html**":

First, we will add the following code on the top of our file, which allows us to load the static files in our template.

```
{% load static %}
```

Then we will add some HTML and call the related file using the Django template helpers (as shown in *figure 11.34*).

```
<div class="logo"><img src="{% static
'BPBOnlineBookShopMongoDBApp/bpb-logo.png' %}" alt="BPB
Publications Logo"></div>
```

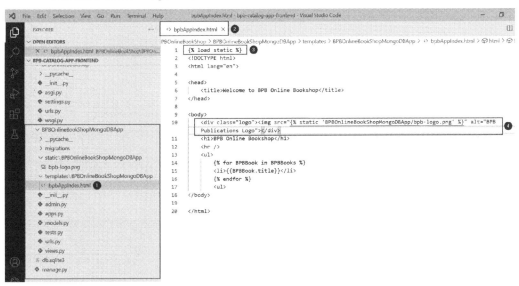

Figure 11.34*: Updating our template view file "bpbAppIndex.html"*

The whole template file code looks like the following:

```
{% load static %}
<!DOCTYPE html>
<html lang="en">

<head>
    <title>Welcome to BPB Online Bookshop</title>
</head>

<body>
    <div class="logo"><img src="{% static
'BPBOnlineBookShopMongoDBApp/bpb-logo.png' %}" alt="BPB
Publications Logo"></div>
    <h1>BPB Online Bookshop</h1>
    <hr />
    <ul>
        {% for BPBBook in BPBBooks %}
        <li>{{BPBBook.title}}</li>
        {% endfor %}
        <ul>
</body>

</html>
```

5. We can now run the server using the following command (as shown in *figure 11.35*):

```
python manage.py runserver
```

C:\Windows\System32\cmd.exe - python manage.py runserver

```
D:\bpb-catalog-app-frontend\BPBOnlineBookShop>python manage.py runserver  ❶
Watching for file changes with StatReloader
Performing system checks...

System check identified no issues (0 silenced).
November 28, 2021 - 14:09:40
Django version 3.2.8, using settings 'BPBOnlineBookShop.settings'
Starting development server at http://127.0.0.1:8000/  ❷
Quit the server with CTRL-BREAK.
```

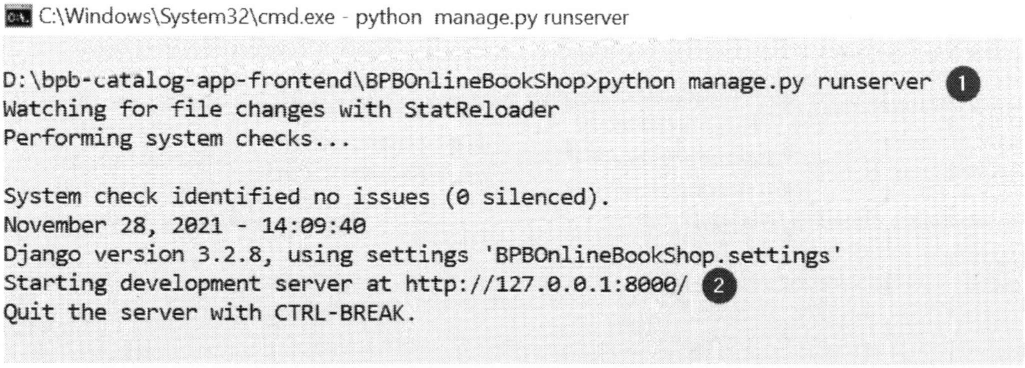

Figure 11.35: Django run server command—starting our app

6. If we open our browser, we will see our app will show the HTML and the title of the books fetched from the MongoDB collection documents along with the BPB publication logo, as shown in *figure 11.36*:

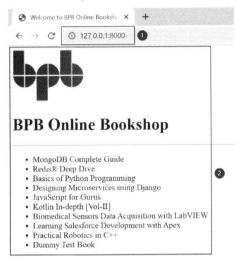

Figure 11.36: Our app running in browser—with logo

Step 7 – Designing our frontend with CSS Flex (Flexible Box Layout)

Let us follow this layout to create our frontend design, as shown in *figure 11.37*:

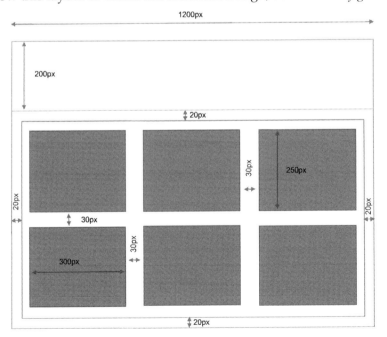

Figure 11.37: Frontend app layout to follow

As we follow this design, we need to add the HTML accordingly and also write the CSS.

We will use **<div>** and use CSS Flex (Flexible Box Layout) to create our front end, as shown in the figure above.

1. Now, we can create a new CSS File with the name "**style.css**" under the **Static** folder of our app. The location in our case would be: "**static\ BPBOnlineBookShopMongoDBApp\style.css**". This is the same location where we have copied our logo file, as shown in *figure 11.38*:

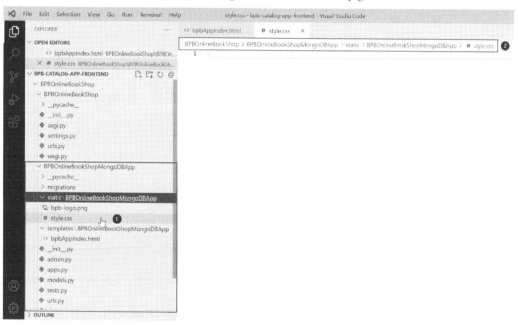

Figure 11.38: *Creating a new CSS file*

2. Let us write some CSS code in this newly created **style.css** file. Here, we will use CSS Flexbox (Flexible Box Layout) to style our frontend.

But even before adding CSS code, we have to do some modifications to our template HTML file.

- Include the CSS file in the template
- Replace **<ul>** and **<li>** with **<div>** with class names

The following is a modified code of the HTML template file "**bpbAppIndex. html**", which includes the required preceding two changes:

```
{% load static %}
<!DOCTYPE html>
```

```
<html lang="en">

<head>
    <title>Welcome to BPB Online Bookshop</title>
    <link rel="stylesheet" href="{% static
'BPBOnlineBookShopMongoDBApp/style.css' %}">
</head>

<body>
    <div class="main-container">
        <div class="header-container">
            <div class="logo"><img src="{% static
'BPBOnlineBookShopMongoDBApp/bpb-logo.png' %}"
                    alt="BPB Publications Logo" /></div>
            <h1>BPB Online Bookshop</h1>
            <hr />
        </div>
        <div class="body-container">
            <div class="items">
                {% for BPBBook in BPBBooks %}
                <div class="item">
                    <div class="book-image-container"></div>
                    <div class="book-title">{{BPBBook.title}}</div>
                    <div class="more-details-button"></div>
                </div>
                {% endfor %}
            </div>
        </div>
    </div>
</body>

</html>
```

The following is the CSS, which we write in our **style.css**:

```
.main-container {
  margin: 0 auto;
  max-width: 1200px;
```

```
    }

    .header-container {
      background: #ffffff;
      height: 200px;
    }

    .body-container {
      width: 1200px;
      background: #fafafa;
      margin: 20px;
    }

    .items {
      display: flex;
      flex-wrap: wrap;
      justify-content: center;
    }

    .item {
      width: 300px;
      height: 250px;
      border: 1px;
      border-style: solid;
      border-color: blueviolet;
      margin: 15px;
      text-align: center;
      padding: 10px;
    }

    .book-image {
      display: inline-block;
      width: 150px;
      height: 150px;
    }

    .book-title {
      margin-top: 5px;
      font-family: Georgia, 'Times New Roman', Times, serif;
```

```
        font-weight: bold;
        font-size: 14px;
    }
```

3. We can now run the server using the following command if it is not running:

   python manage.py runserver

   If your server is already started, then if you refresh the browser page, the layout will look as follows (*figure 11.39*):

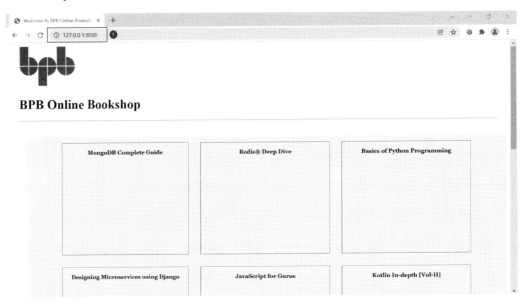

Figure 11.39: *Refreshing the page—new frontend layout*

Step 8—Adding book pictures to our frontend app

Now, we will add the book cover pictures above the book title inside the **<div>** with a class "**book-image-container**".

In order to do so, we need to first run our backend application which we had created with PHP and MongoDB earlier in *Chapter 8, MongoDB Step by Step Practical Application Development Using PHP* of this book. To do that, we just need to be sure that our WAMP server is running and our backend application is accessible using the browser URL:

If you have not started the WAMP server, please start the WAMP server first.

Step 8.1—Start WAMP server

You should start the WAMP server by typing "**wamp**" on the search area of the taskbar. Opening the WAMP server will launch the WAMP server on your Windows machine, as shown in *figure 11.40*:

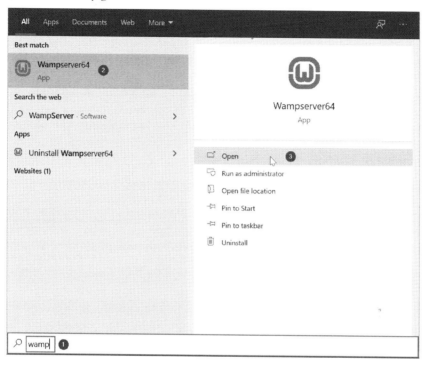

Figure 11.40: Launching WAMP server

Once the WAMP server has been successfully started, you will see the WAMP server icon (in green) in the taskbar tray. When you run the WAMP server, it usually takes a few seconds to start all the services such as Apache, MySQL, and so on, and the icon changes from red to orange and finally to green. If the WAMP icon is green, it means that all the services have been successfully started, and now you can use the WAMP server, as shown in *figure 11.41*:

Figure 11.41: WAMP server—all services have been started successfully

Step 8.2—running localhost

Once the WAMP server has started on your machine, you can start working with the local server, which has Apache and PHP installed. As we have the required environment ready, we can run localhost.

To run localhost, just open your favorite browser like Google Chrome and type: **http://localhost/** and then press *Enter*. This will open up a new page, and you will be shown the WAMP server default page on your localhost. Here, you will get all the information about the version of the WAMP server, server configurations, which has a list of various software running in the background along with their version details such as Apache web server and PHP, as shown in *figure 11.42*:

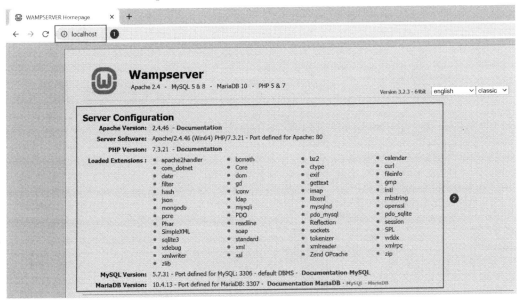

Figure 11.42: *WAMP server—localhost*

If you are able to see this page, then this means that your WAMP server has been successfully started.

Now try to open the PHP-based backend application using the URL: **http://localhost/bpb-catalog-app-backend/**.

You should see the backend dashboard while you browse this URL, as shown in *figure 11.43*:

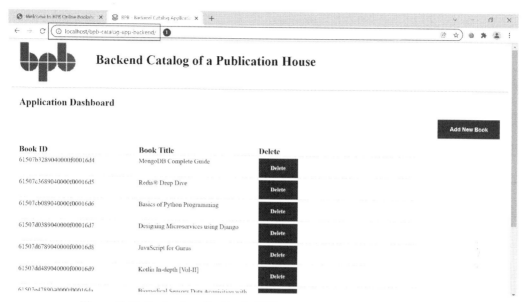

Figure 11.43: Backend application in PHP—running using the WAMP server

Once we are able to open our backend application, it means we can now use the backend application URL to display the book cover images.

Step 8.3—Coding part

Now, we need to update our HTML Code in "**bpbAppIndex.html**" as follows:

```
{% load static %}

<!DOCTYPE html>
<html lang="en">

<head>
    <title>Welcome to BPB Online Bookshop</title>
    <link rel="stylesheet" href="{% static 'BPBOnlineBookShopMongoDDApp/
style.css' %}">
</head>

<body>
    <div class="main-container">
        <div class="header-container">
            <div class="logo"><img src="{% static
'BPBOnlineBookShopMongoDBApp/bpb-logo.png' %}"
                alt="BPB Publications Logo" /></div>
```

```
            <h1>BPB Online Bookshop</h1>
            <hr />
        </div>
        <div class="body-container">
            <div class="items">
                {% for BPBBook in BPBBooks %}
                <div class="item">
                    <div class="book-image-container"><img class="book-
image"
                            src="http://localhost/bpb-catalog-app-
backend/images/{{BPBBook.coverimage}}" /></div>
                    <div class="book-title">{{BPBBook.title}}</div>
                    <div class="more-details-button"></div>
                </div>
                {% endfor %}
            </div>
        </div>
    </div>
</body>


</html>
```

If we see carefully in the above HTML code (template), we will find the under the image **src** attribute the value is as follows:

http://localhost/bpb-catalog-app-backend/images/{{BPBBook.coverimage}}

In which the **{{BPBBook.coverimage}}** will be appended to the URL from the database according to the book cover page.

Let us now refresh the browser, and we will see the book cover images appear in the frontend application. This will show the book's images, and these book images are rendered from our backend application which we created earlier in this book using PHP, as shown in *figure 11.44*:

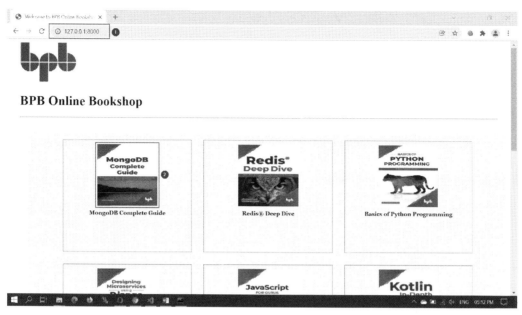

Figure 11.44: Our frontend application in Django—showing books images—these book images are rendered from our backend application which we created earlier in this book using PHP

Now our next step is to create a link (or button) that will take us to the book details page on click.

To do so, let us update our HTML and CSS.

HTML

```
{% load static %}
<!DOCTYPE html>
<html lang="en">

<head>
    <title>Welcome to BPB Online Bookshop</title>
    <link rel="stylesheet" href="{% static 'BPBOnlineBookShopMongoDBApp/
style.css' %}">
</head>


<body>
    <div class="main-container">
        <div class="header-container">
            <div class="logo"><img src="{% static
```

```
'BPBOnlineBookShopMongoDBApp/bpb-logo.png' %}"
                    alt="BPB Publications Logo" /></div>
            <h1>BPB Online Bookshop</h1>
            <hr />
        </div>
        <div class="body-container">
            <div class="items">
                {% for BPBBook in BPBBooks %}
                <div class="item">
                    <div class="book-image-container"><img class="book-
image"
                        src="http://localhost/bpb-catalog-app-
backend/images/{{BPBBook.coverimage}}" /></div>
                    <div class="book-title">{{BPBBook.title}}</div>
                    <div class="more-details-button"><a href="/book-
details">More Details</a></div>
                </div>
                {% endfor %}
            </div>
        </div>
    </div>
</body>

</html>
```

CSS

```
.main-container {
  margin: 0 auto;
  max-width: 1200px;
}

.header-container {
  background: #ffffff;
  height: 200px;
}

.body-container {
```

```css
  width: 1200px;
  background: #fafafa;
  margin: 20px;
}

.items {
  display: flex;
  flex-wrap: wrap;
  justify-content: center;
}

.item {
  width: 300px;
  height: 250px;
  border: 1px;
  border-style: solid;
  border-color: blueviolet;
  margin: 15px;
  text-align: center;
  padding: 10px;
}

.book-image {
  display: inline-block;
  width: 150px;
  height: 150px;
}

.book-title {
  margin-top: 5px;
  font-family: Georgia, 'Times New Roman', Times, serif;
  font-weight: bold;
  font-size: 14px;
}

.more-details-button {
  margin-top: 20px;
}
```

```css
.more-details-button>a {
  background-color: darkorchid;
  color: white;
  padding: 10px 15px;
  text-decoration: none;
}

.more-details-button>a:hover {
  background-color: blueviolet;
  color: white;
  padding: 10px 15px;
  text-decoration: none;
}
```

If we refresh our browser, we will see that our changes are reflected, and we can see the "**More Details**" button below the book title, as shown in *figure 11.45*:

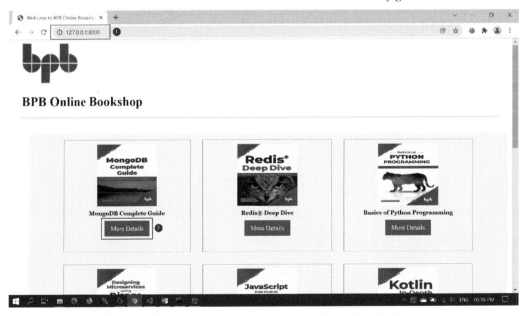

Figure 11.45: Our frontend app—showing the "More Details" button

Our frontend application main page is almost complete, but now the next step is to link the "**More Details**" button to the book details page. For this step, we need to first append the "**Book ID**" to the button link so that we can refer to the Book ID while we are navigating to the book details page.

Step 9—Adding more details functionality to our frontend app

In this step, we will add the "**More Details**" functionality to our app. In this, once the **More Details** button is clicked, then it will open the details page related to the specific book.

Let us try to append the following in the link:

/{{BPBBook._id}}

With this change the HTML of the button **<div>** gets updated as follows:

```
<div class="more-details-button"><a href="/book-details/{{BPBBook._id}}">More Details</a></div>
```

Now, if you will refresh the browser, it will give you the error, and our application will break, as shown in *figure 11.46*:

Figure 11.46: Our frontend app breaks due to the updated link code of the "More Details" button

We can even see the same error in the command prompt or console from where we are running our frontend application, as shown in *figure 11.47*:

Figure 11.47: Command Prompt—app console showing the errors

This means that we cannot move ahead before fixing this issue. So, we need to fix this issue before we move ahead in the frontend app development.

Step 10—Fixing underscore attribute issue for Django using the Django template tags

As you can see that, the above issue arises because we are trying to get the MongoDB document ID (_id) by referencing the MongoDB object (**BPBBook**).

So in our case, **BPBBook._id** will not work as this is Django-specific nomenclature that we need to follow.

To fix this issue, we need to use the Django template tags so that we can get the MongoDB document ID in our template.

1. For this, we need to create a directory in our Django app with the name "**templatetags**". So in our case, the path would be: **BPBOnlineBookShopMongoDBApp/templatetags/**, as shown in *figure 11.48*:

Figure 11.48: *Creating a new directory named "templatetags" inside our app folder*

2. The next step is to create a blank `__init__.py` into the "**templatetags**" directory. The purpose of this file is to make the Django framework know that this "**templatetags**" is a Module, and Django will automatically treat this as a

Module. So in our case, the path would be: **BPBOnlineBookShopMongoDBApp/ templatetags/__init__.py**, as shown in *figure 11.49*:

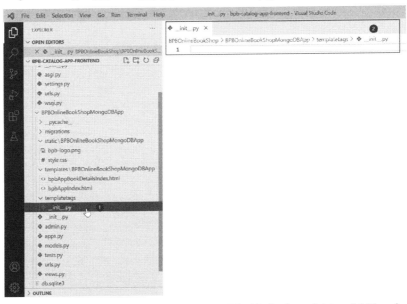

Figure 11.49: *Creating a new file named "__init__.py" inside the "templatetags" folder of our app*

3. After we finish creating our blank **__init__.py** file next step is to create a new file that will contain the Template Tag code; for this purpose, we will create a new file in the "**templatetags**" directory with the name "**custom-mongodb-tags.py**". So in our case, the path would be: **BPBOnlineBookShopMongoDBApp/ templatetags/ custom-mongodb-tags.py**, as shown in *figure 11.50*:

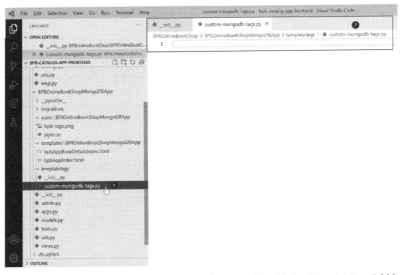

Figure 11.50: *Creating a new file named "custom-mongodb-tags.py" inside the "templatetags" folder of our app*

4. Now, we will add the Template Tag related code in this file which is as follows:

```
from django import template

register = template.Library()

@register.filter(name='bpbfrontendapp')
def bpbfrontendapp(obj, attribute):
    return obj[attribute]
```

The purpose of this code is to use the template library and register a new filter with the name "**bpbfrontendapp**". The function will have the same name in this code, "**bpbfrontendapp**", this function will take the two arguments one is an "**Object**", and the second one is the "**attribute**", which is a key. So this function will fetch the key's value, or you can simply say attribute's value and return to the template from where it is called.

1. We have to use this Template Tag filter functionality in our Home Page template, So for this, we need to open our template file, which is: "**bpbAppIndex.html**"

   So first step is to add the following code:

   {% load custom-mongodb-tags %}

   This code will load this Template Tag module in our Template View file, and using this; we can then refer to this custom Template Tag module function and filter.

2. We can use the Template Tag filter in our link, and the following is the code for that:

   ```
           <div class="more-details-button"><a href="/book-details/
   {{ BPBBook|bpbfrontendapp:'_id' }}">More Details</a></div>
   ```

   So basically, we are referring to the "**bpbfrontendapp**" filter, which will filter this value using the template Tag function and pass it back to the template. So, in this case, the real value of MongoDB Document ID will be returned, and the error will go.

   The following is the full HTML code for "**bpbAppIndex.html**":

   ```
   {% load static %}
   {% load custom-mongodb-tags %}
   <!DOCTYPE html>
   <html lang="en">
   ```

```
<head>
    <title>Welcome to BPB Online Bookshop</title>
    <link rel="stylesheet" href="{% static
'BPBOnlineBookShopMongoDBApp/style.css' %}">
</head>

<body>
    <div class="main-container">
        <div class="header-container">
            <div class="logo"><img src="{% static
'BPBOnlineBookShopMongoDBApp/bpb-logo.png' %}"
                    alt="BPB Publications Logo" /></div>
            <h1>BPB Online Bookshop</h1>
            <hr />
        </div>
        <div class="body-container">
            <div class="items">
                {% for BPBBook in BPBBooks %}
                <div class="item">
                    <div class="book-image-container"><img
class="book-image"
                            src="http://localhost/bpb-catalog-
app-backend/images/{{BPBBook.coverimage}}" /></div>
                    <div class="book-title">{{BPBBook.title}}</
div>
                    <div class="more-details-button"><a href="/
book-details/{{ BPBBook|bpbfrontendapp:'_id' }}">More Details</
a></div>
                </div>
                {% endfor %}
            </div>
        </div>
    </div>
</body>

</html>
```

Now to verify if this functionality has worked and we are not getting the previous error, we need to start our app from the command prompt if it is not running, using the following command:

```
python manage.py runserver
```

If your server is already started, then if you refresh the browser page, the layout will look as follows (*figure 11.51*):

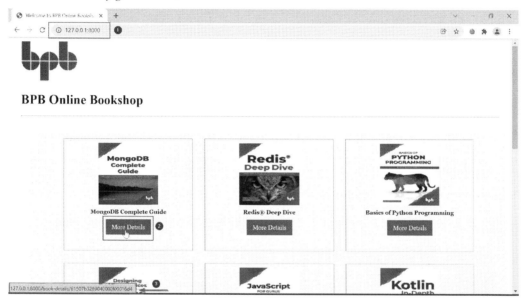

Figure 11.51: *Our frontend app—the error is gone, and we can now see the MongoDB Document object ID appended to the URL*

If you see the above image, you will see that once hovering the mouse to the "**More Details**" button. You can now see that the MongoDB Document ID is appended to the URL, and the error that we were getting earlier has also gone.

Now, we have to create the "**More Details**" page for a specific book. In our next step, we will learn how to create this new page.

Step 1—Creating the more details page

To create a More Details page, we need to perform the few similar tasks that we did for the main page.

So the first thing is to create a route for this new More Details page; for this, we need to open the "**urls.py**" file in our app and then add one new URL, which will take care of routing it to the correct URL and load a related view.

1. In the "**urlpatters**" list we need to add the following code:

```
        path('book-details/<str:bookId>', views.
bpbAppBookDetailsIndex, name='BPB-Book-Shop-Book-Details-Page'),
```

This code has been already explained in the previous section, and we are just adding our URL path, which is "**book-details/<str:bookId>**" in which the "**bookId**" is the additional parameter that is actually a dynamic MongoDB Document ID related to the particular book and is of string type.

We have also specified the related view function (method) "**bpbAppBookDetailsIndex**", which we have to create next in our "**view. py**" file in our app.

The following is the updated code for "**urls.py**" for our app, as shown in *figure 11.52*:

```
from django.urls import path

from . import views


urlpatterns = [
    path('', views.bpbAppIndex, name='BPB-Book-Shop-Home-Page'),
    path('book-details/<str:bookId>', views.
bpbAppBookDetailsIndex, name='BPB-Book-Shop-Book-Details-Page'),
]
```

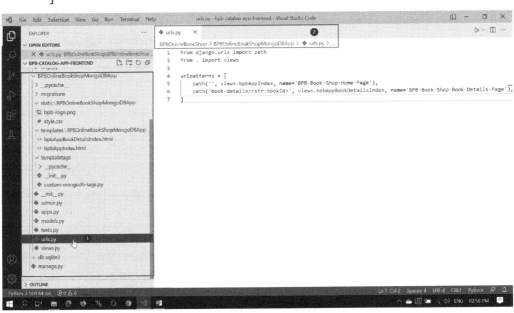

Figure 11.52: Updated "urls.py" file in our app

Before we create a template view file for this path or URL, Let us do some adjustments to our existing "**view.py**" and add the new method related to the new URL accordingly.

2. The first thing is to shift all the PyMongo related code from the existing home page view "**bpbAppIndex**" to the use between all the views now. As we are adding one new view related to the "More Details" page, the following code has to be shifted in the global scope.

```
# Connect to MongoDB Database from the Connection String Defined
in Django Project "settings.py"
PyMongoclient = pymongo.MongoClient(settings.DB_CONNECTION_
STRING)

# Define the Database
dbname = PyMongoclient['BPBCatalogDB']

# Use Collection
collection_name = dbname["BPBCatalogCollection"]

# Create your views here.
```

3. The next update is to add the following line at the top of the file where we are importing a few modules and libraries.

```
from bson.objectid import ObjectId # For MongoDB Document Object
reference in the PyMongo Functions
```

This will be required during the PyMongo find function call, where we would be now referring to the MongoDB document with respect to MongoDB document object ID.

4. Next, we will be defining our new view function, which will be as follows:

```
def bpbAppBookDetailsIndex(request, bookId):

    # Fetch Specific Document from Collection with respect to
Document or Book ID
    BPBBookFromId = collection_name.find_one({"_id" :
ObjectId(bookId)})

    return render(request, 'BPBOnlineBookShopMongoDBApp/
bpbAppBookDetailsIndex.html', {'BPBBookFromId' : BPBBookFromId})
```

This function will take a "**bookId**" as a second parameter from the URL and pass it to the function. Our function will then fetch the relevant document from the database with respect to this ID, and the whole document object is then passed to the template view for further display or process.

In our case, the template for this view would be "**BPBOnlineBookShopMongoDBApp/bpbAppBookDetailsIndex.htm**", which we have to create next.

The following is the updated code for the "**views.py**" file for our app (as shown in *figure 11.53*):

```
from django.shortcuts import render
import pymongo # Import PyMongo
from django.conf import settings # Import the Settings (We will
use DB_CONNECTION_STRING from the settings file)
from bson.objectid import ObjectId # For MongoDB Document Object
reference in the PyMongo Functions

# Connect to MongoDB Database from the Connection String Defined
in Django Project "settings.py"
PyMongoclient = pymongo.MongoClient(settings.DB_CONNECTION_
STRING)

# Define the Database
dbname = PyMongoclient['BPBCatalogDB']

# Use Collection
collection_name = dbname["BPBCatalogCollection"]

# Create your views here.

def bpbAppIndex(request):

    # Fetch All the Documents from Collection
    BPBBooks = collection_name.find({})

    # Pass the Data Object to the Template Output by passing as a
parameter using "Key" : "Value" Style
    return render(request, 'BPBOnlineBookShopMongoDBApp/
bpbAppIndex.html', {'BPBBooks' : BPBBooks})

def bpbAppBookDetailsIndex(request, bookId):
```

```
    # Fetch Specific Document from Collection with respect to
Document or Book ID
    BPBBookFromId = collection_name.find_one({"_id" :
ObjectId(bookId)})

    return render(request, 'BPBOnlineBookShopMongoDBApp/
bpbAppBookDetailsIndex.html', {'BPBBookFromId' : BPBBookFromId})
```

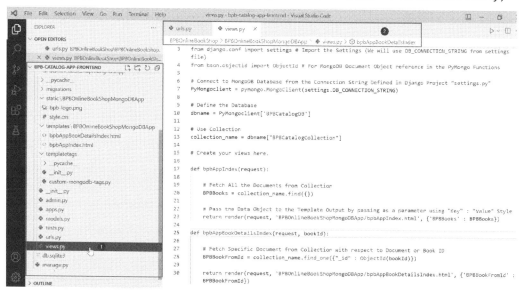

Figure 11.53: *Updated "views.py" file in our app*

After we are done with the above parts, now we have to create the HTML template file to render this new view.

5. For this, we have to create a new HTML template file under our existing app templates folder, which would be: "**BPBOnlineBookShopMongoDBApp/bpbAppBookDetailsIndex.html**" in our case:

The following is the code for the newly created template file (as shown in *figure 11.54*):

```
{% load static %}
<!DOCTYPE html>
<html lang="en">


<head>
    <title>Book Details Page - BPB Online Bookshop</title>
    <link rel="stylesheet" href="{% static
```

```
'BPBOnlineBookShopMongoDBApp/style.css' %}">
</head>


<body>
    <div class="main-container">
        <div class="header-container">
            <div class="logo"><img src="{% static
'BPBOnlineBookShopMongoDBApp/bpb-logo.png' %}"
                    alt="BPB Publications Logo" /></div>
            <h1>BPB Online Bookshop</h1>
            <hr />
        </div>
        <div class="body-container">
            {{BPBBookFromId}}
        </div>
    </div>
</body>


</html>
```

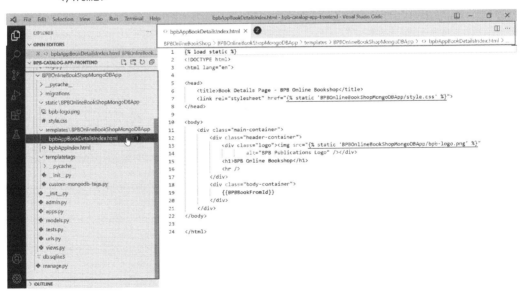

Figure 11.54*: New template file "bpbAppBookDetailsIndex.html" File in our App for More Details Page*

Before we do some fancy stuff with this template file using some new CSS. Let us run it to check if everything is working fine with this page till now.

To do this, we need to run our Django app if it is not running and then first run the app server and then open our frontend application in the browser; these steps have been explained many times in previous sections. Please follow them if you have any confusion in this.

Make also sure that your WAMP server is running and you are able to access the backend application, which is required to serve the images to the frontend application. If it is not running, please start your WAMP server.

After your app has been started and you have opened your frontend application in the browser, you will see the home page of our frontend application.

6. Now to check if everything is working for the new "More Details" page, you need to now click on any of the book's "**More Details**" button (as shown in *figure 11.55*), and this will load the new page that we have created.

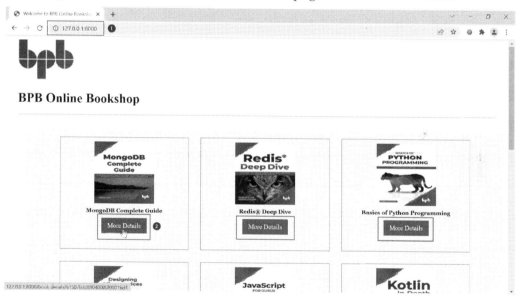

Figure 11.55: Our app's—home page – clicking More Details button

Once your new page is loaded, you can see the new page content as similar to shown in the following screenshot (*figure 11.56*):

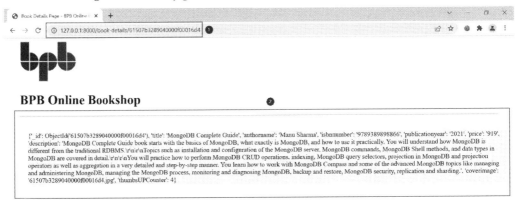

Figure 11.56: *Our frontend app—more details page*

As we can now see that we have all the data present to be displayed in our frontend "More Details" page, we can now do some modifications in the HTML and CSS to display this data beautifully.

Step 12—Designing the More Details page

So let us have a very simple layout for the More Details page, as shown in *figure 11.57*:

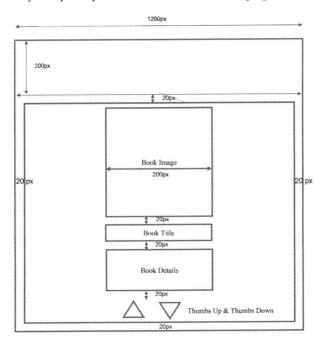

Figure 11.57: *More Details page template layout*

1. We now follow the above layout for More Details page, and the following is the updated HTML for the "**bpbAppBookDetailsIndex.html**" file (as shown in *figure 11.58*):

```
{% load static %}
<!DOCTYPE html>
<html lang="en">

<head>
    <title>Book Details Page - BPB Online Bookshop</title>
    <link rel="stylesheet" href="{% static
'BPBOnlineBookShopMongoDBApp/style.css' %}">
</head>

<body>
    <div class="main-container">
        <div class="header-container">
            <div class="logo"><img src="{% static
'BPBOnlineBookShopMongoDBApp/bpb-logo.png' %}"
                    alt="BPB Publications Logo" /></div>
            <h1>BPB Online Bookshop</h1>
            <hr />
        </div>
        <div class="book-details-body-container">
            <div class="book-details-book-image-container"><img
class="book-details-book-image"
                    src="http://localhost/bpb-catalog-app-
backend/images/{{BPBBookFromId.coverimage}}" /></div>
            <div class="book-details-book-title">{{BPBBookFromId.
title}}</div>
            <div class="book-details-book-other-
details"><b>Description</b> :
                {{BPBBookFromId.description}}<br /><b>Price</b> :
{{BPBBookFromId.price}}</div>
            <div class="more-details-book-thumbs-up-down-
container"><b>Thumbs Up Count</b> :
                {{BPBBookFromId.thumbsUPCounter}} <b>Thumbs Down
Count</b> : {{BPBBookFromId.thumbsDOWNCounter}}</div>
        </div>
```

```
            </div>
       </body>

       </html>
```

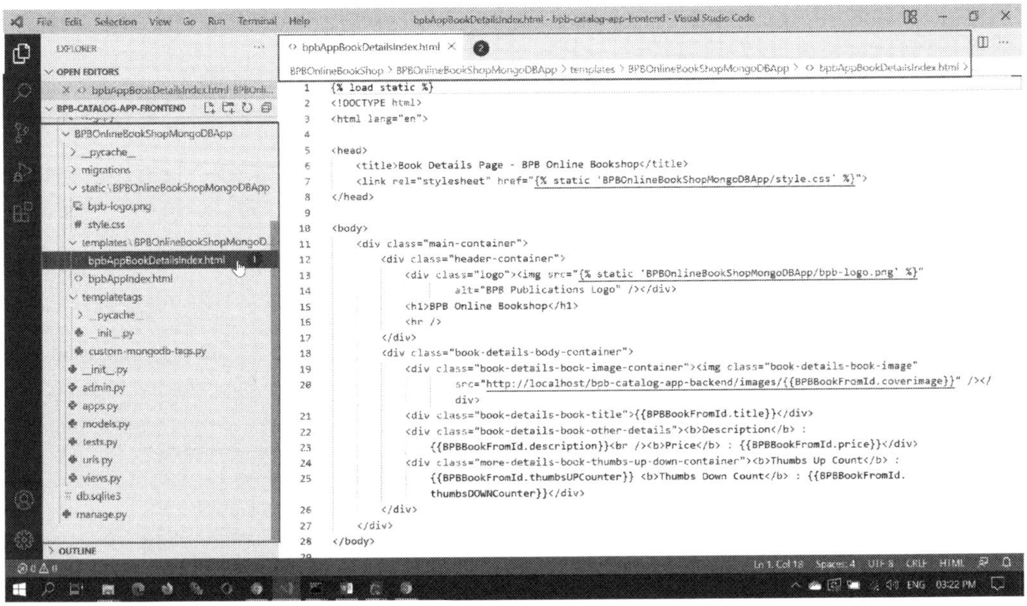

Figure 11.58: More Details page—updated HTML view file—bpbAppBookDetailsIndex.html

2. We have also updated the CSS according to this new layout. So following is the updated code at the end of our existing CSS file, which is located under the "**static**" folder of our app (as shown in *figure 11.59*):

```css
/* More Details Page CSS Starts Here */


.book-details-body-container {
  text-align: center;
}


.book-details-book-image {
  display: inline-block;
  width: 200px;
  height: 200px;
  margin-bottom: 20px;
}
```

```
.book-details-book-title {
  font-family: Georgia, 'Times New Roman', Times, serif;
  font-size: 20px;
  font-weight: bold;
  margin-bottom: 20px;
}


.book-details-book-other-details {
  font-family: Georgia, 'Times New Roman', Times, serif;
  font-size: 12px;
  max-width: 1000px;
  margin-left: auto;
  margin-right: auto;
  text-align: left;
  margin-bottom: 20px;
}
```

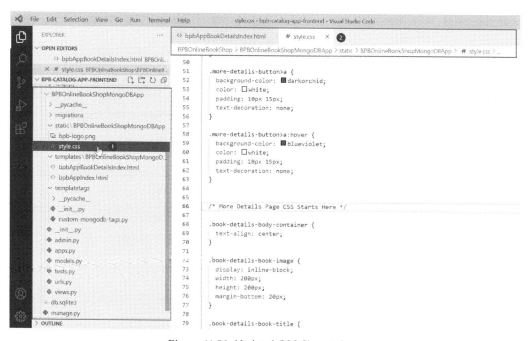

Figure 11.59: Updated CSS file—style.css

Let us run it to check if everything is working fine with this page till now.

To do this, we need to run our Django app. If it is not running and then first run the app server and then open our frontend application in the browser, these steps have been explained many times in previous sections. Please follow them if you have any confusion in this.

Make also sure that your WAMP server is running and you are able to access the backend application, which is required to serve the images to the frontend application. If it is not running, please start your WAMP server.

3. After your app has been started and you have opened your frontend application in the browser, you will see the home page of our frontend application. Please navigate to the More Details page by clicking the "**More Details**" button of any of the listed books. Once you do this, you will be able to see the More Details page with the new layout, as shown in *figure 11.60*:

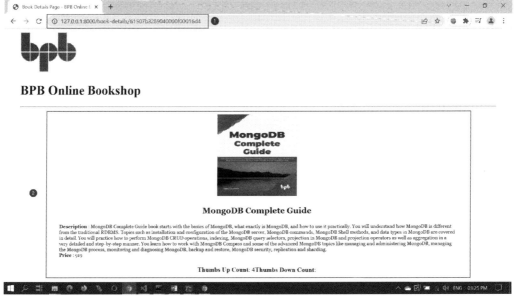

Figure 11.60: *More Details page—updated changes are shown in the browser*

We need to do a few of the changes in this layout to make it perfect:

- If there is no count for "Thumbs Up" or "Thumbs Down", then show "0" instead of blank.

- Use some Icons to show the "Thumbs Up" or "Thumbs Down"

In the last step of this application, we will make our "Thumbs Up" and "Thumbs Down" looks nicer.

Step 13—Making "Thumbs Up" and "Thumbs Down" looks nicer

There are now two things that we need to do in this step that we mentioned in the last step.

1. To make our "Thumbs Up" and "Thumbs Down" looks nicer. In this step, we will use Google Font "**Material Icons**". For more information, you can refer to this URL: **https://fonts.google.com/icons**

2. To add Google font "**Material Icons**" we just need to include the following line inside the **<head>** tag of our Template HTML file:

```
<link rel="stylesheet" href="https://fonts.googleapis.com/
icon?family=Material+Icons">
```

   Adding this line will call the external CSS file, which will help us to use the CSS classes related to Google icons to be used in our template.

3. Now, we need to do some more modifications in the HTML file where we are showing the "Thumbs Up" and "Thumbs Down" text in a container **<div>** with class "**more-details-book-thumbs-up-down-container**" inside this <div> we will modify the existing code and use Google icons. The following is the updated code for the same:

```
<div class="more-details-book-thumbs-up-down-container">
    <div class="more-details-book-thumbs-up"><i
class="material-icons">thumb_up</i>
        {{BPBBookFromId.thumbsUPCounter}}</div>
    <div class="more-details-book-thumbs-down"><i
class="material-icons">thumb_down</i>
        {{BPBBookFromId.thumbsDOWNCounter}}</div>
</div>
```

4. As we have added the new **<div>,** we have to add a few CSS to make it perfect, and the following is the updated CSS for this part:

```
/* Thumbs Up and Thumbs Down */

.more-details-book-thumbs-up-down-container {
  display: flex;
  flex-direction: row;
  align-content: center;
  justify-content: center;
  flex-wrap: nowrap;
}
```

```
.more-details-book-thumbs-up, .more-details-book-thumbs-down {
  margin-right: 20px;
  margin-left: 20px;
  font-size: 30px;
}
```

5. As you will refresh your browser screen now, you will be able to see that
    instead of "Thumbs Up" and "Thumbs Down" text. Now, the Google Icons
    are appearing, which is making it look very nice, as shown in *figure 11.61*:

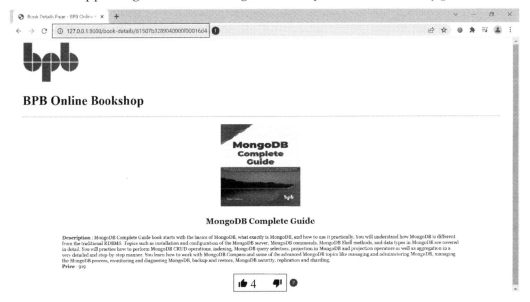

Figure 11.61: More Details page—updated screen showing icons

The only thing which is not looking nice is the "Thumbs Down" icon that is
not showing anything; as for this book, there is no entry of thumbs down in
our database, so there would be many cases where either the "Thumbs Up"
or "Thumbs Down" will have no values in the MongoDB document.

Like there is no "Thumbs Up" value for a "Dummy Book" in our MongoDB collection, as shown in *figure 11.62*:

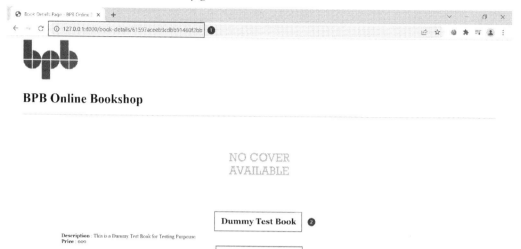

Figure 11.62: *More Details page—icons showing blank counter values*

To tackle this scenario, we need to work on our last part, which is as follows:

If there is no count for "Thumbs Up" or "Thumbs Down" then show "0" instead of blank.

For this, we need to add a simple "if" condition to our template HTML file in the **<div>**, which consists of these icons.

Let us do some modifications, and we will be using Django template helpers to perform this.

6. We will just use the simple if condition to check if the value of "Thumbs Up" or "Thumbs Down" exists in the collection then only display the values else display the 0 value for this and following is the updated template HTML code for the same:

```
<div class="more-details-book-thumbs-up-down-container">

        <div class="more-details-book-thumbs-up"><i
class="material-icons">thumb_up</i>
```

```
                    {% if BPBBookFromId.thumbsUPCounter %}
{{BPBBookFromId.thumbsUPCounter}} {% else %} 0 {% endif %}

                    </div>

                    <div class="more-details-book-thumbs-down"><i
class="material-icons">thumb_down</i>

                    {% if BPBBookFromId.thumbsDOWNCounter %}
{{BPBBookFromId.thumbsDOWNCounter}} {% else %} 0 {% endif %}

                    </div>
              </div>
```

7. If you now refresh the browser and see the "Book Details" page, then it will show value as "0" whenever there is no count for the "Thumbs Up" or "Thumbs Down" in the MongoDB collection, as shown in *figure 11.63*:

BPB Online Bookshop

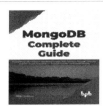

MongoDB Complete Guide

Description : MongoDB Complete Guide book starts with the basics of MongoDB, what exactly is MongoDB, and how to use it practically. You will understand how MongoDB is different from the traditional RDBMS. Topics such as installation and configuration of the MongoDB server, MongoDB commands, MongoDB Shell methods, and data types in MongoDB are covered in detail. You will practice how to perform MongoDB CRUD operations, indexing, MongoDB query selectors, projection in MongoDB and projection operators as well as aggregation in a very detailed and step-by-step manner. You learn how to work with MongoDB Compass and some of the advanced MongoDB topics like managing and administering MongoDB, managing the MongoDB process, monitoring and diagnosing MongoDB, backup and restore, MongoDB security, replication and sharding.
Price : 919

Figure 11.63: More Details page—icons showing "0" values instead of blank

The same will be now shown for the "Thumbs Up" in the "Dummy Book" as it has no value for "Thumbs Up", as shown in *figure 11.64*:

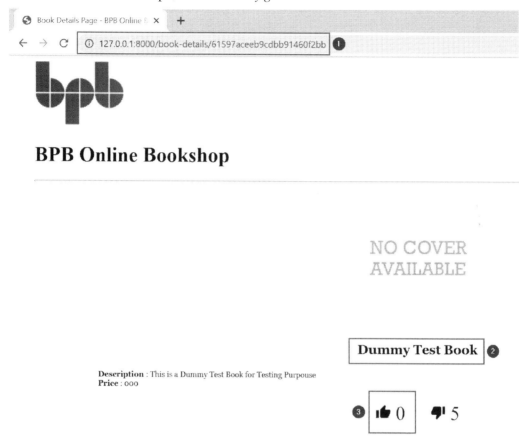

Figure 11.64: More Details page—icons showing "0" values instead of blank

Following is the updated final code for template HTML and CSS.

HTML—for file "bpbAppBookDetailsIndex.html"

```
{% load static %}
<!DOCTYPE html>
<html lang="en">


<head>
    <title>Book Details Page - BPB Online Bookshop</title>
```

```html
    <link rel="stylesheet" href="{% static 'BPBOnlineBookShopMongoDBApp/
style.css' %}">
    <link rel="stylesheet" href="https://fonts.googleapis.com/
icon?family=Material+Icons">
</head>

<body>
    <div class="main-container">
        <div class="header-container">
            <div class="logo"><img src="{% static
'BPBOnlineBookShopMongoDBApp/bpb-logo.png' %}"
                    alt="BPB Publications Logo" /></div>
            <h1>BPB Online Bookshop</h1>
            <hr />
        </div>
        <div class="book-details-body-container">
            <div class="book-details-book-image-container"><img
class="book-details-book-image"
                    src="http://localhost/bpb-catalog-app-backend/
images/{{BPBBookFromId.coverimage}}" /></div>
            <div class="book-details-book-title">{{BPBBookFromId.
title}}</div>
            <div class="book-details-book-other-
details"><b>Description</b> :
                {{BPBBookFromId.description}}<br /><b>Price</b> :
{{BPBBookFromId.price}}</div>
            <div class="more-details-book-thumbs-up-down-container">
                <div class="more-details-book-thumbs-up"><i
class="material-icons">thumb_up</i>
                    {% if BPBBookFromId.thumbsUPCounter %}
{{BPBBookFromId.thumbsUPCounter}} {% else %} 0 {% endif %}
                </div>
                <div class="more-details-book-thumbs-down"><i
class="material-icons">thumb_down</i>
                    {% if BPBBookFromId.thumbsDOWNCounter %}
{{BPBBookFromId.thumbsDOWNCounter}} {% else %} 0 {% endif
                    %}
                </div>
            </div>
        </div>
```

```
        </div>
    </div>
</body>

</html>
```

CSS—for file "style.css"

```
.main-container {
  margin: 0 auto;
  max-width: 1200px;
}

.header-container {
  background: #ffffff;
  height: 200px;
}

.body-container {
  width: 1200px;
  background: #fafafa;
  margin: 20px;
}

.items {
  display: flex;
  flex-wrap: wrap;
  justify-content: center;
}

.item {
  width: 300px;
  height: 250px;
  border: 1px;
  border-style: solid;
  border-color: blueviolet;
  margin: 15px;
  text-align: center;
```

```
    padding: 10px;
  }

  .book-image {
    display: inline-block;
    width: 150px;
    height: 150px;
  }

  .book-title {
    margin-top: 5px;
    font-family: Georgia, 'Times New Roman', Times, serif;
    font-weight: bold;
    font-size: 14px;
  }

  .more-details-button {
    margin-top: 20px;
  }

  .more-details-button>a {
    background-color: darkorchid;
    color: white;
    padding: 10px 15px;
    text-decoration: none;
  }

  .more-details-button>a:hover {
    background-color: blueviolet;
    color: white;
    padding: 10px 15px;
    text-decoration: none;
  }

  /* More Details Page CSS Starts Here */

  .book-details-body-container {
    text-align: center;
  }
```

```css
.book-details-book-image {
  display: inline-block;
  width: 200px;
  height: 200px;
  margin-bottom: 20px;
}

.book-details-book-title {
  font-family: Georgia, 'Times New Roman', Times, serif;
  font-size: 20px;
  font-weight: bold;
  margin-bottom: 20px;
}

.book-details-book-other-details {
  font-family: Georgia, 'Times New Roman', Times, serif;
  font-size: 12px;
  max-width: 1000px;
  margin-left: auto;
  margin-right: auto;
  text-align: left;
  margin-bottom: 20px;
}

/* Thumbs Up and Thumbs Down */

.more-details-book-thumbs-up-down-container {
  display: flex;
  flex-direction: row;
  align-content: center;
  justify-content: center;
  flex-wrap: nowrap;
}

.more-details-book-thumbs-up, .more-details-book-thumbs-down {
  margin-right: 20px;
  margin-left: 20px;
  font-size: 30px;
}
```

322 ■ *Full Stack Development with MongoDB*

Conclusion

In this chapter, we have learned the practical step-by-step development of a frontend application developed using Python and MongoDB. We started this chapter with an overview of our frontend development using Python, Django, PyMongo, and MongoDB and basic requirements. Later in this chapter have learned how we can build the various functionalities of the frontend application like displaying the book catalog list and displaying the book cover images, total number of "Thumbs Up" and "Thumbs Down" for that particular book using the Python and its Django framework with the help of Python's official MongoDB driver. In this chapter, all the sections have been explained in a step-by-step practical manner so that by the end of this chapter, you feel more confident in dynamic python application development with MongoDB.

Questions

1. What is a frontend application?

2. What is the Django framework?

3. How you can install Django?

4. What is PyMongo?

Index

Made in the USA
Middletown, DE
06 July 2022

68614006R00199